THE PRAISES OF ISRAEL

PSALMS 107–150

THE PRAISES OF ISRAEL

Volume Three

Psalms 107-150

Dudley Fifield

First Published 2010

ISBN 978-0-85189-179-8

© 2010 The Christadelphian Magazine and Publishing Association Limited

Printed and bound in England by:

CROMWELL PRESS GROUP
TROWBRIDGE
WILTSHIRE BA14 0XB

CONTENTS

INDEXES TO ALL THREE VOLUMES

PREFACE

THIS work on the Book of Psalms was written over a period of some twenty-five years; Psalms 107–150 being the product of recent study. Consequently it is possible that readers will detect a development in style between earlier and later studies. The writer is, after all, twenty-five years older!

Originally they appeared in the pages of *The Bible Student* and we are grateful to the Editors of that magazine for agreeing so readily to their reproduction.

Inevitably, given the period of time involved, our thinking on some of the Psalms has changed. It would, however, have been a monumental task to have made substantial changes in those that were written in earlier years. We have therefore, apart from some minor editing, left them in their original form.

Because they were written in this way there is also some repetition of thought and ideas. However, as readers are most likely to read the Psalms on an individual basis, 'dipping in' as it were, this might prove to be more of a benefit than a disadvantage.

When this venture began it was not anticipated that the study of all 150 psalms would be completed, or that they would be published in book form. I am grateful to the Christadelphian Magazine and Publishing Association, the Editor and his staff for making this possible.

I should also like to express my gratitude to my son, Brother Stephen Fifield, whose computer expertise has helped me considerably in the production of these studies.

This is the third volume of a three-volume work. This final volume contains Psalms 107–150.

PSALM 107

PSALM 107 is the first in what is commonly accepted as the Fifth Book of the Psalms. Nevertheless one cannot escape the conclusion that it has a very close connection with the two preceding psalms (105 and 106) and forms with them what has been described as "a trilogy of songs" encompassing a specific period in Israel's history.

It will be remembered that parts of both Psalms 105 and 106 were incorporated into the song that David sang on the occasion that the ark of God was brought to Zion (see 1 Chronicles 16). It cannot be denied that the psalm speaks of a return of the exiles of Israel from the lands of their enemies (verses 3 and 4) and that the substance of the psalm (verses 4-31) speaks of the various difficulties encountered by the pilgrims on their journeys.

It must also be recognised, however, that the redemption described in this psalm is a direct reference to the prayer contained in verse 47 of Psalm 106. The close link between the two psalms can be clearly seen also by the similarity of language used in their opening words: "O give thanks unto the LORD ..." Compare also:

Psalm 106	Psalm 107
"... redeemed them from the hand of the enemy" (verse 10).	"... redeemed from the hand of the enemy" (verse 2).
"... gather us from among the heathen" (verse 47).	"... gathered them out of the lands" (verse 3).
"... scatter them in the lands" (verse 27).	"... out of the lands" (verse 3).
"... they waited not for his counsel" (verse 13).	"... contemned the counsel of the most High" (verse 11).
"... he regarded their affliction" (verse 44).	"... they cried [cry] unto the LORD in their trouble [Hebrew, 'affliction']" (verses 6,13,19,28).

Historical Background

However, although there is a close association between the two psalms it does not follow that Psalm 107 must have been written by David. It could have been written later by another who, in the circumstances in which he found himself, meditated on David's earlier psalm because of the appropriateness of its message to his situation. This we believe to be the case and the internal evidence points to the days of Hezekiah as the probable historical background to the psalm. So Psalm 106 (verses 34-46) describes the manner in which the people of Israel, because they failed to drive out the people of the land, but adopted their practices and way of life, were delivered into their hand. The nations ruled over them, oppressed them and brought them into subjection. They were mingled amongst them. This was especially true of the period of the Judges and continued to a degree into the beginning of David's reign. Thus David, moved by the ark of the covenant now residing in Zion, reflects on the history and sins of his people up to that time (Psalms 105 and 106). He prays that God, in His mercy, would gather all Israel together that, in the city which He had chosen to put His name, they might all in unity worship the One who had delivered them from the hands of their enemies.

Thus it was that in the days of Ahaz and Hezekiah the sins of the people of Judah had brought a similar calamity upon them. By the hand of the Assyrian over 200,000 of the inhabitants of the land had been carried away captive. This information is to be found in the inscriptions of Sennacherib preserved in what is known as the Taylor Cylinder in the British Museum (*Old Testament Problems*; J. W. Thirtle, pages 134 and 135). Whether the figure is accurate or exaggerated does not affect our understanding of the psalm. It is enough to say that a large number of the people had been carried into captivity and others scattered abroad amongst the surrounding nations. Just as the bringing of the ark to Zion provided a crucial moment for all Israel to unite, so it was that after the destruction of the Assyrian army, when God magnified Hezekiah in the sight of the nations so that many brought gifts to the Lord and presents to the king

(2 Chronicles 32:23), a similar opportunity was provided for those who were carried away captive to return. Those who faced the perils of the journey looked for a city of habitation, a dwelling place with their God in Zion (verses 4,7,32,36).

Thus the Psalmist seeks God's blessing on those who would travel back to Jerusalem to worship: "Then they cried unto the LORD in their trouble, and he delivered them out of their distresses" (verses 6,13,19,28), for this cause: "Oh that men would praise the LORD for his goodness, and for his wonderful works to the children of men!" (verses 8,15,21,31).

The *Cambridge Bible* points out that by generalising these verses, the AV has obscured the fact that those referred to are the redeemed of verses 2 and 3. They are also the redeemed of Psalm 106:10 who the Lord delivered out of the hand of the enemy when He saved them from the bondage of Egypt: in other words the people of Israel. Thus the historical background of the psalm, while having an incipient fulfilment in the events of Hezekiah's days, looks beyond to the return from their captivity in the land of Babylon to that great ingathering of God's people when the Lord Jesus Christ will reign enthroned in Zion.

Structure of Psalm

After a brief introduction (verses 1-3), we have four vivid and dramatic word pictures drawn from the experiences of men in extreme danger from which they are delivered by the goodness of God –

(a) Travellers lost in the wilderness, finally brought to the dwelling they seek (verses 4-9).

(b) Exiles who, like men imprisoned in a dungeon, are finally granted the freedom they desire (verses 10-16).

(c) Men sick unto death, chastised because of their sins, restored to health (verses 17-22).

(d) Mariners, fighting a dreadful storm, brought to a safe haven (verses 23-32).

There is a change of character in the final section of the psalm. The word pictures and the refrains that conclude them disappear and the writer reflects on what he has written (verses 33-42), concluding with a final word of exhortation (verse 43).

Verses 1-3

We have already commented on these verses but it must be emphasised again that the theme is national deliverance, not individual salvation. That the experiences described can be referred to an individual's personal circumstances is true, but that is not the primary purpose for which the psalm was written.

The final regathering of Israel is, of course, one of the great themes of the Old Testament scriptures, and the limited fulfilment that the words had in Hezekiah's times and in the return from Babylon is totally eclipsed by the great work that remains to be accomplished.

However, it needs to be appreciated that the psalm is not describing the manner of Israel's deliverance, either from Babylon or the final regathering in the last days. There are no details given of the way in which they come into the land. Rather, the emphasis is on the privations they suffered in their exile and on their journey, their longing for deliverance, and the way God responds to their cry for relief and grants them the succour for which they long. It is because of this that the illustrations given can apply to God's servants in every age who cry unto Him in their distress.

The Wilderness

Those who wandered in this dry and arid place knew all the privations of the desert. They looked, as if in vain, for a city to dwell in. They were hungry and thirsty. However, the reference is not only to physical deprivation, but also to the manner in which they longed for the blessings of the covenant. This becomes apparent, for when safely delivered the psalm tells us of them: "He satisfieth the longing soul, and filleth the hungry soul with goodness" (verse 9).

The Prisoners

Ancient prisons were usually unlit vaults and they present a dramatic picture of the plight of those who were experiencing the misery of exile from their homeland. It was as if the very shadow of death hung over them for they were without hope of deliverance (verse 10). The reason for their suffering was because they had rebelled against the words of God (verse 11). This echoes again the language of Psalm 106 where the same Hebrew word translated "rebelled" is rendered "provoked" in verses 7,33 and 43. What reason then to give thanks and to rejoice before their God when He delivered them out of the prison house.

The Sick unto Death

It is because of their foolishness in embracing iniquity and transgression that they have been brought into affliction (verse 17). Food repels them – they are at the very doors of death (verse 18). Then in their extremity they cry unto the Lord who saves them out of their affliction, for He sends His word and heals them. Note the way in which the word of God is almost personified, given an independent existence as though it were an angel of God sent to heal and deliver from the pit (verse 20, RV). This, and similar passages (see for instance Psalms 33:6; 119:89; 147:15), form a background to our understanding of the record in John 1 with its teaching on the word made flesh (verse 14).

The wonder of God's deliverance was such that it would produce in them a spirit of thankfulness in which they would offer sacrifices, and in the overflowing joy that filled their hearts, tell of all that the Lord had done for them (verse 22).

Sailors Caught in a Storm

It is hard to imagine a more graphic portrayal of a storm at sea than that described in this psalm. It bears comparison with the records of Jonah 1 and Acts 27. The mariners, although accustomed to crossing the ocean in pursuit of their business and trade, are nevertheless helpless before the might and fury of the wind and sea. Note that the storm is evidence of the sovereignty of God. It is at His command that the wind and waves have risen (verse 25). He speaks the word and it is done (Genesis 1:3; Psalm 105:31,34). In the outworking of His purpose, all the storms of life are at His behest – He is in control. It is worth reflecting that if it were not for times of trouble and

901

adversity we would not see His wonders in the deep. We would not appreciate what great things He has done for us. So, tossed with tempest, swept hither and thither by the waves, "their soul is melted because of trouble. They reel to and fro, and stagger like a drunken man, and are at their wits' end" (verses 26,27).

Their navigational skills are of no avail. All their experience of the turbulence of the sea is rendered useless by the ferocity of the storm: "Then they cry unto the LORD in their trouble." He calms the winds and stills the waves (verses 28,29) and brings them to "the haven where they would be" (verse 30, RV).

For this cause they publicly declare His praises before the congregation of the people as they assemble for worship, and in the presence of the elders as they meet in council (verse 32). It should be observed that whereas in the first three illustrations the suffering described is imposed upon them through the circumstances in which they find themselves, in this instance they are pursuing their normal trade until they are brought to realise the peril of their situation by the tempestuous seas that rise at God's command. Thus in the daily affairs of life in which they legitimately engage, God's servants sometimes need the storms of life to quicken their desire for the deliverance that only God can provide.

God's Providential Hand

The tone of the psalm changes as the Psalmist considers the way in which God works to bring about the accomplishment of His purpose in gathering His people. It is not always easy to recognise the hand of God at work when we are contemporary with the events. Often it is only when He has completed His purpose and we are able to look back and reflect upon His actions, that we appreciate the manner in which He has worked to accomplish it. So it is that all the verbs in this final section of the psalm (verses 33-41) are in the past tense, as referring to what has been accomplished in the experience of the psalmist. He speaks of rivers turned into thirsty ground (RV), and fertile lands smitten with barrenness because of the wickedness of the inhabitants (verses 33,34). The word translated "barrenness" is rendered "a

902

salt desert" by the RV and this directs our attention to Deuteronomy 29. There Moses warns the people of the danger of being influenced by the abominations of the surrounding nations with their idols of wood, stone, gold and silver. He tells them that the consequences of such unfaithfulness would be "that the whole land thereof [should become] brimstone, and salt, and burning, that it is not sown, nor beareth, nor any grass groweth therein, like the overthrow of Sodom and Gomorrah" (verse 23). Note also that because the anger of the Lord would be kindled against the land, they would be rooted out and cast into another land (verses 27,28). Chapter 30 continues the theme when it speaks of the faithfulness of God and His promise to regather them from amongst the nations where He had scattered them, if they would turn to Him and obey His voice (verses 1-5).

An obvious link between the words of the psalm and the Book of Deuteronomy is established and it is a clear indication that God could have reacted to their wickedness in this way.

So in contrast, the Lord "turneth a wilderness into a pool of water, and a dry land into watersprings. And there he maketh the hungry to dwell, that they may prepare a city of habitation" (Psalm 107:35,36, RV).

Isaiah 34 and 35

A similar connection with Deuteronomy is to be found in other parts of scripture and the language of Isaiah 34 and 35 in particular should be noted – not only for its allusions to Deuteronomy 29 but also for its links with this psalm.

Isaiah 34 describes the judgements of God upon the nations of the earth (verses 1-4). They are represented by the nation of Edom which is typical of the wickedness and hatred of things divine that is characteristic of them all (verses 5,6). It is, says the prophet, "the day of the LORD's vengeance, and the year of recompences for the controversy of Zion" (verse 8). The result is that the land is turned into a wilderness, "and the streams thereof shall be turned into pitch, and the dust thereof into brimstone, and the land thereof shall become burning pitch" (verse 9; Deuteronomy 29:23).

903

This arid and parched land becomes the habitation of unclean birds and beasts, as from generation to generation it lies waste (verses 10-15). When we move to chapter 35 however, we have a startling and amazing contrast, for in this barren wilderness God is going to provide a highway. (Remember the king's highway through the land of Edom – Numbers 20:17.) There in the wilderness, waters will break out and streams in the desert. The parched land will become a pool and the thirsty land springs of water (verses 6-8). Why? Because, "the ransomed of the LORD shall return, and come with singing unto Zion; and everlasting joy shall be upon their heads: they shall obtain gladness and joy, and sorrow and sighing shall flee away" (verse 10, RV).

Like Psalm 107 it is the great ingathering of God's people, the past deliverance of Israel from captivity being an incipient fulfilment of that final consummation of all that God has promised.

The Chastening Hand of God

The writer of Psalm 107, having established his theme of the redeemed of the Lord gathered out of the lands where they had been scattered, now reflects on the manner in which their God, having chastened them – for they were diminished and brought low through the oppression of their enemies (verse 39) – eventually scatters and brings to confusion those who afflicted them. He gathers and keeps His people as a shepherd does his flock (verses 40,41).

Final Exhortation

"The righteous shall see it, and rejoice: and all iniquity shall stop her mouth. Whoso is wise, and will observe these things, even they shall understand the lovingkindness of the LORD."   (verses 42,43)

When God finally vindicates His people, then they will know that they have not put their trust in Him in vain. Their joy and gladness will be contrasted with the silence of all who have mocked Israel's God and blasphemed His holy name.

The psalm speaks primarily of God's people Israel, yet the assurance that it gives is true also for all His servants in every age who are numbered amongst the redeemed. Although they too may have travelled across the wilderness of this world, and on occasions been afflicted with spiritual maladies, and shut up in the prison house, and tossed by the storms and tempests of life, because they are wise they will observe and understand the work of God in their lives. They will appreciate all that He has done for them in the bonds of the covenant.

"Who is wise, and he shall understand these things? prudent, and he shall know them? for the ways of the LORD are right, and the just shall walk in them: but the transgressors shall fall therein."   (Hosea 14:9)

PSALM 108

PSALM 108 bears the inscription, "A Song or Psalm of David". It is unlikely, however, that David is responsible for its inclusion in the Psalter in its present form as it is composed of portions of two earlier psalms of David brought together by a later writer because of their appropriateness to the situation in which he found himself. Verses 1-5 of the song are taken from Psalm 57 (verses 7-11) and the remainder of the psalm (verses 6-13) from Psalm 60 (verses 5-12). There are some minor textual variations but these do not appear to be of great significance and the general meaning of the words themselves is not affected.

Commentators generally have little to say about the psalm. Some suggest that the two psalms were brought together for liturgical purposes; others affirm that it is the work of an anonymous author written against the background of an unknown event, perhaps after Judah's return from captivity. Our own reflections, however, lead us to the conviction that it was written in this form in the days of Jehoshaphat against the background of the confederacy of Moab, Ammon and Edom that came against Judah to battle (2 Chronicles 20:1).

As far as the exposition of the original words of David is concerned, we refer readers to what we have already written in Psalms 57 and 60. We shall, however, draw attention to the historical backgrounds of those psalms which have some relevance to their reproduction in Psalm 108.

The Reign of Jehoshaphat

Our belief that the psalm is associated with the days of Jehoshaphat is based on the historical record of his reign recorded in 2 Chronicles (chapters 17 to 20). These chapters describe how Jehoshaphat "walked in the first ways of his father David" and "sought to the LORD God of his father, and walked in his commandments" (17:3,4). At his instigation the princes and Levites taught the people from the book of the law (verses 7-9). As a result he prospered and the kingdom was established in his hand:

"And the fear of the LORD fell upon all the kingdoms of the lands that were round about Judah, so that they made no war against Jehoshaphat."   (verse 10)

Foolishly Jehoshaphat made an alliance with the house of Ahab (chapter 18), thereby incurring the wrath of God (19:2). However, good was found in him and he carried out further religious reforms throughout his kingdom and, as a result of his efforts, many of Judah were brought back to the Lord God of their fathers (19:3,4). In keeping with the meaning of his name (Yah is the Judge), Jehoshaphat proceeded to appoint judges throughout all his kingdom, instructing them to remember they were not to judge for their own ends, but for the Lord, and that consequently they were to judge righteously, taking no gifts and showing no respect of persons (verses 5-11). However, calamity seemed about to overtake the kingdom, for there gathered against them a great company of the surrounding nations, Moab, Ammon and Edom amongst them, and in preparation for the impending attack they were encamped in Engedi (20:1,2). Jehoshaphat and all the people of Judah, recognising how great their plight was, prayed to the Lord their God (verses 3-13). Jahaziel, a Levite of the sons of Asaph, moved by the Spirit of the Lord encouraged the people, assuring them that they were not to be afraid or dismayed because of this great host for the battle was not theirs but God's. Consequently they were to stand still and see the salvation of the Lord, for He it was who would gain the victory (verses 14-19). The subsequent verses describe the reaction of Jehoshaphat and the people and the remarkable victory won on behalf of His people by the God of Israel.

Psalms 57 and 60 – Historical Links

Both psalms fall into a group of five that carry the title "a Michtam of David" (Psalms 56-60). Psalm 60 indicates that the purpose of these psalms was "to teach" and the idea behind the term translated "an inscription"

(Septuagint) is 'that which is engraved upon the heart'. Such lessons learned from David's personal experiences were intended not only for his own spiritual education, but for all who would meditate on that which was written. Both psalms would therefore be treasured by godly men. Psalm 57 also has a superscription "Al-taschith", which means 'destroy not', and indicates that the psalm was written at a time of great trouble and extreme danger. We would therefore conclude that Psalm 108 was written against just such a time of peril.

Historically the psalm was written when David fled from Saul and took refuge in the wilderness of Engedi, shortly after the distressed and the disaffected in Israel gathered themselves to him at the cave of Adullam (1 Samuel 22:1,2).

The connection between Psalm 57 and the events of Jehoshaphat's reign may not be immediately apparent. Psalm 108 opens with the words "My heart is fixed". So also it is recorded of Jehoshaphat that he had prepared his heart (RV, "set" – same word as that translated "fixed") to seek God (2 Chronicles 19:3). This, however, could hardly be regarded as conclusive in establishing a connection between the two.

Much more appropriate to the circumstances of Jehoshaphat's day is the emphasis in Psalm 57 upon praising God with singing and melody and by the playing of psaltery and harp (108:1,2). The Psalmist cries:

"I myself will awake early. I will praise thee, O LORD, among the people: and I will sing praises unto thee among the nations." (Psalm 108:2,3)

So it is recorded of Jehoshaphat and the people of Judah that after the Levites, of the children of the Kohathites, and of the children of the Korites, had stood up to praise the Lord God of Israel with a loud voice on high that they rose early in the morning, and went forth into the wilderness of Tekoa. After speaking words of encouragement, Jehoshaphat consulted with the people, and singers were appointed to go forth before their army and to say, "Praise the LORD; for his mercy endureth for ever" (2 Chronicles 20:19-21).

"And when they began to sing and to praise, the LORD set ambushments against the children of Ammon, Moab, and mount Seir, which were come against Judah; and they were smitten."   (verse 22)

With the enemy destroyed and the threat removed all Judah returned to Jerusalem with joy:

"And they came to Jerusalem with psalteries and harps and trumpets unto the house of the LORD. And the fear of God was on all the kingdoms of those countries, when they had heard that the LORD fought against the enemies of Israel."   (verses 28,29)

Another factor that might be relevant is that David's coming to the cave of Adullam follows his sojourn amongst the Philistines (1 Samuel 21). His flight to Achish at Gath arose directly out of the hatred of Doeg the Edomite (verse 7). This hatred, as subsequent events were to show, was directed not only at David but also against Israel's God (1 Samuel 22:17-23).

Of the verses included in Psalm 108 from Psalm 60 it is perhaps sufficient to quote the concluding part of the psalm to demonstrate how appropriate they are to the events recorded in 2 Chronicles 20:

"Who will bring me into the strong city? who will lead me into Edom? Wilt not thou, O God, who hast cast us off? and wilt not thou, O God, go forth with our hosts? Give us help from trouble: for vain is the help of man. Through God we shall do valiantly: for he it is that shall tread down our enemies."   (Psalm108:10-13)

In the historical information at the head of Psalm 60 we are told that it was written when Joab smote 12,000 of Edom in the valley of salt. This situation arose as, under David's command, they fought with Syria. It would appear that the Edomites, seeing an opportunity to take advantage of this northern conflict, invaded Israel in the south. Joab was quickly despatched to deal with the danger. It seems, however, that Joab's victory was not decisive and both David and Abishai became involved in the campaign which appears to have lasted for several months before it was brought to a satisfactory conclusion (see 2 Samuel 8:13,14; 1 Chronicles 18:12; 1 Kings 11:15,16). In the opening words of Psalm 60 David recognises the attack from the south, with its initial success, as an indication of God's displeasure with His people: "O God, thou hast cast us off, thou hast scattered us, thou hast been displeased; O turn thyself to us again" (verse 1).

It would appear that David's success and prosperity had produced a spirit of complacency and through the attack of the Edomites his God sought to teach him how dependent he was upon Him to maintain his way before Him.

The latter part of the psalm, that reproduced in Psalm 108, speaks of the ultimate victory of God's people when Moab, Edom and Philistia are brought into subjection (see verses already quoted above).

Conclusion

Like David, Jehoshaphat was keenly aware of the fact that God was at work in his life. As David had prospered, so had he. As David had been taught that in God only was help to be found, so he also recognised that the great confederacy gathered against him was the result of his foolish alliance with the House of Ahab. Consequently in the Lord only was deliverance to be found. The danger was imminent and the thought of his heart, remembering the inscription at the head of Psalm 57, was "destroy not". David's flight from Saul brought him into the strongholds of Engedi, and it was here that the great host gathered against Jehoshaphat was encamped. Thus his meditations led him to Psalm 57, and moved by it, he sought in the playing of the instruments and the singing of God's praises to put the words of the psalm into practical effect.

Psalm 60, written concerning the attack by Edom on Israel, and being one of the same group of 'Michtam' psalms as Psalm 57, would naturally come within the purview of his thought and the ultimate defeat of all those surrounding nations, of which the psalm spoke, would have been a source of comfort to him in his extremity. As God had done for David so He would do for him also.

We do not say that Jehoshaphat wrote Psalm 108 himself. When we wrote of Psalm 83, which was also written against the background of 2 Chronicles 20, we suggested that Jahaziel, who played such an important

910

part in the events of that chapter, might well have been the author of that psalm. Might he not also have been the one who, in the confidence of Jehoshaphat, brought together the relevant parts of Psalms 57 and 60 to form Psalm 108 and celebrate the victory which God had won on behalf of His people? It remains, however, a psalm of David, for all the words written were originally his.

PSALM 109

THIS is an imprecatory psalm. An imprecation is a curse and we have already commented, albeit briefly, on the problems sometimes caused by the use of language that appears to be inconsistent with the teaching of the New Testament in our consideration of Psalm 35. That psalm, together with Psalms 69 and 109 are the most notable examples of this type of language although it is not confined to them. But though the sentiments of the three psalms are similar in many respects, those of Psalm 109 go beyond the other two in that the curses expressed involve not only the individual to whom they are addressed but also his wife and children (verses 9,10,12,13). Indeed the language is so extreme that if read without understanding it cannot fail to shock and astonish the reader.

It must be emphasised that in the scriptural record of his life David is never portrayed as showing a vindictive spirit towards those who wronged him. On two occasions when his implacable enemy Saul was delivered into his hand he allowed him to escape unharmed:

"The LORD judge between me and thee, and the LORD avenge me of thee: but mine hand shall not be upon thee ... The LORD therefore be judge, and judge between me and thee, and see, and plead my cause, and deliver me out of thine hand."   (1 Samuel 24:12,15)

In a foreshadowing of the spirit of the Lord Jesus, "he ... committed himself to him that judgeth righteously" (1 Peter 2:23).

Indeed the very psalms themselves show a spirit that is completely void of any desire for personal vengeance:

"They rewarded me evil for good to the spoiling of my soul. But as for me, when they were sick, my clothing

912

was sackcloth: I humbled my soul with fasting; and my prayer returned into mine own bosom. I behaved myself as though he had been my friend or brother: I bowed down heavily, as one that mourneth for his mother."

(Psalm 35:12-14)

"For my love they are my adversaries: but I give myself unto prayer. And they have rewarded me evil for good, and hatred for my love."   (Psalm 109:4,5)

Again, David's words breathe the very spirit of the Lord's teaching on the Mount:

"Love your enemies, bless them that curse you, do good to them that hate you, and pray for them which despitefully use you, and persecute you."

(Matthew 5:44)

What then is the answer to the problem? There are two suggestions that seem to be relevant. The first applies to all such psalms whereas the second is, in one sense, only appropriate to our understanding of Psalm 109, yet on reflection is seen to be an extension of the first suggestion.

God's Recompense

Kay (*The Psalms with Notes*) in an Appendix devoted to this particular question draws attention to the words of Solomon's prayer in 2 Chronicles 6:

"If a man sin against his neighbour, and an oath be laid upon him to make him swear, and the oath come before thine altar in this house; then hear thou from heaven, and do, and judge thy servants, by requiting the wicked, by recompensing his way upon his own head; and by justifying the righteous, by giving him according to his righteousness."   (verses 22,23)

Kay points out that there was nothing vindictive or contrary to the spirit of meekness in this prayer. Retribution was asked for, but only because it was good for the nation as a whole. If the unjust had been allowed to triumph over the just then that would have undermined the very foundations upon which the theocracy was built. It would have been a stumbling block to the righteous and it would have hardened the wicked in their sin. The imprecatory psalms must therefore be viewed as the outpourings of a spirit motivated by a love of truth and righteousness, and a zeal for the maintenance of God's honour. This spirit is not foreign to the New Testament "for our God is a consuming fire" (Hebrews 12:29) and "the wrath of God is revealed [by the Gospel] from heaven against all ungodliness and unrighteousness of men, who hold the truth in unrighteousness" (Romans 1:18). Sin is hateful to God and must ultimately be destroyed. Thus these psalms speak of the antagonism between God's kingdom and the pride and arrogance of men.

> "They 'to whom the word of God came' in old time were by these Psalms placed under a necessity of either departing from iniquity or pronouncing sentence on themselves." (*The Psalms with Notes,* pages 468,469)

Who is Cursing Who?

The second suggestion which, at first sight, appears to apply only to Psalm 109 requires us to take particular note of the use of the pronouns in the psalm. The first five verses express the outpouring of David's heart as he beseeches God to deliver him from the slander and malice of his adversaries, who in their hatred have rewarded him with evil for good. At verse 6, however there is a change in the pronouns from 'my' and 'they' to 'him', 'his' and 'he.' At first sight it would appear that we are reading the words of David: the outpouring of his heart before God to take vengeance on those that hated him – in particular one individual who presumably was the leader of, or spokesman for, his enemies. This changed form of address (i.e., 'him', 'his', and 'he') continues from verse 6 through to verse 19. The remainder of the psalm is a renewal of David's prayer to God. However, it has been suggested that the curses pronounced are not David's but are actually the words of his adversaries wherewith they sought to curse him. Perowne (*The Psalms*, Volume 2) points out that it is not unusual in Hebrew to omit the word 'saying' before a quotation. A classic example is to be found in Psalm 2 (verse 2) where the translators have inserted the word "saying" to give the sense although it is not to be found in the Hebrew text. Thus verse 5 of Psalm 109 would read: 'And they have rewarded me evil for good and hatred for my love, saying' – and then follow the words of the curse.

In pursuit of this, various writers have suggested that the individual who so cursed David was Doeg the Edomite, Ahithophel or particularly Shimei the son of Gera. In the case of Shimei, attempts have been made to draw parallels between the records in 2 Samuel 16 and Psalm 109. It must be admitted that this idea has a certain attraction about it, but it does not appear to this writer to get to the root of the matter for, we feel sure, the words of verses 16-19 must be the words of David himself.

The Law of Malicious Witness

We believe that the words of the curse (verses 6-15) did not originate in the heart of David, but they are indeed an expression of the dreadful and deep-seated hatred of his enemies. However, they become the words of David as he pleads his cause before God. It is a plea that the ruin they sought to bring upon him might be turned back upon their own heads, and at this point the thrust of the first suggestion regarding divine recompense is seen to be at the root of this psalm as well. The law of malicious witness (Deuteronomy 19:16-19) provided for the situation where a man falsely accused his brother and testified lies against him. When they stood before the judges and the truth of the matter was established, then that which the wicked man would have done to his brother was to be done unto him. Note that the opening words of the curse are in the setting of a formal court of law:

"Set thou a wicked man over him: and let Satan [an adversary or an accuser] stand at his right hand. When he shall be judged, let him be condemned: and let his prayer become sin." (Psalm 109:6,7)

Compare Zechariah 3 where Joshua the high priest stands before the Lord and Satan stands at his right hand to resist him. Evidently it was the custom for the accuser to stand at the right hand of the accused. The venomous and bitter malediction called on God, the Judge, to cut him off in the midst of his days, that his children should be fatherless and his wife a widow. Not only so, but his children were to become vagabonds (wanderers like Cain, Genesis 4:12); none were to feed them or to show them

915

favour or mercy. His posterity was to be cut off; his family name blotted out of the annals of the nation of Israel.

Thus in the setting of the court these wicked and deceitful men who had spoken with lying tongues against him were found to be guilty of false witness, and that which they had sought to bring upon David they brought down on their own heads. So David cries:

"Because that he remembered not to shew mercy, but persecuted the poor and needy man, that he might even slay the broken in heart. As he loved cursing, so let it come unto him: as he delighted not in blessing, so let it be far from him. As he clothed himself with cursing like as with his garment, so let it come into his bowels like water, and like oil into his bones. Let it be unto him as the garment which covereth him, and for a girdle wherewith he is girded continually. Let this be the reward of mine adversaries from the LORD, and of them that speak evil against my soul." (verses 16-20)

Whoever these men were they had deliberately chosen this policy of cursing. Like oil and water, which should have stood for blessing, they had allowed this vitriolic spirit to permeate throughout their whole being (see Numbers 5:22). They had given it a home in their hearts and banished all thought of blessing. It had become such a habit of mind that it clung to them like a garment. And all this is spoken against the Lord's anointed, motivated by a hatred of the godly life he lived and an antagonism towards the revealed will of God which they saw as a threat to their worldly ambitions.

Judas Iscariot

It has become fashionable in recent times to reassess the character of Judas Iscariot; to suggest that he was not really the villain that he is portrayed to be in the New Testament. These attempts, however, are usually motivated by a wish to undermine the veracity of the Gospel records and, more often than not, are accompanied by a woeful lack of knowledge of what the scriptures really have to say about this man.

916

Surely the words of Peter in the first chapter of Acts give a definitive verdict on the character and actions of this man:

"For it is written in the book of Psalms, Let his habitation be desolate, and let no man dwell therein: and his bishoprick (AV margin, 'office or charge') let another take." (verse 20)

Peter brings together the words of two psalms (69:25 and 109:8), both of them imprecatory psalms which express in the most authoritative way God's final judgement on this man. Moreover if the argument we have developed be accepted, Psalm 109 gives us a remarkable insight into the motivation of this man. Whatever the initial attraction which drew him to the Lord Jesus Christ, it is evident that he became a bitter and disillusioned man. The words of the curse reveal his final conclusions about the Lord Jesus. He did not believe him to be the promised Messiah and he could not accept that he was the Son of God. Do the words of verse 14, "Let not the sin of his mother be blotted out" give us an insight into his changed conviction about the birth of the Lord Jesus? In his mind this man had betrayed him and he could imagine no other fate for him than that his name should be blotted out and that his memory should be cut off in the earth (verses 13,15). It is surely not without significance that Psalm 55, which also prophesies the relationship between Judas and the Lord Jesus (verses 12-14) should include: "The words of his mouth were smoother than butter, but war was in his heart: his words were softer than oil, yet were they drawn swords ... But thou, O God, shalt bring them down to the pit of destruction: bloody and deceitful men shall not live out half their days" (verses 21,23). Thus did God recompense Judas according to his words and his deeds.

PSALM 110

IT has been our experience in the study of the Psalms that scholarly writers can usually be relied upon to state the facts about both the Hebrew and Greek texts of the scriptures. There are, on occasions, variant readings of those texts and again they can usually be depended upon to point out what these are. Beyond that, of course, we must be prepared to use our own understanding of the word of God to determine the true meaning. It came therefore as a surprise when we came to consider Psalm 110 to discover that many ancient and modern commentators had misstated the facts about the opening words of this psalm: "The LORD said unto my Lord ..." The Lord who speaks is Yahweh, whereas David's Lord is 'adoni' which means basically 'to rule', hence a sovereign or a master. It is a term of honour and respect used over 190 times in the Old Testament to acknowledge the dignity of a person of superior status. It is always used of men and never of God. However, many writers mistakenly insist that the word is in fact 'adonai' which is, of course, a divine title that is used only of God and never of men. On this basis they proceed to teach the doctrine of the Trinity and we feel it to be important that readers should be aware of this incorrect use of scripture which will be found in many works of reference. *

Another feature of many orthodox writers is a strange reluctance to accept the Davidic authorship of the psalm, even though we have the authority of the Lord Jesus and the Apostle Peter to affirm it (see Mark 12:35-37; Acts 2:33-36). This arises very largely out of the embarrass-ment

---

* A detailed argument with many examples will be found in *The Doctrine of the Trinity: Christianity's Self-Inflicted Wound* by Anthony F. Buzzard and Charles F. Hunting (pages 47-58) (International Scholars Publications).

918

caused to them by the warrior priests of verse 3 and the slain resulting from the pouring forth of the wrath of God in verses 5 and 6. They do not accept our understanding of the second coming of the Lord Jesus or of the judgements of God preceding the establishment of God's kingdom. Their problem is that the psalm ascribes these events to David's "Lord" and the Lord Jesus Christ corroborated the current view of the Messianic significance of the psalm in his challenge to the Jews. They are unable to find any event in the reign of David on which to hang the words of the song, so they are driven to acknowledge that it is wholly predictive in its substance. While happy to use the opening words in an attempt to support their unscriptural views on the Godhead, they sometimes go to extreme lengths to disassociate the Lord Jesus from its content.

Historical Background

To an extent we share the view expressed above that the psalm is wholly predictive. Messianic psalms usually have a historical background from which the predictive element of the psalm springs. This means that all the detail of such a psalm does not necessarily refer to the Lord Jesus Christ and often it is the attitude of the writer that foreshadows his spirit in a typical way.

While we cannot relate the substance of this psalm to any specific events in the life of David, we believe that we can identify the time in David's life when he wrote it. In 2 Samuel 6 we have the record of how David brought the ark of the Lord to the tabernacle that he had prepared for it in Zion. In connection with this momentous event we are told that the king was girded with a linen ephod and that having offered burnt offerings and peace offerings he blessed the people in the name of the Lord of Hosts and gave them, both men and women, a cake of bread and a flagon of wine (verses 17-19). David played the part of a priest and not only so, but he re-enacted the actions of Melchizedek (Genesis 14:18,19). In other words, he showed a remarkable insight into the purpose of God and revealed an understanding of the truth that ultimately the one who should reign on Zion's throne on God's behalf should be both king and priest – this, remember, before God had revealed the details of the covenant that He

919

would make with him. The record of that covenant and of David's reaction to it is contained in the next chapter (2 Samuel 7). What is of particular interest, in considering the circumstances in which this psalm came to be written, is the manner in which David went into the tabernacle and sat before the Lord, presumably before the ark of the covenant (verses 18-29). There David meditated upon the wondrous things which God had spoken to him; he poured out before the Lord his heartfelt feelings of thankfulness and joy that He should have chosen him and promised such marvellous and amazing things that were to be accomplished in one who would be both son of David and Son of God (2 Samuel 7:12,14). The corresponding chapter in 1 Chronicles records that David said: "(Thou) hast regarded me according to the estate of a man of high degree, O LORD God" (17:17). Young's Literal Translation says, "(Thou) hast seen me as a type of the man who is on high". It was surely at this time, during this sequence of events, that the Lord gave this psalm to David. It is, as has been suggested, wholly predictive and it is given to us as a message received directly from God. The word rendered "said" means literally 'an oracle', and it is used exclusively in the Old Testament of words spoken by Him. It is used on hundreds of occasions in the phrase, "saith the LORD".

"Sit Thou at My Right Hand"

Psalm 110 is undoubtedly the most often quoted Old Testament scripture in the pages of the New Testament. One writer claims to have discovered over thirty such references. He does not list them and certainly we cannot find anywhere near that figure. We have, however, identified approximately twenty, the most obvious of which are listed here: Matthew 22:44; 26:64; Mark 12:36; 14:62; 16:19; Luke 20:42,43; Acts 2:34,35; 7:55; Romans 8:34; Ephesians 1:20; Colossians 3:1; Hebrews 1:3; 5:10, etc.; 8:1; 10:12; 12:2; 1 Peter 3:22.

In these opening words David acknowledged the superior status of the one of whom God would say, "I will be his father, and he shall be my son"; the one in whom he came to appreciate his kingdom would be established forever in a day when God would give him the nations for an inheritance and the uttermost parts of the earth for a possession. To sit at the right hand of God is to share the throne of God.

It was with these words that the Lord Jesus brought his public ministry to a close (Matthew 22:41-46; Mark 12:35-37; Luke 20:41-44). Having withstood their persistent questioning, much of it intended to trap him in his words, or to produce an answer that would give them cause to accuse him before the authorities, the Lord Jesus puts this one question to them, 'If Messiah be the Son of David, why does David address him as Lord?' In the answer to this question there was encapsulated everything that the Lord Jesus, during his ministry, had presented himself to be. If the truths expressed above regarding David's greater Son were properly assessed and applied to the Lord Jesus, there could only be one possible outcome. They would have been compelled to recognise him for everything that he claimed to be. Their confusion and embarrassment is well expressed in the words of the Gospel records: "No man was able to answer him a word". Each of the synoptic Gospels tell us, in this context, that from that day forth no man asked him any more questions The public ministry was over; the challenge had been made. It was for them to search their hearts and decide whether this man was indeed the Messiah. In his words the Lord Jesus gave them the most solemn warning. Although they might succeed in killing him, he would yet, by resurrection, sit at God's right hand, and a day would come when his enemies would be trampled under his feet.

The eminence of the Lord Jesus as next only to God his Father was established by this scripture. This status which he now enjoys is eternally his; it is in no way diminished by the fact that he is to return to the earth to establish the throne of David. The fact that he sits at God's right hand is to be understood as a token of the fact that he has won his victory over sin and death and in this respect his work of salvation has been accomplished successfully. He is, of course, for ever active on behalf of his brethren but in relation to the establishment of the throne of David, he sits, as it were, until that day when God will make his enemies his footstool.

The Lord Jesus at his defence before the high priest brought together the words of the psalm and the prophecy of Daniel (7:13,14): "Hereafter shall ye see the Son of man sitting on the right hand of power, and coming in the clouds of heaven" (Matthew 26:64). In that day the Lord shall send the rod of his strength out of Zion and he shall rule in the midst of his enemies (Psalm 110:2). Note that the rod is not a sceptre, but a rod of chastisement like that used by Moses to bring the plagues on Egypt. It is used to bring the nations into subjection that they might recognise his authority and sovereignty:

"Thou shalt break them with a rod of iron; thou shalt dash them in pieces like a potter's vessel. Be wise now therefore, O ye kings: be instructed, ye judges of the earth. Serve the LORD with fear, and rejoice with trembling." (Psalm 2:9-11)

"Thy People Shall be Willing"
It is not only his day of exaltation in the sight of the nations, but also of all those who through the ages have chosen to be associated with him:

"Thy people shall be willing in the day of thy power, in the beauties of holiness from the womb of the morning: thou hast the dew of thy youth."
(Psalm 110:3)

We are reminded of the manner in which the people of Israel, together with the governors, offered themselves willingly in the days of Barak and Deborah for the battle against Jabin and Sisera when God wrought a great victory (Judges 5:2,9). So now the king's people associated with him in the day of his power are "freewill offerings" (RV margin), or as the text means literally, 'willingnesses', the plural encompassing the spirit that pervades them all. In the days of their weakness they gave themselves as living sacrifices (Romans 12:1), but now in the magnificence of Spirit nature, with gladness of heart they wholeheartedly follow their king. The word translated "power" means literally 'army' (Strong). The *Cambridge Bible* says, "Thy people shall give themselves willingly in

922

the day of thy muster". In his work on *The Epistle to the Hebrews,* Brother John Carter has a quotation (source not indicated) which is most appropriate:

"Round him is gathered a host, at once priests and warriors, in holy vestments – a nation of warriors in arms, following so gladly that they are called 'willingnesses.' Language, vague in its magnificence, speaks of an eternal youth, fresh as the dew and vast and glorious as the illimitable dawn, from which it derives its origin. In brief and rapid touches there follows the subjugation of the head of a vast confederacy of different countries."   (Second edition, page 54)

They are described as clothed in "the beauties of holiness", or with the RV margin, "In holy attire ... thy youth are to thee as the dew". They were decked as with the holy garments for glory and beauty with which Aaron was adorned (Exodus 28:2). They are the children of the resurrection made strong with the strength of everlasting youth, who shall run and not grow weary and walk and not faint – from the womb of the dawn of that morning without clouds, numberless as the drops of dew "in the star-like splendour of holy spirit nature" (Brother John Thomas).

They are "'as dew from the LORD' (Micah 5:7) – countless, as the dew drops (2 Samuel 17:12), – (which) were born 'not of the will of man' (John 1:13), but by the will of 'The Father of Lights', who 'begat them by the word of Truth' (James 1:17,18)" (Kay, *The Psalms with Notes*).

The wonder of that resurrection morn is expressed beautifully by the prophet Isaiah:

"Thy dead men shall live, together with my dead body shall they arise. Awake and sing, ye that dwell in dust: for thy dew is as the dew of light (RV, margin), and the earth shall cast out the dead."   (26:19)

For a New Testament parallel to Psalm 110, see Revelation 19:11-16.

The Order of Melchizedek

"The LORD hath sworn, and will not repent, Thou art a priest for ever after the order of Melchizedek."

(Psalm 110:4)

We have already commented on the spiritual perception of David when he re-enacted the role of the king-priest Melchizedek. All that we know of the life of this man is contained in three verses in the Book of Genesis (14:18-20). It is truly remarkable that "the three verses in Genesis and the one in the Psalm provide the apostle with the evidence by which he establishes the temporariness and ineffectiveness of the Levitical priesthood, and also, by contrast, the character of the priesthood of Christ" (Brother John Carter, *The Epistle to the Hebrews* – page 66, 2nd Edition). We do not intend to deal at length with the use of Psalm 110 in the Epistle to the Hebrews or with the apostle's exposition of the priesthood of Melchizedek and in this connection we refer readers to Brother John Carter's work.

Enough to say that he is described as being without father and without mother (Hebrews 7:3) to emphasise the truth that his priesthood, unlike the Levitical order, did not depend upon natural descent. It was not passed on from father to son neither was it transmitted to a line of successors.

Could anything be more emphatic?

"The LORD hath sworn, and will not repent, Thou art a priest for ever after the order of Melchizedek."

(Psalm 110:4)

The king by divine decree is also a priest. Of course, the 'oath' did not make God's word more reliable, but God who cannot lie condescended to men to confirm His word in this way. Aaron was not inaugurated into the priesthood by an oath but he was called of God to his office (Hebrews 5:4). In other words, he was bidden of God to undertake this function. The Lord Jesus, however, was not so bidden but he was acknowledged and recognised as such by his intrinsic worth when he took upon himself the divine nature. See the contrast between the quotation from Psalm 110 and the words that follow regarding the days of

924

his flesh in Hebrews 5 (verses 6,7). So because he "continueth ever" he has "an unchangeable priesthood" (see also Hebrews 7:20-24).

The truth that the Lord's anointed should be both king and priest was, of course, always an integral part of the purpose of God both explicitly and implicitly. The promise to Abraham spoke of one who should possess the gates of his enemies and in whom all families of the earth should be blessed. That the blessing involved the forgiveness of sins, a priestly function, is made clear in both Old and New Testaments (see Psalm 32:1; Acts 3:26; Galatians 3:8).

It is also implicit in the Seventy Weeks Prophecy of Daniel 9: Messiah the Prince is cut off that he might make reconciliation for iniquity. Zechariah speaks of the man whose name is the Branch who shall sit and rule upon his throne and who shall be a priest upon his throne (6:12,13), and it is our hope that we shall be numbered amongst that glorious company of the redeemed who will be made kings and priests unto God (Revelation 5:9,10).

The Final Conflict

Characteristic of many psalms, there is a dramatic change of scene as the king goes forth to war and the Lord (Adonai) at his right hand is depicted as coming down to assist and support him in the conflict. In the previous psalm (109), the wish of his enemies was that an adversary should stand at his right hand to accuse him (verse 6). God, however, had vindicated His servant by standing at his right hand to deliver him (verse 31). So now, as Messiah had shared His throne, the Lord stands again at his right hand for the approaching warfare, for they are one in mind and purpose. The outcome is certain; the tenses of the verbs "show that it is to be regarded, according to a common Hebrew idiom, as a 'prophetic' perfect. The victory is still future, but the Psalmist regards it as already won" (verses 5,6, *Cambridge Bible*).

The AV translation of verse 6 obscures the fact that the word rendered "heads" is not plural but singular (see RV) and we could amend the text to read, 'He shall wound the head ...' The reference to Genesis 3:15 and the fatal blow

925

to the head of the serpent is clear. Thus the corporate power of sin manifested in this vast confederacy of nations is destroyed.

In the last verse of the psalm there is yet another abrupt change of theme. "He shall drink of the brook in the way: therefore shall he lift up the head" (verse 7). Note that the word translated "brook" means literally 'the winter torrent' and it reminds us of the suffering of the Lord Jesus when he crossed the Brook Kidron to the Garden of Gethsemane. It is a reference to the days of his flesh when he offered up prayers and supplications with strong crying and tears to Him that was able to save him from death. Though he was a Son, he learned obedience by the things that he suffered. He shared our human experiences and conquered sin in that arena in which in all others it reigned supreme. It was this victory that qualified him to be a priest forever after the order of Melchizedek (Hebrews 5:6-10).

A final word regarding this psalm. In his book *Reflections on the Psalms,* C. S. Lewis points out that the psalm is one of those appointed in *The Prayer Book* for Christmas Day and finds in this fact an anomaly. He comments, "The note is not 'Peace and goodwill' but 'Beware He's coming'" (page 122, 1958 Edition). The writer cannot be described as 'a babe or suckling', yet he demonstrates how sometimes even men learned in the wisdom of this world can perceive the obvious while yet choosing to ignore the significance of the words, not only for themselves but for the world at large.

PSALMS 111 & 112

PSALM 111 is the first of a group (111-118) that begin with the words "Praise the LORD" (Hallelujah). The last six of this sequence constitute what the Talmud refers to as "the Hallel", or sometimes "the Egyptian Hallel", which was sung at the great festivals of the Jewish year. We comment on these in our consideration of Psalm 113.

It has been suggested that Psalms 111 and 112 might have been sung as an introduction to the Hallel, but whether or not this is so there can be no doubt that there is a very close connection between the two psalms. They are both alphabetical psalms, each consisting of twenty-two lines and in both the order of the Hebrew alphabet is strictly preserved. This is not the case with other alphabetical psalms such as Psalms 27, 34 and 37, for instance. So exactly does the structure of the two psalms correspond that in each, the first eight verses consist of two lines each and the last two verses of three lines each (Perowne, *Psalms*, Volume 2).

The two psalms, however, do not only correspond to each other in structure but also in thought and in language. An interesting and instructive exercise is to set them in parallel columns and to compare the language used. It will be found that there is a striking similarity in the phraseology used as verse is contrasted with verse. By way of illustration compare the following:

111:10 with 112:1 ("feareth the LORD")

111:2 with 112:1 ("delighteth")

111:3 with 112:3,9 ("righteousness endureth")

111:4 with 112:4 ("gracious and full of compassion")

111:4 with 112:6 ("remembrance")

111:7,8 with 112:7,8 (God's character reflected in the godly)

927

There is, however a difference in emphasis between the two psalms, for whereas Psalm 111 speaks of the work of God and extols His majesty and excellence, Psalm 112 tells of the effect of those qualities in the life of a godly man. Interestingly the godly of Psalm 112 is singular and not plural, and although the lessons and blessings described in it are no doubt relevant to the righteous generally, we can only conclude that it is referring primarily to the Lord Jesus Christ.

Historical Background

Writers generally suggest that it is not possible to recognise either the author or the historical setting for these psalms. The comment in the *Speaker's Commentary* is typical: "The contents are of so general a nature that they give no clue to the author, or to their date" (page 430, 1878 Edition).

However, some verbal links between Psalms 111, 112 and 2 Chronicles 30 noted by Kay (*The Psalms with Notes*), suggest that there is a case to be made for linking both psalms with Hezekiah's Passover. At first sight the link appears to be somewhat tenuous, but the fact that most of the connections fall within the space of five verses gives added weight to the association between the passages. The verses from Chronicles are reproduced below with the relevant Hebrew equivalents in the Psalms indicated by italics:

"But Hezekiah prayed for them, saying, The good LORD pardon every one *that prepareth his heart* (*his heart is fixed* – 112:7) *to seek* (*sought out* – 111:2) God, the LORD God of his fathers, though he be not cleansed according to the purification of the sanctuary. And the LORD hearkened to Hezekiah, and healed the people. And the children of Israel that were present at Jerusalem kept the feast of unleavened bread ... with great *gladness:* and the Levites and the priests *praised the LORD* (*Praise the LORD* – 111:1,10; 112:1) day by day, singing with loud instruments unto the LORD. And Hezekiah spake comfortably unto all the Levites that taught *the good knowledge* (*a good understanding* – 111:10) of the LORD: and they did eat throughout the feast seven days, offering peace offerings, and making confession to the LORD God of their fathers. And the whole assembly took counsel to keep other seven days: and they kept other seven days with *gladness* (note the emphasis on *gladness* and *singing* – compare 112:1, *Blessed – the happiness*)". (2 Chronicles 30:18-23)

Note also, "The LORD your GOD is gracious and merciful" (2 Chronicles 30:9) compared with Psalms 111:4 and 112:4; and "the Levites arose and *blessed* the people" (30:27) with Psalm 112:2 (*blessed*).

If, however, these verbal links are not thought to be substantial enough to establish the link with Hezekiah's Passover, the case is strengthened significantly by observing that the words of Psalm 111:4 are a direct reference to the record of the Passover in the Book of Exodus. Literally, 'He hath made a memorial for his wonderful works' (*Cambridge Bible*; see Exodus 12:14; 13:9).

The reference, however, encompasses not only the Passover but also the name of God of which He said when He revealed Himself to Moses, "this is my name for ever, and this is my memorial unto all generations" (Exodus 3:15). The deliverance from Egypt including the Passover was, of course, a manifestation of that name and all that it represented (see also Psalm 135:13).

Again, there is clear reference in both psalms to the words of the prophet Isaiah (chapter 26) which reflect the historical circumstances of Hezekiah's reign: "Thou wilt keep him in perfect peace, whose mind is stayed on thee: because he trusteth in thee" (verse 3). The phrase "stayed upon thee" occurs in both psalms translated as "stand fast" (Psalm 111:8) and "established" (Psalm 112:8).

Note also that the references to "His seed" and "the generation of the upright" (112:2) echo the words of Isaiah 53, generally accepted as having as its background the sickness of Hezekiah: "Who shall declare his generation?" (verse 8), and "He shall see his seed" (verse 10).

Another Characteristic

It should not be overlooked that while there is no historical connection, it does appear that in the

929

compilation of the Psalms there was purpose in including the eight Hallelujah psalms immediately after Psalm 110. The key verse there is, "Thou art a priest for ever after the order of Melchizedek" (verse 4), and the phrase "for ever" runs like a golden thread through this group of psalms (see 111:3,5,8-10; 112:6; 113:2; 115:18; 117:2; 118:1-4,29). In Psalm 111 it is to emphasise the unchanging nature of God, the steadfastness of His purpose and the abiding faithfulness of His word. In Psalm 112 it speaks of the blessing of the righteous man who puts his trust in God.

It has been suggested, on the basis of language in Isaiah's prophecy, that Hezekiah at this time, like David before him, in faith adopted the function of a king-priest, thus further confirming the link with Psalm 110. Attractive as the idea might be there is no evidence in the historical record to support it.

Psalm 111

A feature of Psalm 111 is the emphasis upon the works of God (see verses 2-4,6,7). The works of the Lord are the grounds of the Psalmist's outpouring of praise:

"I will praise the LORD with my whole heart, in the assembly of the upright, and in the congregation."

(verse 1)

It was with singleness of purpose that the writer, from the very depths of his being, expressed his thanks for all the wonderful works whereby God had blessed His people and made Himself known in their midst. The words rendered "assembly" and "congregation" present an interesting contrast. The first conveys the idea of a company of people in close deliberation. Strong says, "to sit down together, to settle, to discuss". It suggests an intimacy of association and it is the upright who share this blessing together (see also Malachi 3:16,17). The word "congregation" however speaks of the general assembly of the people as they gathered together for worship. It is as though the Psalmist would have us know that both in private with those who shared his spiritual aspirations and in public with the multitude gathered together, his heart ever overflowed with praise and thankfulness.

In these works of God his heart rejoiced, "for they are sought out of all them that have pleasure therein" (verse 2). Of the words translated "sought" and "pleasure" the *Speaker's Commentary* says, "Searched into and studied and thus fully understood to be inimitably great", and "delightful or fully satisfying, precious, incomparable, in the judgement of those who best understand them" (see Psalm 119:45,94,155).

The emphasis upon the works of God in this psalm, given the association with the passover suggested above, would appear to be primarily, but not exclusively, a reference to the deliverance from Egypt and the manifestation of God's power and might at that time. So there is an emphasis also upon the name of God, for by those acts His name was made known, the characteristics of His moral excellence demonstrated. Thus it was that in extolling the works of God at the time of the Exodus that the Levites in the days of Nehemiah cried: "So didst thou get thee a name, as it is this day" (Nehemiah 9:10; see also Exodus 14:4,17,18). Thus His righteousness endures forever and He is gracious and full of compassion; all His works are verity and judgement and are done in truth and uprightness (Psalm 111:3,4,7,8; see Exodus 34:6,7).

The mercy and compassion of God was shown in the manner in which He had given meat to His people and kept His covenant in remembrance. He had given His people the heritage of the nations in dispossessing the Canaanites and bringing them into the land He had promised to their father Abraham (Psalm 111:5,6).

The word translated "meat" means literally 'prey' and some have suggested that it has only been used to preserve the alphabetical structure of the psalm. Surely there is more to the word than this? The children of Israel faced with a barren waste murmured against Moses and Aaron, comparing the fleshpots of Egypt with the lack of provision to be found in this wilderness. There was little here to provide prey for the hunter that they might eat.

The Lord's response was first to send the quails and then to provide the manna:

931

"At even ye shall eat flesh, and in the morning ye shall be filled with bread; and ye shall know that I am the LORD your God." (Exodus 16:12)

The quails demonstrated that God was able to provide flesh in abundance, but this was not the way in which they should be fed. The manna told them that there would be no need to concern themselves with hunting for food. Like the prey they might have sought, God would provide day by day all that they required.

Perhaps there is a reflection of these thoughts in Psalm 34, emphasising also that God's provision for His people is a continuing experience:

"O fear the LORD, ye his saints: for there is no want to them that fear him. The young lions do lack, and suffer hunger: but they that seek the LORD shall not want any good thing." (verses 9,10)

Note that the word rendered "meat" in Psalm 111 is specifically related to the prey of lions in Nahum (2:11,12).

The deliverance from Egypt was a token to God's people that His covenant was sure and would never be forgotten. His promise to Abraham was always held in remembrance (see Exodus 2:24; 6:5). Equally, the fact that He had brought them into this land in fulfilment of His word was an assurance that ultimately they would possess the land for ever. By all His works on behalf of His people He had revealed Himself as a God awesome in His holiness and terrible in His majesty – a God to be feared (Psalm 111:9).

What then should be the reaction of His people in the light of their understanding of all that the name of their God conveyed?

"The fear of the LORD is the beginning of wisdom: a good understanding have all they that do his commandments: his praise endureth for ever."
(verse 10)

Wisdom is the application in life of the knowledge of God gained from His word. He has revealed Himself as a God to be feared. Wisdom then begins with the fear of the Lord, and in the keeping of His commandments an experiential knowledge is gained of His character. "Insight is the reward of obedience" (*Cambridge Bible*). In the words of scripture:

"If any man will to do his will, he shall know of the doctrine, whether it be of God, or whether I speak of myself."   (John 7:17)

God's praise stands forever and all those attributes of His character, revealed in His name, are worthy of praise and must be reflected in the lives of His servants. They must "shew forth the praises of him who hath called (them) out of darkness into his marvellous light" (1 Peter 2:9). It is these qualities, reflected in the life of the godly, that are the subject of the psalm that follows.

Psalm 112

As already intimated, this song speaks of the righteous in the singular, pointing unmistakably to the Lord Jesus Christ in whom all these qualities are seen to perfection. That this is indeed the case is reinforced by the manner in which the words of Psalm 111 (verse 3) are repeated twice in this psalm: "His righteousness endureth for ever" (verses 3,9) – a concept that is true of the 'King of Righteousness' alone in its primary significance and of those who follow him only in a derivative sense (see Psalm 24:5). The opening and closing words of this psalm have a distinct similarity with the opening and concluding words of Psalm 1:

Psalm 112	Psalm 1
"Blessed is the man that feareth the LORD, that delighteth greatly in his commandments" (verse 1).	"Blessed is the man that walketh not in the counsel of the ungodly ... but his delight is in the law of the LORD" (verses 1,2).
"The desire of the wicked shall perish" (verse 10).	"The way of the ungodly shall perish" (verse 6).

Psalm 1 is of course another psalm that speaks of "the man" who was the perfection of manhood, and it is appropriate that Psalm 112 should reproduce the language of that song in this way. Psalm 112 also refers to the material prosperity of the righteous man (see verse 3). However, the context speaks so powerfully of spiritual blessings that one cannot escape the conclusion that we

933

are intended to understand these words as referring to the true riches that all men of God seek to acquire. Not withstanding this fact, it might still remain true that the description of "wealth and riches (being) in his house" is intended to convey also the reality of the blessings of the kingdom age, of which these material things are a token.

The connection between this and the preceding psalm is immediately apparent, for the first verse of this psalm takes up the thought of the last verse of Psalm 111 and expands and develops its meaning. As the fear of the Lord is the beginning of wisdom, so the man who fears God knows a happiness and contentment beyond anything that the material things of life can offer. "Blessed (happy) is the man that feareth the LORD, that delighteth greatly in his commandments" (verse 1).

The words are especially true of the Lord Jesus Christ for he loved righteousness and hated iniquity (Psalm 45:7). This was one of the factors that enabled him to conquer sin; this was a quality that he inherited from his Father that made him different from all other men. It was because he delighted in His commandments that, although tempted like all men, he was without sin. Because of his victory, "His seed shall be mighty upon earth: the generation of the upright shall be blessed" (verse 2). The words "seed" and "generation" gather together a host of allusions to the redeemed, the spiritual progeny of the Lord Jesus (Psalms 22:30; 24:6, RV; Isaiah 53:8,10; Galatians 3:29; etc.).

There is also a contrast with Nimrod who began to be a "mighty" (same word) one in the earth (Genesis 10:8). He was the founder of Babel, ever the symbol of human arrogance and enmity towards God. As the great and mighty of this world have sought to build their empires by cruelty and violence, so God will ultimately vest all power and authority in those who fear Him and delight in His commandments. This contrast between the wicked and the godly is a theme to which the Psalmist returns at the conclusion of his song (verses 9,10).

Herein is the hope of the righteous, for "Unto the upright there ariseth light in the darkness" (verse 4). It is suggested that properly the idea of the Hebrew is that God

rises as a light to illuminate the darkness that threatens
to envelop His servants. The darkness of this world with
its constant reminders of human wickedness will finally
be dispersed when unto those who fear God's name "the
Sun of righteousness arise(s) with healing in his wings"
(Malachi 4:2).

There is also a connection with Isaiah's prophecy
(Chapter 58) where the prophet seeks to impress upon the
people of Judah the real significance of the Day of
Atonement and the Year of Jubilee (see verses 3-5). He
cries in verse 6:

"Is not this the fast that I have chosen? to loose the
bands of wickedness, to undo the heavy burdens, and to
let the oppressed go free, and that ye break every yoke?
Is it not to deal thy bread to the hungry, and that thou
bring the poor that are cast out to thy house? when thou
seest the naked, that thou cover him; and that thou hide
not thyself from thine own flesh?"

To the man that does these things God says:

"Then shall thy light break forth as the morning ...
and if thou draw out thy soul to the hungry, and satisfy
the afflicted soul; then shall thy light rise in obscurity,
and thy darkness be as the noonday."   (verses 8,10)

These thoughts are reflected in our psalm:

"A good man sheweth favour, and lendeth." (verse 5)

"He hath dispersed, he hath given to the poor."

(verse 9)

Ultimately He who is light will shine forth to pierce the
darkness of this world, but even now when darkness
threatens God's light will penetrate the clouds that would
obscure our way and illuminates our pathway, for He is
"gracious and full of compassion".

Because the "good man" manages his affairs with
judgement (verse 5), always being careful that in his walk
he does no harm and causes no offence to others, he lives
with a quiet assurance that God will bless him in all his
ways. His trust in God is steadfast, his heart fixed.
Because of this he knows no fear of what men might seek
to do or of the evil that they might speak against him
(verses 7,8). He is able to maintain this calm and quiet

935

spirit, with which he faces all life's vicissitudes, for he has also an absolute confidence in his eternal security. He will not be moved for ever for he is remembered of God (verse 6). The world and all that it represents is his enemy and it is doomed (verse 8). God will exalt the godly and honour him in that day when he shall receive the gift of righteousness from the God of his salvation (verse 9).

In that day the wicked shall be filled with a grievous rage at the loss of everything that they held dear. They will behold the exaltation of the righteous and, powerless to challenge the might of God, they will melt away and perish (verse 10).

The Apostle Paul goes to the very heart of the psalm when he quotes it in his Second Epistle to Corinth:

"And God is able to make all grace abound toward you; that ye, always having all sufficiency in all things, may abound to every good work: (as it is written, He hath dispersed abroad; he hath given to the poor: his righteousness remaineth for ever)."

(2 Corinthians 9:8,9)

PSALM 113

AS intimated (see Psalm 111), Psalms 113-118 constitute what, according to ancient Jewish tradition, was known as the 'The Hallel' or sometimes 'The Egyptian Hallel'. It was sung at the three great feasts, at the Feast of Dedication and at the new moons. Interest is usually focussed on the Feast of Passover because of its possible connection with the 'Last Supper'. Of this feast Delitzsch (quoted or referred to by most commentators) wrote:

"In the domestic celebration of the Passover night, the 'Hallel' is divided into two parts; the one half, Psalms 113 and 114, being sung before the repast, before the emptying of the second festal cup; and the other half, Psalms 115-118, after the repast, after the filling of the fourth cup, to which the 'having sung an hymn' in Matthew 26:30; Mark 14:26 ... may refer."

Apparently there were four cups of wine drunk at intervals during the feast and the third of these, known as 'The Cup of Blessing', is suggested as that referred to by the Apostle Paul (1 Corinthians 10:16). While there are undoubted connections between these psalms and that 'dark betrayal night', it has to be said that there has been fierce debate over the question of whether the Lord Jesus partook of the Jewish Passover meal and we do not feel it appropriate to enter into that controversy in our study of the psalms themselves.

Historical Background
We feel that the content of these six psalms is sufficient of itself to convince any unbiased reader that they belong to the life and times of King Hezekiah. Whether any or all were written by that godly man or by someone associated with him is a different question, and that may become

apparent as we study the substance of the psalms. As we shall see there is a close connection between Psalms 113 and 114 and this is almost certainly why they were sung together. Psalm 113 speaks of the love and condescension of God and Psalm 114 of the most striking and wonderful example of it in the deliverance from Egypt. These reflections upon the lovingkindness of God and His power to save must have been a source of great comfort to Hezekiah, and the faithful remnant of Judah, at the time of the Assyrian invasion and in the following spiritual revival.

In the general liturgical use of the Psalms, however, apart from the singing of the 'Hallel', there is evidence that Psalm 114 was also sung in association with Psalm 115.

Structure

It should be remembered that the salvation from the Assyrian threat was in fact a Passover deliverance. Hence the close connection between this psalm and those that follow with the celebration of that feast:

"As birds flying, so will the LORD of hosts defend Jerusalem; defending also he will deliver it; and passing over he will preserve it."   (Isaiah 31:5)

The psalm falls into three sections or stanzas:

1. An exhortation to offer constant and unceasing praise (verses 1-3);
2. A description of Yahweh's glory (verses 4-6);
3. Instances of His providence and condescension (verses 7-9).

Call to Praise and Worship

The words "praise" and "name" dominate the first three verses:

"Praise ye the LORD. Praise, O ye servants of the LORD, praise the name of the LORD. Blessed be the name of the LORD from this time forth and for evermore. From the rising of the sun unto the going down of the same the LORD's name is to be praised."

The call to the servants of the Lord is a reminder that what Israel was intended to be nationally (see Isaiah

938

41:8,9), each member of the nation was to be individually. They were the bondservants of the Most High, dedicated to His service. They are called to praise Yahweh's name and the thrice repeated command to do so gives an added emphasis to the words and stresses the importance of the phrase. God's name is a compendium of all that He is. It is a gathering together of all those qualities, both physical and moral, by which He has made Himself known. It is to be the object of His servants' praise because it is associated with His works; all those wondrous deeds that He has performed on their behalf. It was their privilege; for no other people could claim such a benefit or sound forth His praises as they could:

"For God will save Zion, and will build the cities of Judah: that they may dwell there, and have it in possession. The seed also of his servants shall inherit it: and they that love his name shall dwell therein."

(Psalm 69:35,36)

One of the great truths that God's servants need to learn is that each time there is a manifestation of His power in delivering His people, it is a token to them of the ultimate victory that will be achieved when His purpose is consummated in the earth. In that day all those who through the ages have put their trust in Him will know the everlasting joy that He has promised. So it was that those who had come to know the salvation of God not only sang forth the praises of His name at that time, but also looked forward to that day when His praise should be sung for evermore (verse 2).

This must surely have been the experience of Hezekiah and his contemporaries when God saved them from Sennacherib's host. The historical record tells us that following this deliverance, "Many brought gifts unto the LORD to Jerusalem, and presents to Hezekiah king of Judah: so that he was magnified in the sight of all nations from thenceforth" (2 Chronicles 32:23).

Once again the events of Hezekiah's days foreshadowed the final victory when the Lord Jesus enthroned in Zion will be honoured by all nations, and this truth is reflected in the words of the psalm, for: "From the rising of the sun unto the going down of the same the LORD's name is to be praised" (verse 3). Similar language was used by the Lord Jesus when he healed the Roman centurion's servant:

> "And I say unto you, That many shall come from the east and west, and shall sit down with Abraham, and Isaac, and Jacob, in the kingdom of heaven."
>
> (Matthew 8:11)
> (see also Psalm 102:15-22; Isaiah 59:19; Malachi 1:11)

Yahweh's Glory

He is worthy to be praised for:

> "The LORD is high above all nations, and his glory above the heavens. Who is like unto the LORD our God, who dwelleth on high, who humbleth himself to behold the things that are in heaven, and in the earth!"
>
> (Psalm 113:4-6)

Thus is described the greatness and condescension of Israel's God. He sits enthroned on high; higher than the heavens themselves, for "in respect of God all created things are low, whether in earth or in heaven" (quoted by Kay, *Psalms with Notes*).

Yet although He is so high and so holy He condescends to men who are of low estate:

> "For thus saith the high and lofty One that inhabiteth eternity, whose name is Holy; I dwell in the high and holy place, with him also that is of a contrite and humble spirit, to revive the spirit of the humble, and to revive the heart of the contrite ones."
>
> (Isaiah 57:15)

Literally, the Hebrew says that "He stoops to regard" (verse 6). It is a great paradox that if we were to seek to walk with 'the great and the good' of this world then we would have to exalt ourselves – raise ourselves up (in human terms) to be associated with them in the honour and dignity that they imagine they deserve. Yet to walk with the Most High, who has humbled Himself to deliver us from the power of sin and death and indeed to dwell with those who are of a humble and contrite spirit, he asks us to humble ourselves that we might walk with our God (Micah 6:8, AV margin; see also Exodus 15:11; Deuteronomy 3:24; Psalm 138:6).

God's Providence and Condescension

The first three lines of this last section of the psalm (verses 7-9) are taken almost verbatim from the song of Hannah (1 Samuel 2:8) and have been described as a bridge between that song and the song of Mary (Luke 1:46-55). That Mary based her song (known generally as the 'Magnificat') upon Hannah's is clear from a comparison between the two.

Song of Hannah	Song of Mary
"My heart rejoiceth in the LORD ... because I rejoice in thy salvation" (1 Samuel 2:1).	"My spirit hath rejoiced in God my Saviour" (Luke 1:47).
"There is none holy as the LORD" (verse 2).	"... and holy is his name" (verse 49).
"They that were full have hired out themselves for bread; and they that were hungry ceased" (verse 5).	"He hath filled the hungry with good things; and the rich hath he sent empty away" (verse 53).
"The LORD maketh poor, and maketh rich: he bringeth low, and lifteth up. He raiseth up the poor out of the dust, and lifteth up the beggar from the dunghill" (verses 7,8).	"He hath put down the mighty from their seats, and exalted them of low degree" (verse 52).

Hannah, a barren woman, in her desire for a child besought God to hear her prayer. He granted her request and Samuel was born. His name is commonly understood to mean, 'asked of God'. It has been suggested, however, that his name is more literally Shemuel, meaning 'name of God' or 'son of God' in the sense that he was given to this barren woman by the direct intervention of God. It is difficult to be certain of the precise definition of the name, but the latter suggestion has a fascination about it when we reflect upon Mary's use of Hannah's song, following the angel's declaration that the holy thing to be born of her should be called the Son of God (Luke 1:35).

There was, of course, a great difference between the two births for although Samuel was given of God through the natural processes of procreation, the Lord Jesus was born as a result of the power of the Holy Spirit overshadowing Mary.

In these facts is to be found the sense in which the words of Psalm 113 act as a bridge between the two songs. The words of the psalm quoted from Hannah's song are:

"He raiseth up the poor out of the dust, and lifteth the needy out of the dunghill; that he may set him with princes, even with the princes of his people." (verses 7,8)

To "sit in the dust" (Isaiah 47:1) or on a dunghill (Lamentations 4:5) are metaphors for extreme degradation and misery (see Job 2:8). The description is of one who because of some dreadful malady has been cast out of human society. He would sit in his wretchedness, not allowed to enter into the company or sit in the presence of his fellows.

Yet to those who experience such despair, God says that He will lift them up that they might dwell with princes. He will elevate them to the very highest rank, for they will sit not just with the princes of the earth but with the princes of His people.

A psalm associated with Hezekiah's reign and the events subsequent to the destruction of Sennacherib's host has an appropriate comment in understanding the words of Psalm 113:

"God reigneth over the nations. God sitteth upon his holy throne. The princes of the peoples are gathered together unto the people of the God of Abraham."

(Psalm 47:8,9, RV, with margin)

We have already referred to the manner in which, after the destruction of the Assyrians, Hezekiah was magnified in the eyes of the nations who brought presents to him and gifts for the Lord to Jerusalem (2 Chronicles 32:23). What is not always appreciated, however, is that the spiritual reformation in Judah concurrent with these events was also accompanied by an infusion of Gentile peoples attracted to the worship of the God of Israel.

Psalm 87 speaks of these who demonstrated their desire to be joined to the people of the God of Abraham. They are described as "born in" Zion (verses 5,6) and the Psalmist declares that, "The LORD shall count, when he writeth up the people, that this man was born there" (verse 6).

942

Isaiah (56:1-8) speaks of these proselytes to the Hope of Israel as "the son of the stranger, that hath joined himself to the LORD". They are described as eunuchs and encouraged not to speak of themselves as "a dry tree", possibly because they would have no natural inheritance in Israel. Nevertheless they were not to be discouraged because they had taken hold of God's covenant:

"Unto them will I give in mine house and within my walls a place and a name better than of sons and of daughters: I will give them an everlasting name, that shall not be cut off." (verse 5)

The Lord would bring them to His holy mountain, to His house that would be called a house of prayer for all nations, and there they would be joined to the outcasts of Israel whom God had regathered from the nations. It has a wonderful future fulfilment in the day of the Lord Jesus, but also an incipient fulfilment in those Gentiles who embraced the worship of Israel's God in the days of Hezekiah.

It is the prophet Isaiah again who, using the imagery of a barren woman, describes this spiritual rebirth of both Jew and Gentile:

"Sing, O barren, thou that didst not bear; break forth into singing, and cry aloud, thou that didst not travail with child: for more are the children of the desolate than the children of the married wife, saith the LORD." (54:1)

These words are quoted by the Apostle Paul in his allegory regarding the two covenants. He contrasts those born after the flesh (the married wife) with those born after the Spirit (the barren woman), and speaks of the seed of the desolate as "the children of promise". His assurance is, "Jerusalem which above is free, which is the mother of us all" (Galatians 4:22-31).

So the Psalmist could cry against the background of these momentous events in the days of Hezekiah:

"He maketh the barren woman to keep house, and to be a joyful mother of children." (Psalm 113:9)

The picture is of a barren woman becoming the mother of children – a childless wife made glad by the gift of a

943

family. The reference to a house is surely to be understood in the sense that God made houses for the midwives in Egypt (Exodus 1:21) and established a house for David (2 Samuel 7:11,21).

By general consent, the "Praise ye the LORD" at the conclusion of this psalm belongs to Psalm 114.

PSALM 114

THIS has been described "as the most beautiful of all the Psalms which touch on the early history of Israel" (Perowne, *Psalms* Volume 2, page 325). Certainly the graphic and dramatic power of the language is breathtaking in its force. The psalm is divided into four stanzas of two verses each:

1. The Exodus itself which was the foundation of the nation of Israel.
2. The miracles that marked their progress to the land of promise.
3. All nature trembles before the majesty and power of God.
4. Recognition that God's might is still available for the salvation of His people.

It is emphasised by many writers that God is not mentioned until verse 7 of the psalm and literary factors are introduced to explain the omission. However, in doing this they are overlooking the very close connection that exists between this psalm and that which precedes it. Psalm 113 has, in a most emphatic way, described the mercy and condescension of God and Psalm 114 is a continuation of that theme seen now in the most marvellous demonstration of His power at the time of the Exodus. That God is active on behalf of His people is implied throughout the first six verses of the psalm, but the introduction of one of His titles and the emphasis upon His presence in verses 7 and 8 bring the theme of the song to a dramatic conclusion.

Verses 1 and 2

"When Israel went out of Egypt, the house of Jacob from a people of strange language; Judah was his sanctuary, and Israel his dominion."

The Exodus was the occasion of the birth of the nation of Israel. It was particularly appropriate therefore that God's actions at that time should be recalled now at the time of another Passover deliverance and the birth of a new generation of faithful people, both Jews and Gentiles. The use of the name "Jacob" and the combination of both "Israel" and "Judah" in this passage is significant, for the historical record tells that while some of the Northern Kingdom mocked Hezekiah's invitation to keep the Passover at Jerusalem, there were others of Ephraim, Manasseh, Issachar, Zebulun and Asher who humbled themselves and came to Jerusalem (2 Chronicles 30:10,11,18).

The use of the word "house" also provides a link with the last verse of Psalm 113, establishing the birth of the new generation with the barren woman of that psalm.

Israel were delivered from a people of strange language for they did not understand the tongue of the Egyptians. (see Genesis 42:23). Difference of language emphasises also difference of race and culture. This was particularly true of conquered nations who could not understand the speech of their oppressors (see Deuteronomy 28:49; Isaiah 33:19).

There is a lesson here for those who seek to follow the Lord Jesus Christ, for the world speaks a different language. It has different values and standards, and true believers will find themselves unable to empathise with its ideals and principles which are contrary to the ethical and moral teaching of the Lord Jesus. They must ever be pilgrims and strangers as they look for that city that has foundations to which their citizenship belongs.

Judah was His sanctuary and the fact that the verb is feminine is an indication that it is the land of Judah that is referred to and not the people (Kay, *Psalms with Notes*). The purpose of God's deliverance of His people was that He might dwell among them and exercise dominion over them. He sanctified them that they might be unto Him a kingdom of priests and an holy nation (Exodus 19:5,6). The land of promise itself was to be a sanctuary for, "Thou shalt bring them in, and plant them in the mountain of thine inheritance, in the place, O LORD, which thou hast made for thee to dwell in, in the Sanctuary, O Lord, which thy hands have established". The next words establish the source of the Psalmist's thought: "The LORD shall reign for ever and ever" (Exodus 15:17,18).

Balaam, brought to curse Israel, could only speak the words of God's command:

"The LORD his God is with him, and the shout of a king is among them. God brought them out of Egypt; he hath as it were the strength of an unicorn."

(Numbers 23:21,22)

Verses 3 and 4

"The sea saw it, and fled: Jordan was driven back. The mountains skipped like rams, and the little hills like lambs."

Before the power of One who was mightier than they, the waters of the sea and the river were driven back to make a pathway for His people. The crossing of the Red Sea and the parting of the Jordan encompassed their wilderness journey – the beginning and the end of their pilgrimage to the land of promise. In vivid and dramatic poetic language the sea and the river are personified.

We do not always appreciate what an awesome and frightening experience it must have been when God came down and was manifested in all His majesty at Sinai. Exodus describes the thunders and lightnings and the thick cloud that covered the mountain (19:16). These phenomena were accompanied by an earthquake, for "the LORD descended upon it in fire: and the smoke thereof ascended as the smoke of a furnace, and the whole mount quaked greatly" (verse 18).

The Psalmist describes it in graphic fashion: "The earth shook, the heavens also dropped at the presence of God: even Sinai itself was moved at the presence of God, the God of Israel" (68:8). This convulsion of nature, as the very hills and mountains bowed to the will of their Creator, is likened to the leaping of rams and the skipping of lambs.

Verses 5 and 6

"What ailed thee, O thou sea, that thou fleddest? thou Jordan, that thou wast driven back? ye mountains,

947

that ye skipped like rams; and ye little hills, like
lambs?"

While there is a repetition of the language of verses 3 and
4, it is expressed now in the form of a challenge. What
power had they before the glory of Him who was the
Creator of all things? The Authorised Version misses the
force of the Hebrew, for the verbs are now all in the
present tense and it is as if those ancient waters and hills
were asked to give an account of themselves – to explain,
if it were possible, why "at thy rebuke they fled; at the
voice of thy thunder they hasted away" (Psalm 104:7).

Verses 7 and 8

"Tremble, thou earth, at the presence of the Lord, at
the presence of the God of Jacob; which turned the rock
into a standing water, the flint into a fountain of
waters."

Here is emphasised explicitly what before was only
implicit in the text. It was the Lord (*Adon*) before whose
presence the waters had parted and the mountains
trembled. The word translated "tremble" is particularly
related to the pangs of birth and its use is most
appropriate in this context. The Exodus and all those
events associated with it were the birth pangs of the
Children of Israel. A nation was born, as it were 'in a day',
and now in the days of Hezekiah there had been another
new birth in the spiritual revival of Judah and Israel and
those Gentiles who had joined themselves to the God of
Jacob. The God who at Horeb had turned the rock into
pools of water (Exodus 17:6), and at Kadesh had brought
forth fountains out of the flinty rock (Numbers 20:8-11;
Deuteronomy 8:15), was still able to provide life-giving
water to those who looked to Him in faith. Once again we
have a miracle from the beginning of the wilderness
journey linked with a similar wonder as it drew to a close,
emphasising the continuing goodness of God. He who was
the Sovereign Lord, Creator of heaven and earth,
controlled nature itself and used the elements to carry out
His will. The description of the pool of water at Horeb and
the fountain of water at Kadesh are brought together by

the prophet Isaiah in a passage that was, almost certainly, written against the background of the days of Hezekiah:

"When the poor and needy seek water, and there is none, and their tongue faileth for thirst, I the LORD will hear them, I the God of Israel will not forsake them. I will open rivers in high places, and fountains in the midst of the valleys: I will make the wilderness a pool of water, and the dry land springs of water."   (41:17,18)

PSALM 115

IT is hard to imagine how some of the psalms, given their content and structure, could have been used for liturgical purposes. This is not to say that they were not sung and our difficulty might arise from our inability to appreciate the music of the times and, perhaps, the manner in which the Hebrew language lent itself to a particular form of expression in worship.

This, however, is not a problem with Psalm 115, for it formed part of 'the Hallel' (see chapter on Psalm 113), and writers are almost unanimous in their conclusion that the structure of the psalm is indicative of the manner in which it was sung in the temple worship. There are variations in their approach to the question, but generally speaking it is divided in the following way:

Verses 1-8	Sung by a Levitical choir
Verses 9-11	First line of each verse sung solo, second line a response by the choir
Verses 12-15	Antiphonal singing by sections of the choir (see Ezra 3:11, RV: "they sang one to another")
Verses 16-18	Sung by choir.

Whether or not this was the form in which the psalm was sung, it provides us with a suitable basis on which to consider the structure of the song. We have already indicated (Psalm 113) that we consider all six of the psalms that constitute 'the Hallel' as being connected with the reign of Hezekiah. Psalm 115 is an expression of the manner in which the faithful in Judah presented their plight before their God and encouraged each other to put their trust in Him in the face of the threat presented by Sennacherib and his army.

Prayer for God to Vindicate His Name

"Not unto us, O LORD, not unto us, but unto thy name give glory, for thy mercy, and for thy truth's sake. Wherefore should the heathen say, Where is now their God? But our God is in the heavens: he hath done whatsoever he hath pleased."   (verses 1-3)

In the extremity, the depths of their distress they make their plea to their God, but what is remarkable is the manner in which they make their supplication: "Not unto us", repeated for emphasis, "but unto thy name give glory". It is a plea for God to work for the deliverance of His people. But the reason they cry in this way is not for their own sake, for they recognised that they had no merit of themselves and no right to expect that God would deliver them for their own glory. Rather, they ask Him to manifest Himself on their behalf that He might be seen to be true to His covenants of promise. If He did not act then the heathen might think that His love and faithfulness, those two great attributes emphasised in the declaration of His name (Exodus 34), were empty and meaningless.

It reflects the spirit of Moses when God would have destroyed the people of Israel and made of him a great nation. Moses' response was not for his own glory but for the honour of his God:

"Wherefore should the Egyptians speak, and say, For mischief did he bring them out, to slay them in the mountains, and to consume them from the face of the earth? ... Remember Abraham, Isaac, and Israel, thy servants, to whom thou swarest by thine own self ..."

(Exodus 32:12,13)

All the fortified cities of Judah had fallen to Sennacherib as Rabshakeh, almost certainly a renegade Jew, came to negotiate with Hezekiah's representatives. His cry was, as he blasphemed the God of Israel:

"Beware lest Hezekiah persuade you, saying, The LORD will deliver us. Hath any of the gods of the nations delivered his land out of the hand of the king of Assyria? Where are the gods of Hamath and Arphad? where are the gods of Sepharvaim? and have they delivered Samaria out of my hand? Who are they among all the gods of these lands, that have delivered their land out of mine hand, that the LORD should deliver Jerusalem out of my hand? (Isaiah 36:18-20)

The record in Chronicles tells us that the servants of Sennacherib spoke yet more against God and he sent letters in which he railed upon the Lord God of Israel, claiming that as the gods of the nations had failed to deliver their people and lands so also the God of Hezekiah would never be able to deliver His people out of Sennacherib's hand (2 Chronicles 32:16,17). So indeed the heathen had cried, "Where is their God?"

They mocked the God of Israel for they could see no visual sign of His presence; no image or idol to represent His existence They presumed that because they could perceive no indication of action on behalf of His people, He was no God at all. Yet all this time that they had reproached Him and blasphemed His name He remained, omnipotent, enthroned in heaven, exercising His sovereignty over all the earth. In contrast to the impotence of the idols of the heathen, He did all things according to the counsel of His own will (see Psalm 135:6). Men of faith recognised that what appeared to be inaction on His part in allowing the Assyrian to devastate the land was in fact His chastening hand, for, "Whatsoever He willed, He executed" (verse 3: Kay, *Psalms with Notes*).

The gods of the Nations

What then of the gods of the nations? They were but the work of men's hands! (verses 4-7). Silver and gold they might be, but they were destitute of those basic senses that human life enjoys. They could not speak, or see, or hear, or smell, or handle, or walk. Yet all these faculties were possessed by the God of Israel, in whose image man was made. They could not even utter the low soft moaning of a dove, for "no sound make they with their throat" (verse 7, Kay, *Psalms with Notes*).

Just as their idols were vanity, empty valueless lumps of wood, stone and metal, so also those who put their trust in them were dragged down to live lives that were hollow, and empty, without substance and any real understanding of the things that matter.

"They that make them are like unto them; so is every one that trusteth in them." (verse 8)

The foolishness of those who worshipped idols is expressed in the most compelling manner by the prophets of Israel. Bel and Nebo, the gods of Assyria and Babylon are described by the prophet Isaiah as no more than a burden for weary beasts to carry after they have been proved impotent to save. In contrast, the God of Israel carries His people through all the crises of life and is able to deliver them out of all their distress (Isaiah 46:1-4). The sheer stupidity of the man who cuts down a tree and uses the wood to light a fire to warm himself, to bake bread to eat, and then of the same tree makes an idol and falls down and worships it, is exposed again by the prophet Isaiah (44:9-20; see also Jeremiah 10:1-16).

Trust in the Lord (verses 9-11)

In these verses we have a clear example of the way in which the psalm would have been sung in worship. The first line of each verse would have been sung by the Precentor (the leader of the singers), then the choir would respond with the second line of each verse:

"O Israel, trust thou in the LORD:

He is their help and their shield.

O house of Aaron, trust in the LORD:

He is their help and their shield.

Ye that fear the LORD, trust in the LORD:

He is their help and their shield."

The call is to the people of Israel, the priesthood and the God-fearers (Gentile proselytes; see 1 Kings 8:41,42; Acts 13:16,26, etc.) to put their trust in God. The taunt of Rabshakeh had been, "Let not thy God, in whom thou trustest, deceive thee, saying, Jerusalem shall not be given into the hand of the king of Assyria" (Isaiah 37:10).

The exhortation was to put their trust in God; the response to encourage them to do so was a reminder that God was the help and the shield of all His people.

God's answer to Rabshakeh, through the prophet Isaiah, was, "I will defend this city to save it for mine own sake, and for my servant David's sake" (verse 35). Note that the divine response is in keeping with the prayer expressed in verse 1 of the psalm.

Further Encouragement (verses 12-15)

Developing the thoughts of the previous verses, the Psalmist emphasises that the God who had proved Himself to be worthy of the trust of His people, for He had been ever mindful of them, would continue to show Himself active on their behalf in the blessings He bestowed upon them (verse 12). Those same classes of people described in verses 9-11 would be the recipients of His blessing. They would all, both small and great, be embraced within the blessing, for the Lord would fulfil His promise of old and increase their numbers abundantly (Deuteronomy 1:11). Both they and their children would be blessed, and perhaps we detect a reference here to Hezekiah himself who at this time was still childless (Psalm 115:13,14). The section ends with a triumphant declaration of the privilege that they enjoyed under the blessing of God:

> "Ye are blessed of the LORD which made heaven and earth." (verse 15)

Israel's God is contrasted with the dumb idols of the surrounding nations. But there is here also an echo of the blessing of Melchizedek: "Blessed be Abram of the most high God, possessor of heaven and earth" (Genesis 14:19). These words went far beyond the days of Hezekiah in assuring them of the eternal promises that God had made to their father Abraham.

Eternal Blessings (verses 16-18)

Developing the thought of the previous verse, the Psalmist acknowledges the supremacy of God who dwells in the heavens above where no man can intrude (verse 16). From there He exercises His power and authority and carries out His will and purpose. It is in the pursuit of that purpose that He has given the earth to the children of men (Genesis 1:26-28). Encompassed in that purpose was His promise to the people of Israel and it might appear that the words of verse 17 are foreign to the context: "The dead praise not the LORD, neither any that go down into silence."

However, the words echo the prayer of Hezekiah after he was recovered from his sickness and emphasise the oblivion that death brings (Isaiah 38:18,19). In the extremity of the situation in which they found themselves, the people of Judah saw the sickness of their king as symptomatic of their own spiritual sickness and saw in his impending death their own approaching extinction before the might of Assyria. But their God, who performed all things after the counsel of His own will and purpose, granted to their king extension of days and in his recovery they saw the assurance of their own deliverance and the guarantee of the fulfilment of those eternal promises that He had made to Abraham. So they could exclaim, looking forward to that day: "But we will bless the LORD from this time forth and for evermore" (verse 18).

It remains but to point out that the 'Hallelujah' at the conclusion of this psalm actually belongs to that following.

PSALM 116

A N ancient Jewish tradition associates this psalm with Hezekiah. There is, however, no need to rely on such insubstantial evidence to appreciate that the song revolves around the experiences of this righteous man. The internal evidence and the verbal links with the historical record in Isaiah 37-39, are such as to prove completely convincing. Kay (*The Psalms with Notes,* page 372) has the following list of verbal connections with the chapters from Isaiah's prophecy:

Ps. 116 verse:	Verbal connections	Isaiah
1	"The LORD heard my voice"	38:5
2	"Inclined his ear"	37:17
2	"As long as I live" ("In my days")	39:8
3	"The gates of hell"	38:10
4,16	"O LORD"	38:3
6	"I was brought low" ("fail")	38:14
8	"Mine eyes from tears"	38:5
9	"I shall walk before the LORD"	38:3
9	"In the land of the living"	38:11
11	"I said"	38:10
19	"The LORD's house"	38:20,22

As will be seen when we come to consider the substance of the psalm, the thoughts expressed have an even more obvious reference to Hezekiah for it speaks of an individual who has been in the most dire distress. He has been sick nigh unto death (verses 3,9,15) and from this extreme danger in which he found himself God had delivered him. The psalm is therefore a personal expression of the writer's deep felt thankfulness for the manner in which God had saved him out of the anguish of his soul. It can conveniently be divided into two sections: the first (verses 1-9) beginning with the words, "I love" and the second (verses 10-20) beginning with the words, "I believe". (The Septuagint, mistakenly, actually divides Psalm 116 into two separate psalms at this point). In both these instances there is an unusual form of the verb peculiar to this psalm, for the verb has no object. This appears to be a dramatic device to throw all the emphasis on the acts of loving and believing. The two main sections can be further subdivided for easier understanding.

"I Love" (verses 1 and 2)

The point referred to above regarding the form of the verb is better understood when the revised translation adopted by almost all commentators is accepted: "I love, because the LORD heareth my voice, even my supplications" (verse 1). The absence of an object places an intensity of feeling on the love expressed. It is as though the writer was to say, 'I love with all my heart'. In a sense, although not grammatically correct, it is as though the words, "because the LORD heareth my voice" become the object or, more precisely, the reason for his deep felt emotion. We are reminded of the words of the Apostle John in the New Testament where the same sentiment is expressed: "We love, because he first loved us" (1 John 4:19, RV).

It would appear that Hezekiah was meditating upon the life of David his great ancestor and Psalm 18 in particular, for this song has a number of connections with that earlier work. In particular, these opening words of the psalm are a reminiscence of the first verse of that psalm. It should be noted that the prefix to Psalm 18 describes David as "the servant of the LORD", a title that Hezekiah ascribes to himself in verse 16 of his psalm.

His thankfulness for God's deliverance is of such a character that it is to encompass his whole life: "Because he hath inclined his ear unto me, therefore will I call upon him as long as I live" (verse 2). Literally the Hebrew says 'in my days'. This is, of course, a reference to the fifteen

957

years of added life that was granted to Hezekiah, and attention has already been drawn to the verbal connection with the words of the prophet Isaiah in his 39th chapter (see Kay's notes reproduced above). The assertion that he would call upon the Lord is another recollection of the words of Psalm 18 (verse 3).

Hezekiah's Distress

Having first expressed his love and dedication, the Psalmist now reflects on the circumstances of his distress out of which the Lord delivered him:

"The sorrows of death compassed me, and the pains of hell gat hold upon me: I found trouble and sorrow. Then called I upon the name of the LORD; O LORD, I beseech thee, deliver my soul." (verses 3,4)

Note once again the allusion to Psalm 18 (verses 4-6). Literally the Hebrew says, 'the cords of death compassed (or encircled) me' and in keeping with this thought the Psalmist later describes his deliverance with the words, "thou hast loosed my bonds" (Psalm 116:16). It is as though the writer was thinking of one such as Isaac bound to the altar only to be released from that imminent death and his bonds loosed at God's command.

This thought of the altar and sacrifice is reinforced by the words of Psalm 118: "Bind the sacrifice with cords, even unto the horns of the altar" (verse 27). Inevitably this carries our thoughts to the sacrifice of the Lord Jesus Christ and we remember the way in which Hezekiah's sickness forms the background to Isaiah 53 and foreshadows the experiences of the Lord Jesus (see also 2 Kings 20:8).

Of the word rendered "pains" it has been pointed out that apart from this psalm it occurs only on two other occasions (Psalm 118:5 and Lamentations 1:3). A consensus of the views expressed as to its meaning would point to a rocky defile, hence the idea of constraint or pressure. The passage is alluded to by Peter on the Day of Pentecost where the Greek word translated "pains" is closely associated with the pangs of childbirth (Acts 2:24).

Interestingly, the words "gat hold upon me" are the very words that Moses used when describing to Jethro the travail of the children of Israel in their coming out of Egypt (Exodus 18:8). Remembering that the deliverance from the Assyrian was a Passover deliverance (Isaiah 31:5), could there also be associations with the exodus behind the language of this psalm?

In his distress the Psalmist called upon the name of the Lord and this is the first of three occasions in Psalm 116 where Hezekiah uses this phrase (see also verses 13 and 17. There is a similar triple emphasis in Psalms 113:1-3; and 118:10-12).

It is significant that he should call on the name of Yahweh rather than simply on Yahweh alone. It is an indication that he was aware of all that was involved in that name (Exodus 34:5) by which the Lord had made Himself known.

"The Name of the LORD"
It was those attributes whereby the Lord had made Himself known to Moses and by which He had revealed Himself in the history of His people that were the grounds of Hezekiah's confidence in his prayer. It was these qualities that he had known in his own experience in which he now rejoiced:

"Gracious is the LORD, and righteous; yea, our God is merciful. The LORD preserveth the simple: I was brought low, and he helped me (RV, 'saved me')."

(verses 5,6)

The word translated "simple" conveys the idea of those that are free from worldly artifice (Kay). It is well described in the words of the Apostle Peter:

"Wherefore laying aside all malice, and all guile, and hypocrisies, and envies, and all evil speakings, as newborn babes, desire the sincere milk of the word, that ye might grow thereby: if so be ye have tasted that the Lord is gracious." (1 Peter 2:1-3)

There is a suggestion in the word of a certain vulnerability, as though a lack of wisdom and experience leaves them open to danger. Remember that the young man, void of understanding, who fell victim to the wiles of

959

the harlot came from the ranks of the simple ones (Proverbs 7:6-23). Can it be that those who have that open heart that will most readily respond to the word of God are also amongst the most impressionable of people? Is it for this reason that they need the Lord to preserve them and Peter can add the proviso to his exhortation, "If so be ye have tasted that the Lord is gracious"?

Evidently Hezekiah considered himself to be numbered amongst the simple, for doubts and anxieties had racked his mind in his extremity, but although he was brought low the Lord saved him. The antidote for the simplicity of spirit of which the scriptures speak is to be found in the words of the Psalmist: "The entrance of thy words giveth light; it giveth understanding unto the simple" (119:130).

The consequence of his deliverance was that he found again that tranquility of spirit that he had lost in the midst of his affliction:

> "Return unto thy rest, O my soul; for the LORD hath dealt bountifully with thee. For thou hast delivered my soul from death, mine eyes from tears, and my feet from falling. I will walk before the LORD in the land of the living."
> (Psalm 116:7-9)

Hezekiah finds strength and encouragement in the remembrance of God's mercy. The disquiet and anxiety he had experienced are now put aside as he knows once more that serenity of spirit that belongs to those only who have put their trust in God. The word translated "rest" is in the plural, thus giving emphasis to the fulness and completeness of that rest which he now knew.

The word of the prophet sent from God had been, "I have heard thy prayer, I have seen thy tears: behold, I will add unto thy days fifteen years" (Isaiah 38:5). In his misery and pain Hezekiah had cried, "I shall not see the LORD, even the LORD, in the land of the living" (verse 11). These words are echoed in a positive rather than a negative sense in verse 9 of our psalm.

The actual words are quoted almost verbatim from Psalm 56 (verse 13) except that Psalm 116 substitutes the word "land" for "light". Surely Psalm 27 was also in the writer's mind: "I had fainted, unless I had believed to see the goodness of the LORD in the land of the living" (verse 13). Ultimately it was his faith in the face of dreadful adversity that was the grounds of his salvation and the result was that in the land of the living he now knew the light and the goodness of the Lord.

"I Believed"

The thought of Psalm 27 appears to be picked up in the opening words of the next section of the psalm:

"I believed, therefore have I spoken: I was greatly afflicted: I said in my haste, All men are liars."

(Psalm 116:10,11)

We have already commented on the omission of the object to the verb 'believe', thus giving added emphasis to the act (see verse 1). Perowne (*The Psalms,* Volume 2, page 334) points out that the emphasis is maintained in the words that follow, rendering them, "I, even I, was greatly afflicted".

In his distress he had clung desperately to his faith and as a consequence he had emerged victorious. Now therefore he could speak and pour forth from the very depths of his being his praise and gratitude. The Apostle Paul quotes these words when writing to the Corinthians (2 Corinthians 4:13). The context speaks of the manner in which, for the Gospel's sake, they suffered adversity and were nigh unto death. Nevertheless, by faith they continued to preach the word in the confidence that God could deliver them even from the grave.

In his affliction the Psalmist had learned that it was vain to put his trust in men. There was no strength to be found, either in himself or in other men. In them he had found nothing but treachery, deceit and hypocrisy. They 'played false' and disappointed those who put their trust in them (see Psalm 62:9).

So he had declared in his haste that all men were liars. The idea behind the word "haste" is generally agreed by commentators to carry the significance of alarm; as Kay says of the word, it describes "the precipitancy caused by alarm". Given the earlier suggestion of the Passover deliverance, we cannot fail to observe that this word is used twice in connection with Israel's deliverance from

Egypt. They were to eat the Passover with haste, with their loins girded, their shoes on their feet, and their staff in their hand (Exodus 12:11). Surely, in keeping with the meaning of the word already noted, there was a sense of apprehension about the situation that was to precipitate their flight from Egypt. Later, Moses was to declare that they should keep the Passover because they came out of the land of Egypt in haste (Deuteronomy 16:3). Appropriate to this thought, the Targum reading for verse 11 has "in my fleeing".

May it not be therefore that Hezekiah considered his deliverance in terms of the Passover, the precipitate manner in which he was plucked from the very jaws of death and that as he came out of his affliction he reflected and said in his haste (i.e., his deliverance) that there was no help to be found in man, for in the Lord only was salvation.

Thanksgiving for Deliverance

"What shall I render unto the LORD for all his benefits toward me? I will take the cup of salvation, and call upon the name of the LORD. I will pay my vows unto the LORD now in the presence of all his people."

(verses 12-14)

It was fitting that in his appreciation of all that the Lord had done for him and for the people of Judah, Hezekiah should publicly declare his gratitude in paying his vows and in presenting his offerings of thanksgiving. Not only had God given him extension of life, but also He had delivered them from the hand of Sennacherib and his host. Note that these two events occurred almost simultaneously (see Isaiah 38:4-6).

Zion had drunk "the cup of trembling, even the dregs of the cup of my fury", but now once more God had looked upon His people with favour and symbolically they drank the cup of salvation (Isaiah 51:17-23).

Whether Hezekiah actually drank or poured out a cup of wine as a libation in connection with his thank offerings is a matter of conjecture. It is said that this is "the cup of blessing" that the Lord Jesus took when he instituted the Memorial Feast (Matthew 26:27). However, while there can be no doubt that the Hallel was sung at the Feast of Passover in the days of the Lord Jesus, there is little or no evidence as to when this practice began. As they are psalms of Hezekiah's days, unless he himself was responsible for its institution, it must of necessity be of a later date, perhaps after the captivity.

Lessons Learned

What had Hezekiah learned from all these experiences? From his brush with death had come the realisation that in the Lord only was life to be found. He had come to appreciate that "the grave cannot praise thee, death cannot celebrate thee: they that go down into the pit cannot hope for thy truth" (Isaiah 38:18). He had come to a deeper understanding of the vanity of this mortal life that had nothing to offer that was lasting and abiding.

So through his experiences had come the awareness that in resurrection from the dead only was to be found the perpetual joy of everlasting fellowship with God that he longed for with all his heart. So he could declare: "Precious in the sight of the LORD is the death of his saints" (Psalm 116:15).

What a wonderful truth! What comfort and consolation it offers. We have been redeemed "with the precious blood of Christ" (1 Peter 1:19). Consequently we are numbered amongst His saints, "those that have made a covenant with (Him) by sacrifice" (Psalm 50:5). The Hebrew word translated "saints" is used to describe the love of God towards those upon whom He bestows His mercy and also the love that they show towards Him. Dr. Norman Snaith (*The Distinctive Ideas of the Old Testament*) suggests that the root word might fairly be rendered 'covenant love' and so those who are in the bonds of the covenant have the assurance that their death is precious in God's sight (see also *The Teaching of the Master*, Brother L. G. Sargent, pages 49,50).

Unlike other men they do not die without hope and without God in the world, but covered by the precious blood of Christ they are remembered of God and will be His in the day that He makes up His jewels (Malachi 3:16,17).

963

That God required life-long service was another of the lessons that Hezekiah had learned through his experiences (see Psalm 116:2). So as he reflected on all the benefits that the Lord had bestowed upon him he was moved to cry: "O LORD, truly I am thy servant; I am thy servant, and the son of thine handmaid" (verse 16). The Hebrew word for servant means literally, 'one born in the house'. Thus he recognised that he was a member of 'the household of God' and like the servant of Exodus 21 who had his ear bored with an awl that he might serve his master for ever (verses 5,6), he had committed himself to lifelong service. He refers to his mother also as the Lord's handmaid – again one born in her master's house, a member of 'the household of God'.

She too was a faithful servant and what little we know of her points to this fact. She was the daughter of Zechariah who had understanding of the visions of God and encouraged King Uzziah in those days in which he sought the Lord (2 Chronicles 26:5; 29:1). Remembering the wickedness of Ahaz, Hezekiah's father, we can appreciate the influence that this woman had on her son in his formative years.

We have already drawn attention to the close association between Psalms 18 and 116. There David is described as "the servant of the LORD" as he thanks God in the day that He delivered him out of the hand of all his enemies. Appropriately, Hezekiah meditates on this psalm as he too reflects on the manner in which God had delivered Judah out of the hand of Sennacherib and all his host (Isaiah 37:21-36).

The psalm closes with a repetition of his determination to call upon the Lord and to pay his vows in the presence of the people (verses 17,18). This he will do in the Lord's house in the midst of Jerusalem (verse 19). Here again we have an obvious allusion to the words of God spoken through Isaiah to Hezekiah: "Behold, I will heal thee: on the third day thou shalt go up unto the house of the LORD" (2 Kings 20:5).

The words of these closing verses of the psalm carry us beyond the days of Hezekiah to that future day when the Lord Jesus will stand in the midst of his people and praise

the name of the Lord in the courts of His house. They
stand perhaps as a fitting introduction to the brief psalm
that follows.

The final 'Hallelujah' although appropriate to this
psalm might belong to the next.

PSALM 117

W E quote: "This shortest of the Psalms is one of the grandest. Its invitation to all nations to join in praising Jehovah for His goodness to Israel is virtually a recognition that the ultimate object of Israel's calling was the salvation of the world. It is in the truest sense a Messianic Psalm, and it is quoted in Romans 15:11 as one of the scriptures which foretold the extension of God's mercy to the Gentiles in Christ" (Kirkpatrick, *The Cambridge Bible*, page 692).

The above quotation is reproduced as an introduction to this psalm for it sums up in a most appropriate manner its meaning and the purpose for which it was written.

The psalm consists of just two verses:

"O Praise the LORD, all ye nations: praise him, all ye people. For his merciful kindness is great toward us: and the truth of the LORD endureth for ever."

Background

The circumstance in which the psalm was written and which forms the backcloth of its profound message that ultimately all nations of the earth should be blessed in Christ, was undoubtedly the manner in which Hezekiah was magnified in the sight of the nations following his recovery from sickness and the destruction of the Assyrian host (2 Chronicles 32:23). Herein was foreshadowed the eventual consummation of the purpose of God in the earth.

Israel and the Nations

The call to the nations of the earth is to praise the Lord. All people are to join in this paean of praise and two different words are used which are translated "praise": the first, the usual 'hallel' which means basically 'to celebrate';

the second, 'to shout as with a loud tone'. Perhaps the idea is that the individuals involved should sing with all their might, from the very depths of their being.

The reason they sing the Lord's praise in this way is because they have come to recognise the wonder of His mercy towards Israel that has produced this time of unprecedented blessing for them also.

Mercy and Truth

As is characteristic of this series of psalms, mercy and truth are once again brought together. It is once again an emphasis upon the name of God. He declared Himself to be "abundant in goodness (same Hebrew word as that rendered "merciful" – see note on Psalm 116:15) and truth". His merciful kindness is great towards Israel, for great (Psalm 65:3, 'prevail') though their sins and iniquity may be, His mercy is more powerful; it abounds that the power of sin might be eclipsed (Psalm 103:11,12; Romans 5:20).

The foundation of His merciful kindness is His truth, His faithfulness to the promises that He has made. His loving-kindness towards them is confirmation of the truthfulness of the things He has spoken (see Jeremiah 33:6-9). It is expressed beautifully by the prophet Micah:

"Thou wilt perform the truth to Jacob, and the mercy to Abraham, which thou hast sworn unto our fathers from the days of old."   (7:20)

In the Epistle to the Romans the Apostle Paul brings together four Old Testament passages, including Psalm 117, to illustrate the manner in which the Gentiles will rejoice with His people Israel in the day when God will finally fulfil His promises to them (Romans 15:9-12). Significantly, it is the context of Psalm 117 that is emphasised:

"Now I say that Jesus Christ was a minister of the circumcision for the truth of God, to confirm the promises made unto the fathers: and that the Gentiles might glorify God for his mercy."   (Romans 15:8,9)

Truly with this prospect before him the apostle could exclaim:

"Rejoice, ye Gentiles, with his people."

(verse 10; see Deuteronomy 32:43)

PSALM 118

THIS is the last of the psalms that comprise the 'Hallel' and like the others we believe it to be associated with the experiences of Hezekiah. It speaks unmistakably of one who has been delivered from imminent death and is now able to go up to the house of the Lord to worship (verses 17-20). It also expresses praise and thankfulness for the deliverance of the nation from the hand of their enemies who compassed them about (verses 10-12).

The language of the Song of Moses after the destruction of Pharaoh's host (Exodus 15:2,6,12) is part of the fabric of the psalm and this is particularly significant given that the destruction of the Assyrian was also a Passover deliverance (Isaiah 31:5).

It is a strange thing that notwithstanding the obvious reference to Hezekiah's deliverance from death and the clear connection with the words of the prophet Isaiah (38:1,5,6), the majority of commentators place this psalm after the exile and seek to interpret it in terms of the events surrounding the building of the second temple and Nehemiah's expedition to rebuild the walls of Jerusalem.

We believe that they are not completely mistaken in associating the psalm with events after the exile. The psalm was not written then, but was found to be appropriate by men like Ezra, Nehemiah and the prophets after the exile to the situation in which they found themselves, and consequently they meditated upon it and quoted from it in their circumstances in the same manner in which the writer of Psalm 118 cites the psalms of David.

After the Exile

For Hezekiah the deliverance and blessing that he enjoyed could be likened to the great events of Israel's past: the

969

Passover and exodus deliverance from Egypt; the celebrations when David brought the ark to Zion; the rejoicing at the dedication of Solomon's temple. These were all events that figured large in his mind and are reflected in the language of the psalm.

Thus the words that David sang at the entering in of the ark (1 Chronicles 16:34,35) are repeated at the dedication of the temple (2 Chronicles 5:13; 7:3) and form the opening words of Psalm 118. In like manner Ezra, with a sense of the history of his people, including the events of Hezekiah's day, records how these words were sung when Joshua and Zerubbabel laid the foundations of the second temple (Ezra 3:11). Similarly, David had prayed that God would deliver Israel from the nations for He was the God of their salvation, surely recalling the words of Exodus 15 (verse 2) which significantly also spoke of building a habitation for God (1 Chronicles 16:35). In a spectacular fashion Hezekiah had experienced such a deliverance and the psalm speaks of the manner in which all nations had compassed him about (verse 10). Three times the Psalmist emphasises that in the name of the Lord he would destroy them (verses 11,12). Three times he asserts that the Lord has become his salvation (verses 14,21,25). So also Nehemiah speaks of "all the nations that were about us" (Nehemiah 6:16) and names some of them in an earlier chapter (4:7). Note also that Nehemiah's prayer to "prosper ... thy servant this day" (1:11) is an allusion to the Psalmist's words, "Send now prosperity" (Psalm 118:25).

Both Ezra and Nehemiah knew the psalm and drew strength and comfort from the manner of God's salvation revealed in its words.

Analysis of the Psalm

Recognising its association with Hezekiah and appreciating that it was first sung in his days, we need to consider the circumstances in which it was composed and the occasion on which it was first used as a hymn of praise. It is to be noted that whereas the psalm is primarily in the first person singular, indicating the outpouring of thanks felt by an individual, there are also some verses that speak in the third person plural which appear to be more appropriate to the nation of Israel as a whole (verses 25,26). This should not present any real difficulty if we think of Hezekiah acting as the representative of the nation. Thus he could speak of his own personal experiences, while also expressing the jubilant rejoicing of Judah as a whole in the salvation of their God. Remembering also that this is one of his songs of deliverance (Isaiah 38:20), we can perhaps visualise it being sung at a subsequent Passover feast, possibly as they ascended the hill of Zion in solemn yet joyful procession to the doors of the Lord's house, very much as David had done when he brought the ark to Zion.

We can envisage the scene, the joyful chorus, as all Israel were called upon to praise the Lord for His loving-kindness (verses 1-4). Hezekiah, personally, speaks of the deliverance he has experienced (verses 5-9) and reminds them that the nations are powerless before the might of their God (verses 10-14). Once more the king reflects on his salvation from death (verses 15-18) and, as they approach the temple gates, calls for them to be opened to him as David had done centuries earlier (Psalm 24:7-10), before the song finally reaches its grand conclusion in the temple courts (verses 22-29).

All Israel Join in Praise

The opening words of the psalm recall the words of David when he brought the ark to Zion; they also occur at the dedication of Solomon's temple (see above) and are quoted in several other psalms besides Psalm 118 (Psalms 106:1; 107:1; etc.). Jeremiah also uses the words in a prophecy regarding the way in which God will once again bless His people after their exile (see Jeremiah 33:10,11): "O give thanks unto the LORD; for he is good: because his mercy endureth for ever" (Psalm 118:1).

All Israel are called upon to render thanks unto the Lord: the people generally, the house of Aaron and the Gentile God-fearers who dwelt amongst them (verses 2-4). The form of these verses follows the style of Psalm 115 (verses 9-11) and were no doubt sung in a similar way.

971

Hezekiah's Deliverance

It was out of the midst of his distress (verse 5, RV) that Hezekiah called unto the Lord. The word translated "distress" (*metsar*) means literally 'straitened' and conveys the idea of pressure, of being hemmed in and squeezed (cp. *matsor*, used – as Kay points out – on four occasions as a proper name for Egypt: see 2 Kings 19:24; Isaiah 19:6; 37:24; Micah 7:12 – compare with RV). It would appear that the word describing the bitterness of their experiences in Egypt was used as being commensurate with the nation itself. Thus Hezekiah is describing the strait in which he found himself, besieged by the all-conquering Assyrians, as being similar to their affliction in Egypt. This point is reinforced by the abbreviated form of the name of God that is used, not only in this verse but also in verses 14, 17, 18 and 19.

"Out of the strait pass I called upon Yah; Yah answered me on the open plain" (Kay, verse 5). This form of God's name would recall its use in the Song of Moses, sung to celebrate the destruction of Pharaoh's army (Exodus 15:2) and would, of course, be relevant to Judah's deliverance from the Assyrian. God, as it were, had removed him from the straitness of the siege to a large or wide place where he was able to move without harassment or restriction.

The enlargement was the answer to his prayer. So because God was on his side he would not fear, for he asks, "What can man do unto me?" (verse 6). This is an allusion to the words of Psalm 56:9-11. It is most appropriate, for that psalm is concerned with the time that David dwelt alone among the Philistines in the most straitened of circumstances. It is also quoted in the Epistle to the Hebrews (13:6).

Hezekiah repeats the words of verse 6 (see RV) and then acknowledges that the Lord is on his side as his helper. The AV suggests that God is one amongst many helpers, but the *Cambridge Bible* indicates that it is an idiomatic expression describing not one among many, but one whom in Himself was as a host of helpers. As a consequence he would see his enemies brought low (verse 7).

A lesson had been learned in these troubles that
Hezekiah had experienced. And he repeats the words for
added emphasis:

"It is better to trust in the LORD than to put
confidence in man. It is better to trust in the LORD than
to put confidence in princes." (verses 8,9)

This is not a general expression of a principle, but a lesson
learned in the hard school of experience. During his
sickness Hezekiah had entrusted the negotiations with
Sennacherib to the princes of the realm. The prophet
Isaiah makes it clear that they had dealt treacherously
with the Assyrian king and he for his part had no
compunction in disassociating himself from the agreement
they had made (see Isaiah 28:18,20; 31:1-3; 33:1,7,8).

However strong and powerful the princes of this world
might be it needs to be remembered that they are, like all
men, but dust and when their breath goes forth and they
return to dust then all their schemes, all their proud and
arrogant ambitions for self-advancement crumble like
dust with them (Psalm 146:3,4).

"The LORD is my Strength" (verses 10-14)

It had not been the power of men that had repelled the
enemy, but it had been the might of God. In a series of
trilogies the writer speaks of the danger that had
threatened him from the surrounding nations, of their
destruction in the name of the Lord, who in consequence
had become his salvation.

Three times he exclaims that the nations had
compassed him about (verses 10-12). Three times he
affirms, "In the name of the LORD I will destroy them"
(verses 10-12). There appears to be an anomaly in the
tenses, for whereas the nations that encompassed him are
described in the past tense, the destruction in the name of
the Lord is spoken of in the future tense. There can be no
doubt from the whole tenor of the psalm that the
deliverance spoken of has already taken place. It would
appear therefore that the Psalmist is emphasising his
faith that what God had accomplished in the past He was
still able to do in the future. It was not to be regarded as
a one-off occurrence, but rather a continuing experience

for God had become his salvation (verses 14,21,25; another reference to Exodus 15:2).

The reference to all nations (verse 10) means all the nations that were round about them, and the Assyrian records of the time refer to Edom, Moab and Ammon as contributing to Sennacherib's invasion. It is likely also that other subject nations would have been expected to support him in his armed adventures. They are described as being like bees about him, recalling the language used to describe the Amorites when they put Israel to flight at Kadesh-Barnea (Deuteronomy 1:44). Although they had burned as a fire among thorns and thrust at him to cause him to fall, the Lord had been his helper and the threat had been extinguished (see Micah 7:7,8; this prophet, remember, was a contemporary of Hezekiah). So the Lord was his strength and his song and had become his salvation (Isaiah 12:2; 38:20).

The Joy Shared by the King and the People

The righteous rejoiced in their tents and the reference is almost certainly to those who had come from all over Judah, together with God-fearing Gentiles, to celebrate the feast and were encamped in their tents around Jerusalem (verse 15).

As in the day of their deliverance from the land of Egypt, God had once more manifested Himself on behalf of His people and had become their salvation. Again the language of Exodus is echoed (15:6,12) as in another threefold declaration he proclaims that, "The right hand of the LORD doeth valiantly" (Psalm 118:15,16).

One cannot help but be intrigued by this threefold emphasis that is characteristic of the psalm. Why should words on four separate occasions have been repeated in this way? Could it be that Hezekiah, aware of the prophecy of Amos who prophesied in the days of his great-grandfather Uzziah, had meditated upon the second chapter (verses 4-16) and recalled that, "For three transgressions of Judah, and for four (God would) not turn away the punishment thereof" (verse 4 – similarly for Israel – verse 6)? The words of Amos emphasise a great truth. Remember the parable told by the Lord Jesus of the fig tree and the vineyard (Luke 13:6-9). Three years the vinedresser came seeking fruit and found none. It speaks of God's grace towards Israel for although the vine "cumbered the ground", yet another year was allowed to give it opportunity to bear fruit. The obvious background of the ministry of the Lord Jesus needs no emphasis. The words of Amos are a colloquial expression emphasising the fact that although the iniquity of the people had come to the full, indicated by the words "three transgressions", God had not imposed the punishments that they deserved but He was prepared to allow the cup of their wickedness to overflow. It was for four transgressions that His wrath would be poured forth, for thus the longsuffering of God waited. All this Hezekiah recognised and his trilogies in this psalm are an acknowledgement that Judah had come to the very brink of incurring the overflowing anger of the Lord. But He had acted, putting away their threefold iniquity to deliver both the king from his sickness and the city from the oppression of the Assyrian because of the king's faith and the reforms that he initiated.

Once again the king recalls the extension of life granted to him in an inversion of the words of Isaiah 38:1: "For thou shalt die, and not live":

"I shall not die, but live, and declare the works of the LORD." (Psalm 118:17)

The psalm gives a clear indication that Hezekiah's sickness coincided with the threat from Sennacherib and both deliverances were bound together irrevocably in his mind. Although he had been sorely afflicted by the chastening hand of God, he had been delivered out of the hand of death (verse 18).

Approaching the Temple Gates

Reaching the temple gates the king, no doubt at the head of the procession, calls for the gates to be opened to him that he might go in and praise the Lord (verse 19).

They are called gates of righteousness, for this was the abode of the Eternal God of whom it is recorded that "righteousness and judgment are the habitation of his throne" (Psalm 97:2). From here He reigned over His people and answered them in terrible things in righteousness (Psalm 65:5).

The people are reminded of the sanctity of their God and that the righteous only have the right to enter (Psalm 118:20). The prophet Isaiah echoes the words of the psalm: "Open ye the gates, that the righteous nation which keepeth the truth may enter in" (26:2).

This, of course, was a lesson that David learned:

"LORD, who shall abide in thy tabernacle? who shall dwell in thy holy hill? He that walketh uprightly, and worketh righteousness, and speaketh the truth in his heart." (Psalm 15:1,2)

He is "not a God that hath pleasure in wickedness: neither shall evil dwell with (Him)" (Psalm 5:4).

Entering the temple court they were met by the altar of burnt offering erected on that sure foundation, the rock on which Abraham would have offered Isaac; the unmovable rock on which David had offered his sacrifices in the threshing floor of Ornan the Jebusite (1 Chronicles 21:26; 22:1,2). In the days of Ahaz it had become "a stone of stumbling and a rock of offence" (Isaiah 8:14). Ahaz had removed the altar of burnt offering that he might erect his own altar after the pattern that he had seen in Damascus. He could not, however, remove the sure foundation, the rock on which it had been built and it was ever a cause of stumbling to him – a rock of offence. Now Hezekiah rejoiced in the fact that with the altar restored the stone which the builders rejected had become the head of the corner (verse 22). Closely linked with this verse are the words of the prophet Isaiah:

"Therefore thus saith the Lord GOD, Behold I lay in Zion for a foundation a stone, a tried stone, a precious corner stone, a sure foundation: he that believeth shall not make haste." (28:16)

In the very week that the people had welcomed him to Jerusalem with the words of this psalm (verses 25,26; Matthew 21:8,9), the Lord Jesus challenged the Jews by quoting this scripture with regard to himself (Matthew 21:42-45). The passage is also quoted by Peter before the Council (Acts 4:10-12) and in his First Epistle (2:4-10) where significantly he associates it with both an altar and those who worship at it (verses 5,6).

The Israel of God

It needs to be remembered that everything that God desired Israel to be was fulfilled in the Lord Jesus Christ. He was in himself "the Israel of God" and just as God had spoken of Israel as His firstborn (Exodus 4:22,23; Hosea 11:1; Matthew 2:15), so they prefigured the birth of God's only begotten Son. Bearing this in mind, there is a sense in which the people of Israel were also "the head stone of the corner" for they were at the heart of the outworking of God's purpose amongst the nations. Yet they too, a kingdom of priests intended to represent their God in the earth and to draw all men unto Him, were a stone rejected. Now, however, in the deliverance of Hezekiah and the people of Judah they had been exalted amongst the nations, for:

> "Many brought gifts unto the LORD to Jerusalem, and presents to Hezekiah king of Judah: so that he was magnified in the sight of all nations from thenceforth."
> (2 Chronicles 32:23)

Israel was once more fulfilling its ancient destiny and the stone (Hezekiah?) which the builders rejected was again the head of the corner. These thoughts can, of course, be extended and applied to Israel after the spirit who are no longer "strangers and foreigners, but fellowcitizens with the saints, and of the household of God; and are built upon the foundation of the apostles and prophets, Jesus Christ himself being the chief corner stone" (Ephesians 2:19,20).

It was the Lord's doing and it was marvellous in their eyes for, miraculously, He had delivered them out of the hand of the Assyrian (Psalm 118:23) and they rejoiced in the knowledge that nothing was too hard for Him (Jeremiah 32:17,27).

This day, this special festive day, the Lord had made. It foreshadowed the great day of the Lord yet to come. In the words of the prophet Isaiah they were glad and rejoiced:

> "Lo, this is our God; we have waited for him, and he will save us: this is the LORD; we have waited for him, we will be glad and rejoice in his salvation."   (25:9)

In the Courts of the Temple

Finally the procession enters the court of the temple and the people cry for God to continue the work that He has begun: "Save now, I beseech thee, O LORD: O LORD, I beseech thee, send now prosperity" (verse 25).

The response of the priests from within the temple precincts echoes the blessing of Numbers 6 (verses 24-27):

> "Blessed is he that cometh in the name of the LORD: we have blessed you out of the house of the LORD. God is the LORD, which hath shewed us light."
>
> (Psalm 118:26)

It was with these words, coupled with the "hosanna" ("save now") of the preceding verse, that the multitude greeted the Lord Jesus as he entered Jerusalem (Matthew 21:9). "Hosanna" was effectively a 'God save the king' (*Cambridge Bible*). In their understanding, "He that cometh in the name of the LORD" was the Messiah, and so the disciples joined in the shouts of acclaim adding their understanding of the cry "hosanna" to the shouts of the multitude:

> "Blessed be the King that cometh in the name of the Lord." (Luke19:38)

The fact that they strewed palm branches (John 12:13) and branches of other trees (Matthew 21:8) is an indication that they associated these words with the feast of tabernacles. It is said (Delitzsch) that at the feast of tabernacles it was the custom to compass the morning burnt offering once on the first six days of the feast and seven times on the seventh day. The seventh day was called 'The Great Hosanna' and the prayers offered, including the myrtle, willow and palm branches strewn in the way, were all called 'Hosannas'.

It is at this juncture that the command is given to bind the sacrifice, presumably a burnt offering, with cords to the altar (Psalm 118:27; see 116:3). It is interesting to contemplate that if this, as many suppose, was the psalm sung at the Lord's Passover (see Matthew 26:30) then these were amongst the last words uttered by the Lord Jesus before he entered the Garden of Gethsemane.

So the psalm concludes with a final ascription of praise to the Lord (including a last reference to Exodus 15:2):

"Thou art my God, and I will praise thee: thou art my God, I will exalt thee. O give thanks unto the LORD; for he is good: for his mercy endureth for ever."

(verses 28,29)

PSALM 119

PSALM 119 is arranged in 22 stanzas according to the letters of the Hebrew alphabet which appear at the head of each section. Each stanza consists of eight verses, each verse starting with the letter that appears at its head.

There are ten words used to describe the word of God in the psalm. In English these are: word, saying, testimonies, way, judgements, precepts, commandments, law, statutes, faithfulness.

The meanings of the Hebrew words of which the above are translations are as follows. These are reproduced from *The Psalms with Notes* (by William Kay, pages 381,382) and the *Cambridge Bible* (pages 703,704).

1. "Word" (*dabar*). The expression of God's mind and will generally (equivalent to *logos* – New Testament). Used twenty-three times in the psalm.
2. "Saying" (*imrah*). A promise, communicated orally. Used nineteen times.
3. "Testimonies" (*eduth*). An attestation or affirmation; lasting from age to age to attest God's will, to protect against man's waywardness. Used twenty-three times.
4. "Way" (*derek*). Prescribed lines of conduct. Used thirteen times.
5. "Judgements" (*mishpatim*). Judicial decisions or sentences thus forming a rule applicable to other similar circumstances. Used twenty-three times.
6. "Precepts" (*piqqudim*). Entrusted or deposited with us as a charge. Used twenty-one times.
7. "Commandments" (*mitsvoth*). Directions issued with paternal authority. Used twenty-two times.

980

8. "Law" (*torah*). The whole body of practical teaching; the code of duty. Used twenty-five times.

9. "Statutes" (*chuqqim*). Ordinances or enactments. Something engraved or inscribed. Used twenty-one times.

10. "Faithfulness" (*emunah*). The constancy of God's Law. Used four times (and once translated as "truth" – verse 30).

It should be noted that the last of these words describes the quality of God's word and not the word itself. Some commentators suggest alternatives.

One of these words is used in every verse of the psalm with the exception of verse 122. Because of doubt over the Hebrew text this may also be true of verses 90 & 132.

The fact that ten words are used invites an immediate connection with the 'ten words or commandments' written by the finger of God on the tablets of stone (see Deuteronomy 4:13, RV margin).

Each Hebrew letter stands in its own right as a word and also has a numerical value. The meanings of the letters together with their numerical value are given overleaf. These have been extracted from *Gesenius' Hebrew Lexicon,* although there is some difference of opinion in a few cases. These are indicated as appropriate.

We wonder if each of these words had a special significance for the writer and served as a reminder to him of a particular aspect of his relationship with God (see below: "An Enigma").

Note that verses 1 to 3 form an introduction, and that from verse 4 God is addressed in the third person, making the psalm a continuous prayer and supplication. The only exception is verse 115 where the Psalmist addresses the evildoers who afflict him.

While Psalm 119 is the most perfect example of an alphabetical psalm, there are of course other psalms which are based on the Hebrew alphabet. See, for instance, Psalms 111,112 and Psalms 25 and 34; the two latter psalms being notable for the fact that they both have breaks in the continuity of the alphabet occurring at the same point. (They omit the sixth letter – *vau*; and

Letter		Meaning and numeric value	
א	aleph	Ox	1
ב	beth	House	2
ג	gimel	Camel / fruitful	3
ד	daleth	Door	4
ה	he	Window / wall of defence	5
ו	vau	Nail	6
ז	zain	Weapon	7
ח	cheth	Hedge or fence	8
ט	teth	Goodness	9
י	jod	Hand / guide	10
כ	caph	Hollow of the hand	20
ל	lamed	Ox goad	30
מ	mem	Water	40
נ	nun	Fish	50
ס	samech	Support	60
ע	ain	Eye	70
פ	pe	Mouth	80
צ	tzaddi	Righteous	90
ק	koph	Ear / hearing	100
ר	resh	Head	200
ש	schin	Tooth	300
ת	tau	Sign or mark	400

repeat the sixth from the end – *pe*). This suggests that there is something more to the alphabetical psalms than simply being used as an aid to memory, which they undoubtedly were.

The length of the psalm makes it inappropriate to attempt a verse by verse consideration, particularly given the repetition in thought that exists throughout.

The Author

It is suggested generally that the psalm is a meditation upon the Book of Deuteronomy and that book certainly figures largely in the writer's mind. This suggestion is, however, often connected to an assumption that the author of the psalm was Ezra and in our view this is a totally unwarranted supposition. Indeed there is, probably, no other psalm that has been attributed to such a range of different writers than this. In addition to Ezra we have discovered David, Hezekiah, Jeremiah, Daniel, Nehemiah and an unknown post-exilic Levite as suggested authors; not forgetting the critical view that it belongs to the time of the Maccabees, an idea that can be abandoned without further thought.

We believe that with one exception all the suggestions are based on general considerations and have little or no supporting evidence. Indeed the only real guide to the identity of the writer comes from the psalm itself and this we feel points overwhelmingly to David as the author of the work.

Contrary to the general view that the psalm was written, if not by an old man, then by a man of mature years, we believe that it was composed by David when he was still a young man. This is indicated, we believe conclusively, by the words of verses 9 to 11: "Wherewithal shall a young man cleanse his way? by taking heed thereto according to thy word."

Having posed the question and indicated the answer the writer then applies the words to his own personal experience:

"With my whole heart have I sought thee: O let me not wander from thy commandments. Thy word have I hid in mine heart, that I might not sin against thee."

(verses 10,11)

The words have an immediacy about them; a relevance to the circumstances that the Psalmist found himself in at the time of writing. The words would not have been appropriate for an older man looking back and reminiscing on what he had learnt from his experience of life.

983

The words of the Psalmist, contrasting the depth of the knowledge gained from his meditation on the word of God with that to be obtained from his teachers and the ancients (verses 99,100), lends further weight to the evidence for the youthfulness of the writer.

Historical Background

Given then that it was written by David while still a young man, what other evidence is there in the psalm to establish the time and circumstances in which it was written?

We suggest that the substance of the psalm points to the days that David spent in the royal court when Saul took him from watching the sheep on the hillside and elevated him to a place of honour in the kingdom. Remember David's response when Saul in his envy sent emissaries to suggest to him that the king wished to have him for a son-in-law.

"Seemeth it to you a light thing to be a king's son in law, seeing that I am a poor man, and lightly esteemed?
(1 Samuel 18:23)

We can imagine then how he must have felt when taken from the comparative simplicity of his home in Bethlehem and thrust into what for him was an alien environment. He found himself amongst worldly ambitious men who saw their future best served by ingratiating themselves with the king. This was the atmosphere into which David was plunged and we can envisage how much more dangerous and difficult it became for him as Saul's obsessive hatred grew more and more intense. So he could cry, "I am a stranger in the earth: hide not thy commandments from me" (Psalm 119:19) and, "I am small and despised: yet do not I forget thy precepts" (verse 141). If read against this background, the words of the psalm take on an added significance and assume a meaning that we might otherwise have missed.

The Psalmist is suffering affliction and persecution. He pleads: "Remove from me reproach and contempt; for I have kept thy testimonies" (verse 22; see also verses 28,39,50,67,83,92,110,121,122,143, etc.) His life is threatened. His enemies are powerful and influential men

984

who do not share his love for God or his reverence for His word. They are ruthless and determined; moved by jealousy and anxiety to please the king and within the royal court there is no easy way of escape from their scheming and intrigue.

Thus he writes:

"Princes also did sit and speak against me: but thy servant did meditate in thy statutes."   (verse 23)

"The proud have had me greatly in derision: yet have I not declined from thy law."   (verse 51)

"The proud have digged pits for me, which are not after thy law. All thy commandments are faithful: they persecute me wrongfully; help thou me. They had almost consumed me upon earth; but I forsook not thy precepts."   (verses 85-87)

(see also verses 69,78,95,110,115,150,157,161)

David's Reaction

In these distressing circumstances David found his comfort and consolation in the word of God. The psalm breathes a spirit of love and reverence for the word that permeates throughout all its parts. The psalm, however, also gives us an insight into other aspects of David's response to this situation in which he found himself.

There is for instance a suggestion that, at first, David found the grandeur of the royal court somewhat overwhelming. There was an attraction about it that could have beguiled him and led him astray. He was not immediately aware of the dangers posed by the godless men who surrounded the king. Perhaps, a little naively, he came to the royal palace thinking that he would find there the same love for God and His word that he treasured in his heart. Circumstances soon taught him the reality of the situation and his comments as he reflects upon his experiences are an exhortation to all who seek to follow in the footsteps of that man after God's own heart:

"Before I was afflicted I went astray: but now have I kept thy word."   (verse 67)

"It is good for me that I have been afflicted; that I might learn thy statutes."   (verse 71)

"I know, O LORD, that thy judgments are right, and that thou in faithfulness hast afflicted me."   (verse 75)

His realisation of the true nature of the worldly wealth that surrounded him, and the desire for power and riches that motivated so many of those who surrounded the king, brought to him a deep and abiding insight into those things that really mattered:

"Thy word have I hid (literally, treasured) in mine heart, that I might not sin against thee."   (verse 11)

"I have rejoiced in the way of thy testimonies, as much as in all riches."   (verse 14)

"The law of thy mouth is better unto me than thousands of gold and silver."   (verse 72)

"Therefore I love thy commandments above gold; yea, above fine gold."   (verse 127)

(see also verses 37,129,162)

Living in these circles must have been a difficult and lonely path for David to tread and his reaction was typical of the man. He sought out those, like Jonathan who were of a like mind:

"I am a companion of all them that fear thee, and of them that keep thy precepts."   (verse 63)

Not only so, but he endeavoured by the power of his example to influence others that they might be attracted to his company and the fellowship of those who were of a like mind:

"They that fear thee will be glad when they see me; because I have hoped in thy word."   (verse 74)

Another factor that would have had an enormous effect upon such a man as David was the godless atmosphere that prevailed in the royal court. Even as a young man he was sensitive to sin and wickedness, and like righteous Lot in the city of Sodom who "vexed (literally, tortured) his righteous soul from day to day with their unlawful deeds" (2 Peter 2:8), so he too would have experienced anguish of spirit that wickedness and iniquity flourished where righteousness and justice should have prevailed:

"Horror hath taken hold upon me because of the wicked that forsake thy law."   (verse 53)

986

"Rivers of waters run down mine eyes, because they keep not thy law."   (verse 136)

"I beheld the transgressors, and was grieved; because they kept not thy word."   (verse 158)

Here is a yardstick to measure our reaction to the wickedness of the world in which we live. Do we feel a similar sense of distress because the God we profess to love is ignored; because His word is disregarded and men sink deeper and deeper into a morass of uncleanness and iniquity because of an abysmal decline in moral standards?

In David's case remember it was even more dreadful than that, for those of whom he wrote were fellow Israelites, members of the covenant people of God and consequently the grief and anguish that he experienced was keener and even more deeply felt.

Throughout all this time that he spent in the royal court, with all the difficulties and problems associated with it, David never forgot that he had been anointed by Samuel to be king over Israel and that he had the assurance of God's word that what had been promised would be fulfilled. So his prayer was:

"Stablish thy word unto thy servant, who is devoted to thy fear."   (verse 38)

"Remember the word unto thy servant, upon which thou hast caused me to hope."   (verse 49)

(see also verse 42)

A recurring phrase that runs through the psalm is "according to thy word". It occurs on twelve separate occasions (verses 25,28,41,58,65,76,116,154,156,159,169 and 170) and some of these appear to refer specifically to God's promise that one day David would be Saul's successor.

Yet, although he had this confidence in God's faithfulness, this did not prevent David from crying unto the Lord for that deliverance for which he longed:

"My soul fainteth for thy salvation: but I hope in thy word."   (verse 81)

987

"I am thine, save me; for I have sought thy precepts."
(verse 94)
(see also verses 153,154 and 170)

This is a reflection of how those who confidently wait for the coming of the Lord Jesus nevertheless "give (God) no rest, till he establish, and till he make Jerusalem a praise in the earth" (Isaiah 62:7).

Threads of Thought

We have already established, in considering David's reaction to his circumstances, a number of threads of thought that can be traced through the psalm. These have been primarily concerned with establishing the historical background and the Davidic authorship of the writing.

There are, however, other themes that can be identified and traced through each of the psalm's twenty-two stanzas. Any attempt, however, to link them in a thematic way would appear to be a fruitless exercise. Nevertheless, as we have seen, there are forms of expression that occur throughout the psalm, and the repetition of these words and phrases contributes to the overall impact that this magnificent psalm makes upon the hearts and minds of all those who share the writer's love for the word of God.

As mentioned above, many commentators associate the psalm with the Book of Deuteronomy in particular, and there can be little doubt that this book had made a significant impact on the mind of the writer. However, we believe that it would be overstating the case to regard the whole psalm as a meditation on that book alone. Certainly the spirit of the psalm is captured by the words of the sixth chapter:

"And thou shalt love the LORD thy God with all thine heart, and with all thy soul, and with all thy might. And these words which I command thee this day, shall be in thine heart: and thou shalt teach them diligently unto thy children, and shalt talk of them when thou sittest in thine house, and when thou walkest by the way, and when thou liest down, and when thou risest up. And thou shalt bind them for a sign upon thine hand, and they shall be as frontlets between thine eyes. And thou shalt write them upon the posts of thine house, and on thy gates." (verses 5-9)

When Samuel anointed David in preference to his brothers, it was necessary for the Lord to remind him that "the LORD seeth not as man seeth; for man looketh on the outward appearance, but the LORD looketh on the heart" (1 Samuel 16:7). God declared David to be a man after His own heart. It comes then as no surprise to find that David should open this wonderful soliloquy upon the word of God with the words:

"Blessed are the undefiled in the way, who walk in the law of the LORD. Blessed are they that keep his testimonies, and that seek him with the whole heart."
(verses 1,2)

The word "whole" conveys the idea of unity and completeness. It was the entire man that held God's word in affection and that longed for fellowship with Him. Here is a clear allusion to the words of Deuteronomy 6 and they are characteristic of the psalm, being found on another seven occasions (see verses 10,11,34,69,111,112 and 145). Similar words or expressions carrying the same significance can be found throughout the Book of Deuteronomy.

Again, the injunction of God to His people through Moses in the Book of Deuteronomy was to learn His statutes:

"Hear, O Israel, the statutes and judgments which I speak in your ears this day, that ye may learn them, and keep, and do them." (5:1)

The Hebrew word translated "learn" means literally 'an ox goad'. We can appreciate how this would become associated with the practice of learning for just as the ox would be prodded to move, spurred into action, so the teacher would stimulate and provoke the mind of his pupils by his words. Interestingly, the same Hebrew word (*lamed* – ox goad, see twelfth letter of the alphabet above) stands for both 'to learn' and 'to teach' and is a feature of both Deuteronomy and the psalm (see Deuteronomy 4:1,10,14; 5:1,31; 6:1; 11:19; 14:23; 17:29; 18:9; 31:12,13; Psalm 119:12,26,64,66,68,71,73,108,124 and 135).

David's desire was to learn more of God's word. His prayer was that God would teach him His statutes. Two other key words in relation to teaching and learning are the words "understanding" and "meditate". The word "understanding" occurs eight times (verses 34,73,99,104, 125,130,144 and 169) and means literally 'to separate mentally, to distinguish'. The word "meditate" occurs seven times (verses 15,23,48,78,97,99 and 148) and means literally 'to ponder, to talk with oneself'.

David longed for greater understanding; his consuming passion was to broaden his knowledge, to grow in wisdom and appreciation of God's character:

"O how love I thy law! it is my meditation all the day." (verse 97)

One of the great lessons of the Book of Deuteronomy was "that man doth not live by bread only, but by every word that proceedeth out of the mouth of the LORD doth man live" (8:3). The command had been: "Now therefore hearken, O Israel, unto the statutes and unto the judgments, which I teach you, for to do them, that ye may live, and go in and possess the land ..." (4:1).

It was for this life that David longed – not just this mundane mortal life that is common to all men but that life that is life indeed. It is the only life that, in the last analysis, is worth living at all and which, by the grace of God, will finally blossom into the never-ending life of the kingdom age. "Quicken thou me according to thy word" (verse 25; see also verses 37,40,50,88,93,107,116,149,154, 156 and 159).

Throughout all its parts the psalm breathes the sweet savour of the joy and delight that David felt in the word of God:

"Thy testimonies also are my delight and my counsellors." (verse 24)

"O how love I thy law! it is my meditation all the day." (verse 97)

"Thy testimonies have I taken as an heritage for ever: for they are the rejoicing of my heart." (verse 111)

(see also verses 16,18,35,40,45,47, 70,77,92,113,119,140,162,163,167 and 174)

David found nothing irksome in God's law. He did not feel
that it placed restraints on him that prevented him from
enjoying life to the full. Rather he rejoiced in it, delighted
in it, loved it and treasured it above his chiefest joy. Thus
it becomes all God's servants to seek to develop a similar
attitude towards God's revelation, that therein they too
might find the comfort and consolation that it offers.

David's Bible

We need to remember that at the time David composed
this psalm the written scriptures would probably have
been limited to the five books of Moses, the books of Job,
Joshua and Judges and possibly the book of Ruth, the
Psalms of Moses and the early chapters of Samuel (see 1
Samuel 10:25, RV margin).

More problematical is the availability of these
scriptures to David. We can be reasonably certain that as
the first king of Israel there would have been a copy in the
possession of Saul, in accordance with the command of
Moses (Deuteronomy 17:18-20). The original documents
would have been laid up before the Lord in the tabernacle
and there would need to be copies in each of the forty-eight
Levitical cities to enable them to teach the people the law
of God. The development of the schools of the prophets and
particularly the influence of Samuel, presupposes the
availability of copies for the use of those who attended
these seminaries, possibly David amongst them. That he
sat at the feet of the teachers in Israel is evident from the
words of the psalm itself (verses 99,100). Perhaps a
reasonable conjecture is that David, having been anointed
to be king by Samuel, and perhaps at his instigation, took
the first opportunity to put into practice the command of
Deuteronomy and copied for his own personal use 'The
Book of the Law'.

It has been suggested (by Brother Edward Whittaker,
in "Psalm 119: A Chapter from Life", *Testimony Magazine,*
May 1977) that David composed this psalm at the time of
his persecution by Saul and carried it with him into exile
where it served as a constant reminder to him of that law
in its entirety.

An Enigma

It was not without reason that we reproduced the table above giving the letters of the Hebrew alphabet, together with the meanings of each letter and their numerical value. We asked the question whether each of these letters with its particular meaning had a special significance for David and described an aspect of his relationship with God.

The answer is that a significant number of the meanings of the letters are developed in the stanzas they head. The enigma is that this does not appear to be true of all twenty-two stanzas and we are left pondering if those that do conform to this pattern do so coincidentally (something we regard as unlikely), or if the problem lies in our own inability to discern the development of thought arising from the heading – a much more likely possibility. We give below the more obvious connections in thought between the alphabetical heading and the substance of the stanza.

Letter 9 *teth* (goodness)

"Thou hast dealt well with thy servant" (verse 65)

"Teach me good judgment and knowledge" (verse 66)

"Thou art good, and doest good" (verse 68)

"It is good for me that I have been afflicted" (verse 71)

Letter 15 *samech* (support)

"Uphold me according unto thy word" (verse 116)

"Hold thou me up, and I shall be safe" (verse 117)

Letter 16 *ain* (eye)

"Mine eyes fail for thy salvation" (verse 123)

Letter 17 *pe* (mouth)

"The entrance of thy words giveth light" (verse 130)

"I opened my mouth, and panted" (verse 131)

Letter 18 *tzade* (righteousness)

"Righteous art thou, O LORD, and upright are thy judgments" (verse 137)

"Thy testimonies that thou hast commanded are righteous" (verse 138)

"Thy righteousness is an everlasting righteousness" (verse 142)

"The righteousness of thy testimonies is everlasting" (verse 144)

Letter 19 *qoph* (ear / hearing)

"I cried with my whole heart; hear me, O LORD" (verse 145)

"I cried unto thee" (verse 146)

"I prevented the dawning of the morning, and cried" (verse 147)

"Hear my voice according unto thy lovingkindness" (verse 149)

It might be said, with some justification, that just six instances out of twenty-two is not a particularly convincing statistic. Nevertheless, the fact that David did develop his thoughts around the alphabetical heading on these occasions does raise the question as to why he did not follow this pattern throughout. Were there other connections raised in his mind that were not strictly based on the meaning of the letter? For instance, the passage quoted earlier from Deuteronomy chapter 6 contains as many as six words that correspond to the meanings denoted at the head of the stanzas. None of these are to be found in the list of meanings given above.

Again we ask why it is that the ten words used to describe the word of God throughout the psalm are found in every verse save one (or three depending on the reading of the Hebrew text)? We could reasonably expect that one or other of the words would have been found in every verse. Is the omission(s) deliberate, intended to convey some aspect of thought that we have not discerned? It must remain yet another aspect of the enigma of the psalm as any attempt to answer the question on our part would be futile conjecture.

Some Final Thoughts

If further proof were to be needed for the Davidic authorship of the psalm, then a glance at the marginal references will indicate a rich source of connections to other psalms written by David later in his life. The thoughts and expressions that were penned at this early period remained with him and were the foundation of that Godly life that was characteristic of him, albeit with some sad lapses.

It is worthy of note that nowhere in the psalm is there specific reference to the sacrifices and offerings of the law. The nearest we get is to be found in the words of verse 108 which speaks of "the freewill offerings of my mouth" – that is, the sacrifice of prayer and praise (see Hebrews 13:15; Hosea 14:2).

Observing the precepts and commandments of the law would of course have involved the offering of sacrifice and the observance of its ritual, but the emphasis is upon the moral and ethical teaching that God enjoined upon His servants and one wonders if Samuel had impressed the lesson upon David at the time of his anointing. It was, after all, Saul's failure to recognise what God really required of men that led to his rejection and the choice of David:

"Hath the LORD as great delight in burnt offerings and sacrifices, as in obeying the voice of the LORD? Behold, to obey is better than sacrifice, and to hearken than the fat of rams." (1 Samuel 15:22)

There is no sense of waywardness in the life of the writer of this wonderful psalm and although the last verse might seem to suggest that David had departed from God's ways like a lost sheep, a little reflection will convince us that this is not really so:

"I have gone astray like a lost sheep; seek thy servant; for I do not forget thy commandments." (verse 176)

The reference is to the circumstances in which he found himself, not to his spiritual waywardness. Driven from the court of Saul he became a fugitive who wandered in the wilderness like a sheep separated from the flock of God. His prayer was that God would seek him out in the midst of all the dangers he faced, for he had not forgotten God's commandments. He carried that word with him in his heart and it was his source of strength and comfort in all the distress and adversity that faced him.

David knew that in God's word he had an eternal inheritance that no man could take from him, for his God who had promised was faithful and true:

"Thy testimonies have I taken as an heritage for ever; for they are the rejoicing of my heart. I have inclined mine heart to perform thy statutes, for ever, even unto the end."   (verses 111,112, RV)

INTRODUCTION TO PSALMS 120–134
THE SONGS OF DEGREES

MOST commentators suggest that the fifteen Psalms of Degrees that comprise what has been termed 'A Little Psalter' are of a late date and were probably written in the days of Nehemiah and Ezra. This view is based primarily on the verbal links which they feel can be established between the psalms and the Books of Nehemiah and Ezra. That the verbal links exist cannot be denied, but we find it strange that the possibility that these men of God were actually quoting the psalms because of their relevance to the circumstances of their own days never seems to be considered. We are convinced that this is the case, and once this is accepted it becomes evidence not of a late date for their composition, but proof of a much earlier date of origin for they had become known and accepted as part of the canon of Hebrew Scripture.

The Origin of the Psalms

Of the fifteen psalms, four are ascribed to David, one to Solomon and ten are anonymous. Each of them carries the prescription "A Song of degrees" (RV, "A Song of Ascents"). In his book *Old Testament Problems*, J. W. Thirtle lists the primary suggestions that have been made as to the meaning of the inscription (pages 6-10).

1. They are regarded as 'Songs of the Return' being associated with the homeward journey of the exiles from captivity – hence the ascent from Babylon (see Ezra 7:9). Remembering that there was an even greater (in terms of numbers) return from captivity in the days of Hezekiah, it is not surprising that there is a similarity of language between the songs and the later writings of the return from Babylonian captivity. However, in contradistinction to this view, it should be noted that Psalm 122 presupposes the

existence of the temple and in Psalm 134 the services of the temple are regarded as being fully operational.

2. More widely held is the view that the psalms were sung by pilgrims as they journeyed to Jerusalem to keep the feasts. The psalms thus become 'stages' or 'stations' on their journey. The content of the psalms does not lend itself to the view that this was the reason for which they were written. Nevertheless, it might well be true that later generations adopted the psalms for this purpose although this fact is irrelevant as far as determining the origin of the psalms is concerned.

3. Gesenius suggests that there is a particular "step-like structure" marked in some of the psalms. But even if this could be substantiated, which other writers deny, it would apply only to their literary or metrical form and would not help us to determine their historical background.

4. Again, it is said that they refer to the fifteen steps that led from the Court of Israel to the Court of the Women in the second temple. Levites were said to stand on this flight of steps, reciting or singing these psalms on the first day of the Feast of Tabernacles. Delitzsch claims that this has no historical basis but again, even if true, it does not help us to establish the origin of the psalms.

Thirtle maintains that the psalms are temple hymns designed to be used in worship and that the changes in pronouns, from the first person to the third for instance, is an indication that they were intended for antiphonal (part) singing. This seems a reasonable assumption and, for this writer, it is hard to disagree with the conclusions reached by Thirtle in his work mentioned above (pages 13-19). He refers to the titles as 'Headlines' of a literary not musical nature, and as "the bush" (Luke 20:37) would refer to Moses at the burning bush so "the degrees" (or 'steps' as the word means literally) refers to the occasion in the life of Hezekiah when the shadow of the degrees on the sundial of Ahaz moved backwards ten degrees. This sundial may well have been composed of a flight of steps (see number 4 above) and fifteen years were added to the king's life. The psalms are then connected with the great events in the life of Hezekiah, for the siege of Jerusalem by Sennacherib and the king's sickness were synonymous events and the deliverance from both, linked as they are in time, is reflected in the substance of the psalms.

The Greatness of Hezekiah

Just how great a man Hezekiah was is not always appreciated. Like his father David he had a preoccupation with the house of the Lord. At the beginning of his reign he opened the house and cleansed it after the desecration of his father Ahaz. He restored its services and was instrumental in initiating a spiritual revival in Judah.

When stricken with his illness his greatest concern was not that he might die, but that he was cut off from the service of Yahweh, his God. He was unable to go up to the house of the Lord to offer the sacrifices of praise (see Isaiah 38:11; 2 Kings 18:4-6; 2 Chronicles 30:1,26). The sign of the degrees was not just that fifteen years would be added to his life, but also that on the third day he should go up to the house of the Lord (2 Kings 20:8,9; Isaiah 38:8). His primary purpose in life was related to the worship of his God in the temple. So he could exclaim:

"We will sing my songs to the stringed instruments all the days of our life in the house of the LORD."

(Isaiah 38:20)

This does not mean that Hezekiah, or for that matter any of his contemporaries, wrote the anonymous psalms in this group of songs. He (or they) might well have written some of them, or indeed all of them, but they were gathered together because of their appropriateness to the circumstances of his life, and in them he saw a reflection of the deliverance that God had wrought in his life. Thus more than four of the psalms could be from the pen of David, but the number of the psalms collected together was a reflection of the fifteen years that were added to Hezekiah's life and bore the title "the degrees" or 'steps' because of the manner of the sign he was given.

It is a lovely thought that perhaps these songs were sung continuously throughout the day and the night (see

Psalm 134), an idea supported by the words of 1 Chronicles 9:33.

Perhaps it would be appropriate to conclude this introduction by emphasising that all of these psalms can also be described as 'songs of Zion'. Jerusalem is mentioned five times; Zion, seven times and the temple and its services six times. The name of God is also characteristic of the songs, occurring over fifty times with no single psalm being without it.

Some have seen a pattern in the psalms, combining them for instance into three groups. We cannot say that there is no substance to this approach only that, as far as we are concerned, we find the evidence unconvincing.

PSALM 120

ONE writer has stated that a difference of opinion exists respecting the interpretation of almost every verse and word of this psalm. One presumes that he was speaking of the verbal complexities that Hebrew scholars sometimes get enmeshed in, for it appears to us that the message of the song is not complicated but relatively straightforward when the historical background is appreciated.

The psalm for instance is individual and personal. The writer does not speak for the nation but for himself, and in this instance we feel that the writer can be no other than Hezekiah the king. The background is the siege of Jerusalem by Sennacherib and his allies and the psalm reflects Hezekiah's distress at the straitness of the circumstances of the situation in which he found himself. If there is any difficulty of interpretation with this psalm, then it must lie with our understanding of verse 5 which speaks of dwelling with Mesech and among the tents of Kedar. Of these two peoples the *Cambridge Bible* (page 736) says :

> "Meshech, mentioned in Genesis 10:2 as a son of Japheth, was a barbarous people living between the Black Sea and the Caspian, probably the Moschi of Herodotus (3.94), and Mushki of the Assyrian inscriptions: Kedar, mentioned in Genesis 25:13 as the second son of Ishmael, was one of the wild tribes which roamed through the Arabian desert, 'whose hand was against every man' (Genesis 16:12)."

Because of the geographical distance between these two peoples it would be impossible to dwell amongst both. Consequently the names must be considered as being representative of barbarous people generally and thought of as being probably descriptive of men of Judah who behaved as if they were no different to these barbarous people and ignorant of Israel's God. Such an understanding is perfectly in keeping with the tone of the psalm, given the treacherous and disloyal men by whom Hezekiah was surrounded during his sickness.

The psalm is short and there is no need to subdivide it in any way. In the opening verse the Psalmist calls to mind the manner in which the Lord had delivered him from past distress and finds in these experiences the confidence that He will deliver him from his present trouble. The reason for his anguish of soul is described in verse 2:

"Deliver my soul, O LORD, from lying lips, and from a deceitful tongue."

This language bears a striking similarity with the words of David in Psalm 52 (verses 1-4) which were written concerning the actions of Doeg the Edomite that led to his subsequent flight to dwell amongst the Philistines (1 Samuel 21:10-15). The lies of which David speaks are those that were told concerning him and fostered in the royal court of Saul. Hezekiah faced a similar situation within his own court, and perhaps the reference to Mesech and Kedar was prompted by the fact that it was an Edomite who was the primary cause of David's distress at that time.

During his sickness Hezekiah was unable to deal with the affairs of state as he would normally have done. These were delegated to others and taking advantage of the situation they behaved in a duplicitous manner and sought to further their own interests.

It was, we feel sure, the influence of these men that caused Hezekiah to send all the silver and gold that was in the house of the Lord and in his own house in a vain attempt to dissuade Sennacherib from his intended purpose (2 Kings 18:13-16). They, on their part, had sent a delegation to negotiate with the Assyrian king and felt they had achieved an understanding with him that would ensure their safety (see Isaiah 31:1). He, however, was as untrustworthy as they and had no intention of keeping the covenant that they had made with him.

Notwithstanding their covenant with Sennacherib they had taken further precautions to resolve the situation by seeking an alliance with Pharaoh, king of Egypt (see Isaiah 30:1-7; chapter 31). The treachery of these false and untrustworthy men is condemned by the prophet Isaiah (28:14,15,18-22). The prophet Micah, a contemporary of Isaiah, sums up the spirit of the royal court at that time when he writes:

> "For the rich men thereof are full of violence, and the inhabitants thereof have spoken lies, and their tongue is deceitful in their mouth." (Micah 6:12)

The intrigue and devious behaviour of those who surrounded him in the royal court was a cause of anguish of soul to the king and his prayer was that he might be delivered from the plotting and scheming of these evil men.

The lying lips, however, were not confined to the princes of Judah. Sennacherib had shown in his dealings with the delegation from Judah that he too was a man who had a total disregard for honesty and uprightness. He was prepared to break every promise he had made in his determination to achieve his ends. From him too, Hezekiah needed his God to save him:

> "What shall be given unto thee? or what shall be done unto thee, thou false tongue? Sharp arrows of the mighty, with coals of juniper." (Psalm 120:3,4)

The Psalmist is sure that God will not leave those who practise falsehood unpunished.

He addresses the tongue of the liar. God is the subject of the verbs and it is pointed out by several writers that the question is based on the Hebrew idiom, "God do so to thee, and more also" (1 Samuel 3:17). The answer to the question is that just as the deceitful man has shot his verbal arrows of slander and false accusation (Jeremiah 9:3), so God will respond in kind by piercing him with literal arrows of destruction. He will be consumed as with coals of broom. Broom, the literal meaning of the word translated "juniper", was used to make charcoal which was reputed to produce the greatest heat for the longest

1002

period of time. So God will consume them in the burning fire of divine retribution (Psalm 140:10,11).

We have already commented on verse 5, but as a more literal alternative readers might wish to consider the possibility that the reference is to the warlike men of Kedar whose hatred of Judah is reflected in the judgement pronounced against them in Isaiah 21:16,17. The reference to Mesech could then be to those peoples deported from their homes near the Caucasus and transplanted in and around Samaria – the people we know as Samaritans (2 Kings 17:24-41). These, no doubt, would have been a thorn in the side of Judah and would have been prepared to support Sennacherib in his military campaign.

This view would of course affect our interpretation of verse 6 which would then refer to their warlike character: "My soul hath long dwelt with him that hateth peace." For too long he had dwelt with these hostile peoples who were motivated by a desire for aggression rather than concord. Alternatively we think of those in the royal court who put their trust in alliances with the like of Egypt that they might confront the military power of the Assyrian rather than putting their trust in the God of Israel.

The greatest threat of all remained Sennacherib. Hezekiah had no wish to antagonise this Assyrian tyrant. What he longed for was peace that he might be able to worship his God in that house in which He was pleased to dwell in Jerusalem: "I am for peace: but when I speak, they are for war" (verse 7). Sennacherib was determined to capture Jerusalem. In the face of Hezekiah's desire for peace, his heart was set on war (see 2 Chronicles 32:1,2, AV margin, "his face was to war").

Where then could the king look for deliverance? He was beset with unfaithful men within and by a dreadful and ruthless tyrant without. He had previously found solace in his God and it was to Him that he now turned:

"In my distress I cried unto the LORD, and he heard me. Deliver my soul, O LORD, from lying lips, and from a deceitful tongue." (verses1,2)

PSALM 121

THIS is surely one of the loveliest of all the psalms. It expresses perfect trust in the God of Israel who guards and preserves His people. Written against the background of Rabshakeh's taunts and Sennacherib's letter, it bears comparison with the beautiful prayer of Hezekiah when he spread the letter from the Assyrians before the Lord (Isaiah 38:14-20). Here is a man with complete confidence in the ability of his God to save.

There is perhaps a certain ambiguity about the meaning of the first verse: "I will lift up mine eyes unto the hills, from whence cometh my help." Some understand it, following the rendering of the AV margin: "Shall I lift up mine eyes to the hills? whence should mine help come?" as being a reference to the idolatry that was practised on the mountains of Israel. It becomes therefore a complete denial of the gods of the nations who were powerless to help. The words of Jeremiah (3:23) lend themselves to this view. Translators generally, however, do not support this understanding of the Hebrew text. The Psalmist is rather lifting up his eyes to the mountains (RV) of Zion, the seat of Yahweh's throne, which spoke of His sovereignty, not only over His people but over all the earth (Psalms 87:1-3; 125:1,2; 133:3). In keeping with this understanding, the psalms speak of God's help as proceeding forth from Zion (3:4; 20:1,2; 134:3).

There is no doubt expressed in the second phrase but it is introduced to elicit the response of verse 2: "My help cometh from the LORD, which made heaven and earth." His confidence was grounded in the knowledge that his God was the Creator of heaven and earth and consequently nothing could frustrate His will or withstand His power. Hezekiah's prayer in Isaiah 37 revolves around the same premise:

"O LORD of hosts, God of Israel, that dwellest between
the cherubims, thou art the God, even thou alone, of all
the kingdoms of the earth: thou hast made heaven and
earth."   (verse 16)

The same emphasis is to be found in two of the other songs
of degrees (124:8; 134:3).

It is a frequent epithet in scripture and contrasts with
the gods of the nations, "The gods that have not made the
heavens and the earth ..." (Jeremiah 10:11).

Israel's Keeper

In the last six verses of the psalm the same Hebrew word
is used six times to describe Israel's God and He is
presented either as the keeper or the preserver of His
people. The Revised Version uniformly translates the
word either "keep" or "keeper". The same word is used
many times in Psalm 119 where it is translated, "keep",
"observe", and "take heed" and there is a principle
emphasised by the two uses of the word. When Israel
keeps God's word then He keeps them from evil. It is not
only true of Israel for the Lord Jesus told the ecclesia at
Philadelphia:

"Because thou hast kept the word of my patience, I
also will keep thee from the hour of temptation, which
shall come upon all the world ..."   (Revelation 3:10)

When God appears to be unmoved by the sufferings of His
people and they wait longingly for deliverance and for
some sign that He is active on their behalf once more, the
cry is "Awake, why sleepest thou, O Lord?" (Psalm 44:23).

This, of course, is a figure of speech, for unlike Baal, of
whom the prophet Elijah said mockingly, "peradventure
he sleepeth, and must be awaked" (1 Kings 18:27), the God
of Israel neither slumbers nor sleeps. Following the RV
margin of Psalm 121:3, the Psalmist makes an
exclamation of hope that God will not disregard the
welfare of His people: "Let him not suffer thy foot to be
moved: let him not slumber that keepeth thee."

There would appear to be an allusion in these words to
the Song of Hannah – a particularly appropriate reference
when we consider the fate of the Assyrian host:

1005

"He will keep the feet of his saints, and the wicked shall be silent in darkness; for by strength shall no man prevail. The adversaries of the LORD shall be broken to pieces; out of heaven shall he thunder upon them."

(1 Samuel 2:9,10)

Then with a majestic outpouring of confidence the writer answers this deprecative comment. Israel's God neither slumbers nor sleeps. He is not like a human sentry. He is ever watchful, ever aware of the needs of His people. In His vigilance He smote the host of Assyria while they slept (Isaiah 37:36), for:

"The LORD is thy keeper: the LORD is thy shade upon thy right hand. The sun shall not smite thee by day, nor the moon by night. The LORD shall preserve thee from all evil: he shall preserve thy soul."   (Psalm 121:5-7)

The word translated "shade" is elsewhere rendered "shadow" and we are reminded of Psalm 91 (a psalm of Moses) where an assurance is given that, "He that dwelleth in the secret place of the most High shall abide under the shadow of the Almighty" (verse 1).

Under His shadow there was no need to be afraid, whether by day or night, for He who keeps Israel never sleeps. The danger of sunstroke was ever present. It was widely believed that the moon also could have a detrimental effect. However, these physical effects, from which men needed to be protected, were but metaphors for the unceasing guardian care of God in all the varying circumstances of life. He would protect His servants from all evil and from every kind of calamity – nothing is outside of the protective power of God. This is not an insurance policy against the adversities of everyday life. We share with all men the ills to which flesh is heir. The difference is that in our lives God uses these events to test us, to put us to the proof, to chasten us. In our spiritual lives, however, the guardian care of our Heavenly Father is something in which we can have absolute trust, for it is His good pleasure to give us the kingdom.

The closing words of the psalm reaffirm its overall message:

translated "compact" is used of human association on many occasions and the noun "companion" is derived from it. It has been suggested that the phrase carries the meaning, 'as a city in which companionship together was fostered'. In the eye of the Psalmist the fact that the city was joined together, compacted as an integrated unit, spoke not only of the harmony of the inhabitants of the city but of the unity of the nation as a whole. God's people looked to this city and to here the tribes of Israel came thrice yearly to keep the feasts and to give thanks to their God. These things were "a testimony unto Israel" (RV); a token of the privilege that they enjoyed as the people of God. There are two interesting connections with the Hebrew word rendered "compact" that lend themselves to the picture presented in these verses.

Firstly, the term is used of the joining together of the two shoulder pieces of the ephod which the priest wore and on which was inscribed the names of the twelve tribes of Israel – six on each (Exodus 28:7). Secondly, it is used of the coupling together of the curtains of the tabernacle (Exodus 36:10,13,16,18).

A deeper insight will appreciate that the unity of the city speaks also of the heavenly Jerusalem and of the never-ending fellowship of the kingdom age. This city must have an abiding place in the hearts of God's servants of all ages for all their hopes and aspirations are bound up in its future.

It is in this city also that God will fulfil the covenant made with David when He promised the everlasting stability of his throne. It was in this city that judgement was dispensed by David's royal house. It is here in the age to come that there shall sit "thrones of judgment, the thrones of the house of David". That the reference is to the kingdom age is made clear when the Lord Jesus quoted this psalm to his disciples when they asked him:

"What shall we have therefore? And Jesus said unto them, Verily I say unto you, That ye which have followed me, in the regeneration when the Son of man shall sit in the throne of his glory, ye also shall sit upon twelve thrones, judging the twelve tribes of Israel."

(Matthew 19:27,28)

In the light of Psalm 122, the implications of this statement should not be missed for these are the thrones of the house of David. They, therefore, although not born into the royal line are now, by adoption, members of that royal house. The promise had been: "Also the LORD telleth thee that he will make thee an house" (2 Samuel 7:11). We too, by baptism, are members of that royal house, for with a play upon these promises the Apostle Paul writes:

"(I) will be a Father unto you, and ye shall be my sons and daughters, saith the Lord Almighty. Having therefore these promises, dearly beloved ..."

(cp. 2 Corinthians 6:18–7:1 with 2 Samuel 7:14)

The Peace of Jerusalem

A time would come when the prophet would exhort the people of Judah to pray for the peace of Babylon, for in that peace they should find peace (Jeremiah 29:7). The language echoes the thoughts of this psalm, but how different the circumstances. All that God had promised regarding the city of Jerusalem spoke of that glorious future when David's throne should be established for ever. It was their failure as a nation to maintain this hope in their hearts that had led to this situation. To discipline them, and to further His purpose, God brought them into captivity and stressed the importance of seeking the peace of their captors, that they might find the freedom from strife that would enable them to learn again the lessons of their past history. How they must have prayed for the peace of Jerusalem in that alien land, and how down through the succeeding ages have God's servants, in times of adversity and in the long years of waiting, echoed the words of this psalm:

"Pray for the peace of Jerusalem: they shall prosper that love thee. Peace be within thy walls, and prosperity within thy palaces. For my brethren and companions' sakes, I will now say, Peace be within thee. Because of the house of the LORD our God I will seek thy good." (verses 6-9)

This psalm was surely in the mind of the Lord Jesus as he entered the city at the beginning of the last week of his life:

"And when he was come near, he beheld the city, and wept over it, saying, If thou hadst known, even thou, at least in this thy day, the things which belong unto thy peace! but now they are hid from thine eyes."

(Luke 19:41,42)

In the original text, there is a word play that binds together the words peace (*shalom*), prosperity (*shalvah*) and Jerusalem (*Yerushalayim*). There is a resemblance of sound between the syllables that carries a kind of prophetic significance; that acts as a portent of that wonderful future when the city will be seen in all its glory. It is a prayer that all those who look for salvation in Zion might prosper. Once more the literal and the spiritual merge. For David (and Hezekiah) there was a very real sense in which they looked for peace and prosperity in their own days. However, for those who through the dark ages of Gentile domination have longed for the peace of Jerusalem, that prosperity can only be an abundance of spiritual riches.

It was not for all Israel that David looked for these blessings. Truly all the tribes would come up to worship, but David knew in his heart that perhaps for the majority of worshippers this was a religious formality to which they conformed. They had no real love for the house of the Lord; no real conception of the glories of the future age of which all these things were a portent. So his prayer was for his brethren, his companions, who shared his spiritual aspirations – all those joined in fellowship by the common hope that they held. The Psalmist's final thought was for the house of his God:

"Because of the house of the LORD our God I will seek thy good." (verse 9)

His love of the city was centred on the fact that this was the place the Lord had chosen to dwell. It was to this place that David had brought the ark and from here the Lord of all the earth exercised His sovereignty. It was in this shared confidence that he would make his prayer for the good of his fellows.

PSALM 123

THIS short but beautiful psalm expresses the unfaltering faith of Hezekiah faced by the scorn and derision of Rabshakeh. It opens with the king himself speaking as the representative of the nation and then moves (verse 2) to include all the people of Judah who join with him in his prayer.

The emphasis of the psalm is upon the manner in which they acknowledge their dependence on God and this is illustrated by the repetition of the words that describe their attitude of patient waiting upon Him:

"Unto thee lift I up mine eyes." (verse 1)

"Behold, as the eyes of servants look unto the hand of their masters, and as the eyes of a maiden unto the hand of her mistress; so our eyes wait upon the LORD our God ..." (verse 2)

Here is recognition that He who sat enthroned in the heavens (verse 1) was sovereign and that He was the "governor among the nations" (Psalm 22:28). So these things that had befallen them were at His behest and their eyes were fastened upon Him, as a servant upon the hand of his master, for they depended upon Him and looked for some indication that He was ready to relieve their distress. Their attention to their God, like the servant to his master, was an intimation of their readiness to acquiesce with His will and to obey and submit to His wishes.

The extremity of their plight and the intensity of their faith are seen once more in the repetition of their plea to God to look on them with favour:

"So our eyes wait upon the LORD our God, until that he have mercy upon us. Have mercy upon us, O LORD,

have mercy upon us: for we are exceedingly filled with
contempt." (verses 2,3)

Contempt and derision had been their daily food. They
had heard the scornful boasts of the Assyrian; listened to
his insolent taunts and his mockery of their God (see 2
Kings 18:19-35; 19:22,27,28). Truly they could say:

"Our soul is exceeding filled with the scorning of
those that are at ease, and with the contempt of the
proud." (verse 4)

Psalm 44, a song associated with these same events,
echoes these words:

"Thou makest us a reproach to our neighbours, a
scorn and a derision to them that are round about us.
Thou makest us a byword among the heathen, a
shaking of the head among the people. My confusion is
continually before me, and the shame of my face hath
covered me, for the voice of him that reproacheth and
blasphemeth; by reason of the enemy and avenger."
(verses 13-16)

In Rabshakeh, the ambassador of Sennacherib, we see
a cynical and unscrupulous worldly-minded man; a man
with no thought for Israel's God and who had no qualms
about mocking and deriding Him. Although our
circumstances are quite different, his attitude is a
reflection of the kind of world that we live in today. Men
have no thought for the God we worship and no
compunction about mocking Him and the Lord Jesus
Christ. They live in the false assurance that there is no
God, and even if there is, He is not interested in them (see
Psalm 10:3,4,6,11,13). Those who believe in the word of
God are treated by such men with scorn and derision;
dismissed as 'dinosaurs', clinging to long discarded and
outmoded beliefs.

How should we respond to such people? The whole spirit
of this psalm is captured by the command of Hezekiah to
those who listened from the walls of the city to the
invective that poured out of the mouth of Rabshakeh:

"But they held their peace, and answered him not a
word: for the king's commandment was, saying, Answer
him not." (Isaiah 36:21)

We too must wait upon God and surely here is a circumstance where the words of the Lord Jesus are applicable:

"Give not that which is holy unto the dogs, neither cast ye your pearls before swine, lest they trample them under their feet, and turn again and rend you."

(Matthew 7:6)

PSALM 124

THE psalm has the superscription, "A song of degrees of David". The language of the psalm points to a sudden danger that had providentially been averted. Given the varied circumstances and hazardous nature of David's life when he fled from Saul, those who acknowledge the Davidic authorship usually associate it with this period of his life, but find it difficult to link the psalm with any particular event.

However, the words "Now may Israel say" (verse 1) and the use of the third person throughout the song suggest that its background is to be found in the time when David was king. Tentatively, we suggest that a possible background to the psalm might be found in the time when David fought with the Syrians and the Edomites grasped the opportunity to invade in the south. Joab was despatched to deal with the emergency but was in some difficulty until David and Abishai were able to join him in the conflict. It is not easy to determine the actual course of events from the historical records (2 Samuel, chapters 8 and 10) but Psalm 60, which was written about this situation, suggests that it was a crisis of some magnitude and should be compared with Psalm 124.

Notwithstanding its connection with David, it is not difficult to see why Hezekiah should have included it in his songs of degrees. Its language and thought lend themselves in a wonderful way to the manner in which God delivered His people from the dreadful plight in which they found themselves when faced with the Assyrian threat. From Hezekiah's perspective the psalm could conveniently be divided into two parts:

1. God's deliverance from Sennacherib (verses 1-5).

2. Thanksgiving and confidence for the future (verses 6-8).

Deliverance from Sennacherib

The repetition of the words, "If it had not been the LORD who was on our side" (verses 1,2) is not simply for emphasis. The first time is a recognition that throughout the history of His people God had manifested Himself on their behalf. Without His help they would not have been delivered from the many times of disaster they had faced.

So, the Psalmist says:

"Now may Israel say; If it had not been the LORD who was on our side, when men rose up against us: then they had swallowed us up quick, when their wrath was kindled against us: then the waters had overwhelmed us, the stream had gone over our soul: then the proud waters had gone over our soul." (verses 2-5)

"Now" is not a point of time; rather the Psalmist says, 'for this cause' they could once again be confident that God would deliver them as the nation faced a time of frightening danger. No one had been able to withstand the awesome power of the Assyrian king. Like the river Euphrates overflowing its banks, the Assyrian had swallowed up all the nations of that region. All the fortified cities of Judah had fallen and only Jerusalem remained, for he had reached even to the neck (Isaiah 8:7,8; 37:10-13). Many in Judah had been carried away captive; the Taylor Prism (Sennacherib's account of his military campaigns) mentions a figure of over two hundred thousand. Nevertheless their enemies were but men – the use of the word *adam* heightening the contrast with their God, the Creator of man and indeed, of the heavens and the earth. Like a great monster from the deep they would have swallowed them alive (Jeremiah 51:34). There is an emphasis upon the wrath of their protagonists, and when we read the words of Rabshakeh and Hezekiah's response we can well understand first the frustration that would have been felt by the Assyrians and then the anger (shown in Sennacherib's letter) at Hezekiah's refusal to submit. It has been pointed out that in the Taylor Prism, Sennacherib's disdain for the king is shown by the manner in which he refers to him as "Hezekiah, the Jew", never affording him his royal title. The spirit of the Assyrian is well described in the Lamentations of Jeremiah, although the words are written of a later oppressor:

"All thine enemies have opened their mouth against thee: they hiss and gnash the teeth: they say, We have swallowed her up: certainly this is the day that we looked for; we have found, we have seen it."

(Lamentations 2:16)

The figure of overflowing waters overwhelming everything in their path is of course a common symbol in scripture for trouble and adversity (see Psalms 18:4,16; 69:1,2,15).

So here the stream has become a torrent swollen by a storm and threatens to engulf God's people. This, however, was no natural phenomenon for it was motivated by the pride and hatred of their enemy. "Then indeed had the insolent waters swept over our soul" (Kay, *The Psalms with Notes*).

Before the God of Israel all their proud boasting had availed them nothing. Indeed their tirade against Him had sealed their fate for "the angel of the LORD went forth, and smote in the camp of the Assyrians a hundred and fourscore and five thousand" (Isaiah 37:36).

Thankfulness and Confidence

"Blessed be the LORD, who hath not given us as a prey to their teeth. Our soul is escaped as a bird out of the snare of the fowlers: the snare is broken, and we are escaped. Our help is in the name of the LORD, who made heaven and earth." (verses 6-8)

The imagery of the first section of the psalm is sustained. They poured out their hearts in thankfulness to the One who had not allowed the enemy to swallow them up. They had been delivered, as it were, from the teeth of the lion (Psalm 7:2).

Encircled by the Assyrians in Jerusalem, they had been like a bird about to be snared in a trap. But the trap had not worked and the bird had escaped. The snare was broken; the intentions of the Assyrians were frustrated, for God intervened on behalf of His people.

So they could exclaim, "We are escaped"; the word "we" being emphatic to demonstrate the fact that in the extremity of their plight God had delivered them.

It is interesting to note that in describing these events Sennacherib wrote: "Hezekiah of Judah ... I shut up like a caged bird in Jerusalem, his royal city ... He was overwhelmed by the fear of the brightness of my lordship." His words were written long after the psalm was penned. We wonder whether providentially God caused him to write in this way to demonstrate the veracity of His word.

By His name God had revealed Himself throughout the history of Israel. Once again the qualities of the name had been known to His servants in the salvation wrought. They could look to the future with confidence, in the knowledge that He who had created the heaven and earth was powerful to save and that no power on earth could withstand His will.

PSALM 125

THIS beautiful psalm conveys the spirit of trust and confidence that sustained Hezekiah and all those who shared his faith in the dark days of the Assyrian invasion. Sennacherib and his army were round about Jerusalem. The city was besieged and humanly speaking there was little prospect of relief.

The Everlasting Covenant

Nevertheless they were aware of the everlasting covenant that God had made with David and they maintained their conviction that whatever the outcome of this perilous situation, He would remain faithful to His word. Nothing that men could do would frustrate His purpose. They would have been aware of the prophecy of Isaiah, who had spoken of the wonder of the future age when, "the mountain of the LORD's house shall be established in the top of the mountains ... and many people shall go and say, Come ye, and let us go up to the mountain of the LORD ... and he will teach us of his ways, and we will walk in his paths: for out of Zion shall go forth the law, and the word of the LORD from Jerusalem ... and they shall beat their swords into plowshares, and their spears into pruninghooks: nation shall not lift up sword against nation, neither shall they learn war any more" (Isaiah 2:2-4). All the evidence points to the fact that these words were written early in the ministry of the prophet and certainly before the days of Hezekiah. What then would have been the thoughts of the defenders of Jerusalem as they saw from the walls of the city the hostile and heavily armed Assyrians? There must have been some doubt and perplexity in their hearts as they thought of these promises and the danger in which the throne of David now

1021

stood. Nevertheless, Hezekiah spoke comforting words to the people:

> "Be strong and courageous, be not afraid nor dismayed for the king of Assyria, nor for all the multitude that is with him: for there be more with us than with him: with him is an arm of flesh; but with us is the LORD our God to help us, and to fight our battles. And the people rested themselves upon the words of Hezekiah king of Judah."   (2 Chronicles 32:7,8)

Hezekiah's words of encouragement are reflected in the language of the psalm and it should be remembered also that the prophet Micah, a contemporary of Isaiah, refers to the words of Isaiah 2 and expands upon them, speaking of the day when "they shall sit every man under his vine and under his fig tree; and none shall make them afraid ... (because) the LORD shall reign over them in mount Zion from henceforth, even for ever" (see Micah 4:1-7).

We suggest that these words were written after the destruction of the Assyrian host and were intended as a reassurance that God's words through Isaiah could be trusted implicitly. In the breaking of Sennacherib's army they had seen the evidence that no power on earth could prevent their God from performing the things that He had promised.

Moreover, against the background of Hezekiah's experiences Micah goes on to speak of the one born in Bethlehem who would be ruler in Israel, and would be the peace when the Assyrian came into the land (5:2-5).

Our study of this psalm is not the place to give detailed consideration to events at the time of the end, but we feel that insufficient thought is given to these words of the prophet Micah. Remember that Hezekiah was enthroned in Jerusalem when the Assyrian came into the land and if we consider these events as a pattern of the invasion of the latter day Assyrian then we should look to the Lord Jesus, similarly sitting upon David's throne.

Confidence in God

As the everlasting covenant stands sure so those who put their trust in Israel's God are secure in His care for:

"They that trust in the LORD shall be as mount Zion, which cannot be removed, but abideth for ever. As the mountains are round about Jerusalem, so the LORD is round about his people from henceforth even for ever."

(verses 1,2)

Mountains are symbols of permanence. Zion, in particular, because of its association with God's purpose, represented that which was unmoveable and unchangeable. As Zion cannot be moved, and stands firm upon its foundation, so they that trust in the Lord, and look to Zion and all that it represents, are embraced in that covenant of promise that ensures their eternal future. None of life's storms can affect that prospect if they maintain their trust in God. Jerusalem was surrounded by hills. They spoke of the encircling power of God; the never failing guardianship of the One who would be unto them as a wall of fire round about (Zechariah 2:5). Again the thought is not confined to this present life, for it stretches into the future, ensuring their everlasting destiny. No doubt it was on these very hills that the army of Sennacherib encircled the city but the words of Hezekiah had proved true, "for there be more with us than be with them" (see also 2 Kings 6:17).

But, "the sceptre of wickedness shall not rest upon the lot of the righteous; that the righteous put not forth their hands unto iniquity" (verse 3, RV). The sceptre of wickedness is a reference to the dominance of foreign power that would have prevailed over the land if the Assyrian had been successful. The lot of the righteous is of course the land itself, their heritage, which was divided to them by lot by Joshua (Joshua 18:10) – the righteous in this instance standing for the nation of Israel as a whole in contrast to the ungodly Assyrians.

The words of the prophet Isaiah appear relevant:

"For through the voice of the LORD shall the Assyrian be beaten down, with his rod shall he smite him."

(30:31, with RV margin)

The danger was that if the Assyrian had been successful then prolonged oppression might have led even the righteous to despair and embrace the religion and habits of their conquerors.

1023

True Men and False

"Do good, O LORD, unto those that be good, and to
them that are upright in their hearts. But as for such as
turn aside unto their crooked ways, the LORD shall lead
them forth with the workers of iniquity. Peace be upon
Israel."   (verses 4,5, RV)

When Hezekiah was overcome by his sickness he was
obviously unable to handle the affairs of state and it
became necessary to hand over the business of
government to the princes of Judah. That few among them
shared the faith and confidence of the king is evident from
the denunciations of the prophet Isaiah. In plotting and
scheming, in dealing treacherously, even in their
negotiations with Sennacherib, they must have been a
sore trial for the ailing king (for example, see Isaiah
28:15,18; 29:15,16; 30:10,11,15).

The Psalmist's prayer was that God would look with
favour on all those who were upright in their hearts.
There is a hint here of the hypocrisy and deceit practised
by so many. But it was his earnest desire that those loyal,
sincere and true men who were faithful to their king and
above all to their God, should see good; that they should
see peace upon Israel and enjoy the blessing of freedom
and security from the tyranny of their cruel foe.

In contrast, there were those renegades who had
followed crooked ways. They had left the King's Highway,
called a way of holiness (Isaiah 35:8), and walked in the
byways (Judges 5:6). They had strayed from the straight
path and pursued a course of conspiracy and intrigue. The
consequence was that they would suffer with the enemies
of Judah the very fate they had plotted to avoid.

It was the Psalmist's desire that peace should be upon
Israel. In the closing words of his Epistle to the Galatians
the Apostle Paul appears to have had this psalm and its
message in his mind:

"And as many as walk according to this rule, peace be
on them, and mercy, and upon the Israel of God."

(6:16)

1024

PSALM 126

THERE are many who mistakenly believe that the reference to the captivity of Zion is an indication that this psalm belongs to the post-exilic period.

The Captivity of Zion

Strong's Concordance indicates that while the word can indeed stand for our normal understanding of captivity, it is also used on occasions to represent a time of deprivation, when prosperity and blessing depart. Thus, "the LORD turned the captivity of Job" (Job 42:10; see also Psalms 53:6; 85:1; Jeremiah 33:11). So after the years of difficulty, the particularly dark days of Sennacherib's siege when disaster loomed and they seemed to be without hope of deliverance, the sudden and unexpected destruction of the Assyrian host was to them like a dream (verse 1). Could it really have happened? Was it no more than an illusion? In one night the threat was gone, the burden of dreadful carnage and exile lifted (Isaiah 37:36). So marvellous was it, all accomplished in a day, that we can well understand how they found it difficult to come to terms with the reality of what the Lord had done for them. Truly their mouth was filled with laughter and their tongue with singing (verse 2). The Hebrew word for "laughter" carries us back to another occasion when God had performed that which, in human eyes, was impossible:

"And Abraham was an hundred years old, when his son Isaac was born unto him. And Sarah said, God hath made me to laugh, so that all who hear will laugh with me. And she said, Who would have said unto Abraham, that Sarah should have given children suck? for I have born him a son in his old age." (Genesis 21:5-7)

1025

Significantly, the birth of Isaac and Sarah's joy is the background to the words of Isaiah, when he speaks of the birth of that faithful remnant that sprang out of Judah as a consequence of Hezekiah's reforming zeal and the wondrous salvation that God had wrought:

"Sing, O barren, thou that didst not bear; break forth into singing, and cry aloud, thou that didst not travail with child: for more are the children of the desolate than the children of the married wife, saith the LORD."

(see Isaiah 54:1 and Galatians 4:22-31)

Again the word "singing" (literally, 'shouts of joy', *Cambridge Bible*) is characteristic of those chapters of Isaiah that celebrate the deliverance of Zion in Hezekiah's day (44:23; 48:20; 49:13; 51:11; 55:12).

The Response of the Nations

The joy they experienced and the complete reversal of the situation in which they had found themselves had repercussions also for the surrounding nations:

"Then said they among the heathen, The LORD hath done great things for them. The LORD hath done great things for us; whereof we are glad." (Psalm 126:2,3)

Nations, both near and far, recognised the wonder that had been performed in the land and there must have been some among them who had benefited from the removal of the Assyrian threat. The consequence was that:

"Many brought gifts unto the LORD to Jerusalem, and presents to Hezekiah king of Judah: so that he was magnified in the sight of all nations from thenceforth."

(2 Chronicles 32:23)

Many Gentiles came to worship the God of Israel and stayed to become proselytes (see Psalm 87; Isaiah 56:3-8), and Judah prospered and was honoured in the sight of the nations as never before. The words of Isaiah 2 and Micah 4 must have thrilled the hearts of faithful men as they saw in these events a foreshadowing of the grand consummation of God's purpose in the age to come. As the destruction of the Assyrian had spoken of God's faithfulness to the covenant that He had made with David, so the reaction of the nations gave an assurance that Israel would yet fulfil her ancient destiny (Exodus 19:5,6).

The prophet Joel had written: "Spare thy people, O LORD, and give not thine heritage to reproach, that the heathen should rule over them: wherefore should they say among the people, Where is their God?" (2:17). God's response to the prophet's plea was: "Fear not, O land; be glad and rejoice: for the LORD will do great things" (verse 21).

In recognition of the fulfilment of the words of Joel, the Psalmist declares first the acknowledgement of the nations that God had done great things for them, and then repeats the words to emphasise how this was appreciated also by His people who were filled with gladness at the prosperity they now enjoyed.

Turn Again our Captivity

The last three verses of the psalm open with a prayer that God would turn again their captivity (verse 4). How then do we reconcile these words with the opening words of the psalm? We believe that the answer lies in the fact that the land had been ravaged by the Assyrian invader. The cities of Judah were in ruins; the land had not been cultivated, neither sown nor reaped (see 2 Kings 19:25,26). Thus the joy of deliverance known in Zion when the besieging army was destroyed was tempered now by the knowledge that the desolation left by the scourge of the northern host remained. There was an urgent need for rebuilding, for recovering the ground from its infertility that the blessing of deliverance should be extended to encompass the whole land.

So again the prayer goes forth that God would turn again their captivity as the streams of the south. It was a request that the Lord would restore the prosperity of all the land. The streams of the south, the Negeb, literally 'the dry region' is a reference to the manner in which, after the summer brooks had dried up, they would be filled once again by the autumn rains. So the situation was as though, for the land at large, there had been but the first flow of refreshing streams, and the longing was for the reviving waters of blessing to gush in full flow like the waters of the south in their season.

Turning from the political life of Jerusalem to the agricultural life of the people, the Psalmist expresses his confidence that God would bless their labours even as He had the fortunes of the city:

"They that sow in tears shall reap in joy. He that goeth forth and weepeth, bearing precious seed, shall doubtless come again with rejoicing, bringing his sheaves with him."   (verses 5,6)

There was the assurance that if they applied themselves in the midst of all the difficulties and privations they were now experiencing, then God would respond and crown their efforts with blessing (see also Isaiah 30:23; 32:20).

For two years crops had not been sown and as a result there must have been a shortage of seed. There was a need for sacrifice and self-denial. It was inevitable that they must suffer hardship now, sowing in tears, that they might know the joy of harvest. It would be with "shouts of joy" (as verse 2) that they would gather in the sheaves of wheat.

The word "precious" might be taken to refer to the scarcity of the seed, but there is some doubt as to the precise meaning of the word. Some suggest that it means a weight, others that it refers to the bag in which the seed was carried. Perhaps we can think of these two ideas as coming together and describing the burden of carrying the seed, emphasising again the effort and endeavour that was required for the work of restoration to be successful.

God had given them a sign. For two years they were to eat that which grew of itself in the fields and "in the third year sow ye, and reap, and plant vineyards, and eat the fruits thereof" (2 Kings 19:29). It is a measure of the manner in which God blessed their efforts that the record of Hezekiah's prosperity, during the extension of life granted to him, tells us that he had –

"Storehouses also for the increase of corn, and wine, and oil; and stalls for all manner of beasts, and cotes for flocks. Moreover he provided him cities, and possessions

1028

of flocks and herds in abundance: for God had given him substance very much." (2 Chronicles 32:28,29)

The passage in 2 Kings 19, quoted above, continues with the words:

"And the remnant that is escaped of the house of Judah shall yet again take root downward, and bear fruit upward. For out of Jerusalem shall go forth a remnant, and they that escape out of mount Zion: the zeal of the LORD of hosts shall do this." (verses 30,31)

The sign therefore was that as God would bless the land, He would also bless the people. As they sowed in tears, so also would they reap. The spiritual implication of the words becomes clear and we appreciate that the psalm has a message for us also.

The Message for Us

The figure of sowing and reaping is to be found throughout the scriptures. It has two main applications to us: first of all to the preaching of the Gospel and secondly with regard to the way in which we live our lives. In both instances the emphasis upon weeping and sacrifice, of present hardship for future joy, is relevant.

We must be ready always to give an answer to anyone who asks us of the hope that is within us (1 Peter 3:15). When preaching the word we must be instant in season and out of season (2 Timothy 4:2). We must not be deterred by allowing the everyday circumstances of life to influence us – putting personal comfort and convenience before our responsibility to witness:

"He that observeth the wind shall not sow; and he that regardeth the clouds shall not reap."

(Ecclesiastes 11:4)

Preaching is not always easy, for there are occasions when we must spend long hours preparing, teaching and instructing. Personal convenience must be set aside. Patience is a quality required by both farmer and preacher alike (James 5:7). The reward is the precious fruit of the harvest and to share the joy in heaven over one sinner that repents (Luke 15:7,10). The work can sometimes be hard and exhausting and we might feel sometimes that all our efforts are in vain. We must never forget, however, that it is God who gives the increase (1 Corinthians 3:6) and there will always be some who will hear and receive the word and bring forth fruit (Mark 4:14-20).

The second aspect is the seed we sow day by day by the manner of our living:

"Be not deceived; God is not mocked: for whatsoever a man soweth, that shall he also reap." (Galatians 6:7)

It is a lesson that is essential for us to learn, for we cannot escape the consequences of our actions. By our deeds we sow the seed that will determine the kind of people that we will become. If we sow to the flesh we shall of the flesh reap corruption; but if we sow to the spirit we shall of the spirit reap life everlasting (verse 8). In the very nature of things we walk in the valley of the shadow; we take up our cross to follow the Lord Jesus; we sow in tears in this dark night of the kingdom of men. But we do so in the confidence that though weeping may endure for a night, joy comes in the morning (Psalm 30:5). We look to that day of resurrection, that morning without clouds that heralds the dawn of everlasting day.

Like the husbandman who waits for the precious fruit of the earth:

"Let us not be weary in well doing: for in due season we shall reap, if we faint not. As we have therefore opportunity, let us do good unto all men, especially unto them who are of the household of faith."

(Galatians 6:9,10)

PSALM 127

THE psalm carries the superscription, "A song of degrees for Solomon". The Syriac version ascribes it to David and we might best conclude that it was written by David for Solomon. Indeed it could well be regarded as David's reflections on the closing years of his reign when, after the rebellion of Absalom, there was a period of intrigue and unrest which culminated in Adonijah's attempt to seize the throne. Joab and Abiathar, the priest, were complicit in the conspiracy and it was a deliberate attempt to circumvent the declared will of God that Solomon should be king. The psalm, therefore, provides sound words of advice to Solomon to learn from these events that it was impossible to thwart the purpose of God. Sadly, this was something that he forgot, as is seen in his attempt to kill Jeroboam after God had revealed to him that the kingdom was to be divided (1 Kings 11:9-13,26-40).

The Lord had promised David that He would make him "an house" (2 Samuel 7:11,25-29) and it is this royal house of David that is the substance of the psalm. Not any house, in the general sense, not even the house of the Lord, but the question was through whom should this royal house of David be perpetuated?

So all the effort of Adonijah and his allies was in vain for, "Except the LORD build the house, they labour in vain that build it" (Psalm 127:1). The Hebrew word *banah*, translated "build", is the root from which the Hebrew words for son (*ben*), daughter (*bath*) and house (*beth*) are developed – so we can well understand the concept of a house comprising men and women.

The alertness of the watchman, the diligence of the early riser, and the unremitting efforts of the day culminating in sitting down late for the evening meal were all to no avail. Unless they worked with the blessing of the

1031

divine watchman (see Jeremiah 31:28) all their efforts were futile. They were walking in the light of their own fire and the consequence was that they would lie down in sorrow (Isaiah 50:11).

As the Psalmist expresses it, they would "eat the bread of sorrows". All their endeavours would end in bitterness and disappointment. The word translated "sorrows" is the same as that used in Genesis 3 of the travail of childbirth. A similar word is used to describe the constant toil of mortal life:

"I will greatly multiply thy sorrow and thy conception; in sorrow thou shalt bring forth children ... cursed is the ground for thy sake; in sorrow shalt thou eat of it all the days of thy life."   (Genesis 3:16,17)

Given the background outlined above there is something very appropriate about this connection. Their intention was that the royal line should be perpetuated through Adonijah, but without the divine approval they were, like all mortal men, striving after vanity – doomed to failure and to see all their ambitions and aspirations crumble into dust.

In contrast, those who trust in the Lord and gladly submit to His will can rest secure in the knowledge that God is watching over them, confident that He who neither slumbers nor sleeps is working to bring His purposes to fruition. For, "so he giveth his beloved sleep" (Psalm 127:2). Surely David was reflecting on the earlier circumstances of his life when he fled from Absalom (2 Samuel 15; 16); when after the rigours and hardships of the day they "arrived weary at the Jordan" and refreshed themselves there (16:14, RSV). It was concerning this day in his life that David wrote Psalms 3 and 4, and he expresses his faith and trust in God in these most adverse of circumstances in a most remarkable and beautiful way:

"I laid me down and slept; I awaked; for the LORD sustained me."   (Psalm 3:5)

"I will both lay me down in peace, and sleep: for thou, LORD, only makest me dwell in safety."   (Psalm 4:8)

As God providentially watches over the accomplishment of His purposes, so the man who has implicit trust leaves all in His hands and finds refreshment in calm and sweet repose.

"His beloved" is an allusion to the name that was given to Solomon by the Lord (2 Samuel 12:25). He was called Jedidiah (beloved of Yah) because the Lord loved him. It would appear that this is a fulfilment of the blessing of Benjamin:

> "And of Benjamin he said, The beloved of the LORD shall dwell in safety by him; and the LORD shall cover him all the day long, and he shall dwell between his shoulders." (Deuteronomy 33:12)

Jerusalem, where the temple was built, which was the seat of David's throne was of course in the inheritance of Benjamin, and Solomon, the heir designate, dwelt there in safety. The word "beloved" embraces the one of whom Solomon in all his glory was but a shadow; the one of whom God said, "This is my beloved Son, in whom I am well pleased" (Matthew 3:17) and in whom we too are "brethren beloved of the Lord" (2 Thessalonians 2:13).

It needs to be remembered that as the Lord builds the house of David so also He is active in building up His ecclesia, for we who are members of that body have, as sons and daughters of the Lord Almighty (2 Corinthians 6:18), been adopted into that royal house. Without His blessing all our toil and care is in vain. It is by His good hand that successive generations are raised up to testify for Him and to preserve His truth in the earth. Sometimes we forget that it is not our endeavours, although God needs them, which cause the Truth to prosper. The work of preaching does not require gimmicks or 'ingenious' human schemes to bring men to the knowledge of God's saving grace. Big is not always best and we can be sure that as long as we strive to sow the seed then our Heavenly Father is always active to give the increase.

The Lord's Inheritance

It is important to remember that the theme of this psalm is the royal house of David, for it is in this context that the concluding verses of the psalm speak of the blessing of children.

This is not to say that the words are not true of children generally, but it would be wrong to think that there is any sense in which children are a reward for good works. They are undoubtedly a blessing from God, a gift freely given, but they have nothing to do with the merit of the parents, nor can it be presumed that childless couples are in some way deprived of children because of their unacceptable behaviour.

The Lord had told David, "There shall not fail thee ... a man on the throne of Israel" (1 Kings 2:4). Children, and sons in particular, were therefore a vital part of the covenant that God had made with him:

> "The LORD hath sworn in truth unto David; he will not turn from it; of the fruit of thy body will I set upon thy throne."   (Psalm 132:11)

In a very special sense it was true of David's royal house:

> "Lo, children are an heritage of the LORD: and the fruit of the womb is his reward. As arrows are in the hand of a mighty man; so are children of the youth. Happy is the man that hath his quiver full of them: they shall not be ashamed, but they shall speak with the enemies in the gate."   (Psalm 127:3-5)

It is generally agreed that the proper reading should be "sons" and they are described as God's heritage. Literally, "sons are the LORD's inheritance" (Kay, *The Psalms with Notes*). In other words, they belonged to Him; they were His possession, given on trust.

This was true of all Israel and the prophet Jeremiah appears to have had the language of this psalm in mind when he wrote:

> "I have forsaken mine house, I have left mine heritage; I have given the dearly beloved of my soul into the hand of her enemies."   (Jeremiah 12:7)

Given the divine involvement in the gift of children, there was a special responsibility to ensure that they were instructed in the way of the Lord. This is a responsibility that falls upon those of us that have children, also to whom God has said:

> "Bring them up in the nurture and admonition of the Lord."   (Ephesians 6:4)

1034

The fruit of the womb embraces daughters as well as sons, and the word "reward" means literally 'hire' or 'compensation', perhaps a reflection on the manner in which God blessed barren women who had waited long for the birth of a child (see Genesis 30:2,18 and Jeremiah 31:16).

The figure of arrows in the quiver of a mighty man suggests that as arrows are shot into the distance, so the sons of youth would ensure the perpetuity of the family. The picture is of a warrior surrounded by his sons who support him against all those who would seek to defame him or slander him in the gate (the place of judgement). The emphasis is upon sons of youth particularly, rather than sons of old age (see Genesis 37:3) because they would be grown men able to succour and defend their aged father.

We think of David's greater Son and of the everlasting stability of his house. He too "shall see his seed ... he shall see of the travail of his soul and be satisfied" (Isaiah 53:10,11).

In that resurrection day his youth shall renew their strength as eagles (Psalm 103:5). From the womb of the morning like the dew, sparkling in the sunshine, his children (Hebrews 2:13,14) will surround him, resplendent in the glory of everlasting youth (Psalm 110:3; Isaiah 26:19).

Hezekiah

The words of Isaiah 53 quoted above were written against the background of Hezekiah's sickness and the fact that at that time he was childless. This, of course, is the key to the inclusion of this psalm of David in the songs of degrees.

At the time of the Assyrian threat the king was surrounded by intrigue and princes in whom he could put no trust. The royal house of David was threatened but nevertheless it was vain to be filled with anxious care; there was nothing to be achieved by the watchmen rising early or staying up late. In God alone was help to be found and in this truth Hezekiah rested for, "there is a greater with us than with him" (2 Chronicles 32:7, RV).

He would have been aware of the words of Solomon's prayer, "There shall not be cut off unto thee a man from my sight" (1 Kings 8:25, RV margin) – words reflected in the king's prayer when he was recovered from his sickness. "I said in the cutting off of my days, I shall go to the gates of the grave" (Isaiah 38:10). It was a matter of primary concern to him that he had no son to succeed him on the throne. Manasseh was born in the extension of life granted to him (2 Kings 21:1) and in the face of the threats of Rabshakeh he had no sons to support him against the enemy in the gate. Yet in the confidence that God's promise to David that "there shall not fail thee a man ... to sit upon the throne of Israel" (2 Chronicles 6:16; 7:18) was sure, he took to himself the words of the psalm. "So he giveth his beloved sleep." Such was his trust that God's word would not fail that he could even face the sleep of death, knowing that in ways beyond his understanding God's will would prevail.

We can imagine then his joy when, restored to life and vigour, he regarded himself as one whose youth had been renewed and his children as being children of youth (Isaiah 38:19; 39:7). His faith had been vindicated and David's advice to Solomon generations before had proved true for him also.

PSALM 128

WITH his days prolonged and the Assyrian threat removed, Hezekiah was able to look forward to the remainder of his life. Before him was the promise of domestic happiness and peace upon Israel. It was a time of great blessing and this is a most fitting song to follow that which preceded it. Indeed it might well be considered as a continuation of it written, not now by David, but by Hezekiah himself as he meditates on the substance of Psalm 127. There is a thread of thought that might be summed up as the blessings of the true worshipper; in his work (verse 2), his wife and children (verse 3), his children's children (verse 6) and his city and people generally (verses 5,6).

The psalm presents us with a wonderful cameo of family life as it should be lived. Recognising the divine principles on which it should be based, family life for Israel should have been the basis of both their material and spiritual prosperity. It is not without significance for us too, for our family life should also be the foundation of our ecclesial life, in promoting the spiritual welfare of all the members of the body.

The Blessings of Labour

"Blessed is every one that feareth the LORD; that walketh in his ways. For thou shalt eat the labour of thine hands: happy shalt thou be, and it shall be well with thee."   (verses 1,2)

True happiness is to be found in fearing the Lord and walking in His ways (Psalms 112:1-3; 119:1-3). Fearing the Lord suggests a spirit of reverence and awe that abstains from breaking His commandments; whereas to walk in His ways suggests a positive approach that actively seeks to do the things that please Him.

1037

Such a man shall eat the labour of his hands in contrast to those cursed for their apostasy of whom it was written, "The fruit of thy land, and all thy labours, shall a nation which thou knowest not eat up" (Deuteronomy 28:33). Again there is a spiritual counterpart, for such fruits were regarded in Israel as the special blessing of God (see Genesis 31:42).

We, of course, do not equate the good things of this life with righteousness, but when we translate this principle into the spiritual realm we find that abounding in the work of the Lord does bring its rewards. In terms of preaching we plant and sow but God gives the increase. In the parable of the talents the Lord Jesus said:

"For unto every one that hath shall be given, and he shall have abundance: but from him that hath not shall be taken away even that which he hath."

(Matthew 25:29)

In spiritual terms the more we seek to fear God and walk in His ways the more, under God's blessing, will the qualities He delights in be developed in our lives. The more we neglect to walk in God's ways, the more we shall blunt our spiritual aspirations and stultify our growth in the Truth so that we live in constant danger of our spiritual life withering and dying altogether. In the words of the Apostle Paul:

"He which soweth sparingly shall reap also sparingly; and he which soweth bountifully shall reap also bountifully." (2 Corinthians 9:6)

(see also verses 8-11 citing Psalm 112:9)

In this context see also Psalm 126 (verses 5,6) which is relevant to the background of this psalm.

The Blessing of Wife and Children

Although verses 1-4 might describe the family blessing of any faithful Israelite, it is well to remember the historical background against which these songs of degrees were written. We have suggested that this psalm was written by Hezekiah as a result of his meditations on Psalm 127. If this is the case he is still reflecting upon God's promise to David concerning his royal house. When he was sick and was told that he should die, he had no heir. His boundless joy at the extension of life granted to him was not concerned principally with fifteen years more of mortal life. Firstly, there was the realisation that once more he would be able to go up to the house of the Lord and worship. He would be able to carry on with the spiritual reforms he had initiated for the benefit of his people.

Secondly was the fact that now it was possible for him to beget an heir to sit on David's throne, and his son Manasseh was born three years later. Bearing in mind the limited number of years that were allotted to him, Hezekiah could hardly have been describing the family bliss that he expected in his own experience. After all, he had no expectation at all of seeing his children's children (verse 6). His thought is not primarily of himself but of those who should follow him in the royal line of David, for whom he anticipated this abounding blessing in their family life that thereby David might truly never want a man to sit upon his throne.

The prophet Jeremiah expressed similar sentiments when the Lord spoke through him regarding the surety of the covenant that He had made with David (Jeremiah 33:20,21). In view of the fact that the captivity was to return (verse 26) – for God would never utterly forsake His people – the reality was this:

"As the host of heaven cannot be numbered, neither the sand of the sea measured: so will I multiply the seed of David my servant."   (verse 22)

In this respect the Messianic significance of the song becomes apparent and the manner in which it carries forward the theme of Psalm 127 is made clear:

"Thy wife shall be as a fruitful vine by the sides of thine house: thy children like olive plants round about thy table."   (Psalm 128:3)

His wife would be as the vine, which was a symbol of the beauty and fertility of the land, and was an apt representation of the wife who dutifully supported her husband in all things (see Numbers 13:24; Deuteronomy 8:7,8; Genesis 49:11,12; Judges 9:13). The deeper significance of the imagery is made clear when we remember that Israel was likened to a vine that God brought out of Egypt (Psalm 80:8-11) and in a change of symbol He speaks of Himself in the bonds of the covenant as married to Israel. The purpose of that union was that Israel might bring forth fruit to her husband and a vine that fails to do so is useless, for that is its only purpose. All these thoughts are caught up in the language of John's Gospel where the Lord Jesus speaks of himself as the true vine (15:1-8). The ecclesia, the lamb's wife, is here described as a part of the vine; as the branches drawing their strength and vitality from the main stock of the plant that thereby they might bear much fruit. Another feature of the vine that is also relevant is the fact that it cannot stand on its own but needs to be supported, which is an indication of the manner in which all God's servants in every age depend upon Him to uphold them in the vicissitudes of life

The wife is described as being "in the innermost parts of thine house" (RV). This is normally interpreted as referring to the inmost chamber of the house, which was usually regarded as the woman's quarters. There is, however, an interesting use of the words which develops the spiritual theme we have followed. It is used in 1 Kings 6:16 to describe the erection of the interior walls of the most holy place (Kay, *Psalms with Notes*). Even as now we have boldness to enter into the holiest by the blood of Jesus (Hebrews 10:19), so also we look to the day when our permanent abode with the Lord Jesus will be in that glorious incorruptible state of which the most holy place is representative.

The children are described as olive plants. David described himself as being "like a green olive tree in the house of God" (Psalm 52:8). The prophet Hosea, speaking of Israel in the day of her restoration to favour says, "His branches shall spread, and his beauty shall be as the olive tree" (Hosea 14:6). The olive tree was an "emblem of vitality and vigour" (*Cambridge Bible*) and most commentators quote Thompson (*The Land and the Book*, page 57), where he describes the figure behind the words as that of young olive trees growing up around the parent stem conveying the idea of perpetuating the life of the plant – a very apt figure given the background of the royal house of David and an extension of the thought of verse 5 of the previous psalm.

Truly Hezekiah could cry, "Thus shall the man be blessed that feareth the LORD" (Psalm 128:4).

The Lord Bless Thee out of Zion

How would the man that feared the Lord be blessed? Hezekiah could speak from his own experience. He would bless him out of Zion and he would see the good of Jerusalem all the days of his life (verse 5). Zion was the place that the Lord had chosen as His dwelling place. Although He was everywhere present by His spirit, it was from the mercy seat between the cherubim that He was thought to exercise His sovereignty over all the earth. Having sent the ark of God back, it was to Zion that David looked when he fled from Absalom: "I cried unto the LORD with my voice, and he heard me out of his holy hill" (Psalm 3:4). Again, faced by the threat of evil men who would have deposed him from his throne David cried, "Oh that the salvation of Israel were come out of Zion!" (Psalm 14:7). With both these psalms Hezekiah could readily associate himself for his God had delivered him, and all Israel, from the Assyrian threat. In the extension of life granted to him he would see the good of Jerusalem all the days of his life. For the faithful man of David's royal line there was the assurance that he would see his "children's children, and peace upon Israel" (Psalm 128:6).

"Peace upon Israel" was a covenant blessing (Leviticus 26:6, etc.). So Hezekiah could declare in the consciousness of all that God had done for him:

"Good is the word of the LORD which thou hast spoken. He said moreover, For there shall be peace and truth in my days." (Isaiah 39:8)

PSALM 129

THE psalm falls into two easily discernible sections. The first (verses 1-4), speaks of the manner in which God, so many times in the past, had delivered His people from those that oppressed them. The second (verses 5-8), expresses the confidence that God will continue to do so and bring shame and confusion on all those who hate Zion.

There is no doubt that the psalm has a close affinity with Psalm 124, both in structure and in substance. The superscription to Psalm 124 tells us that it is a psalm of David and this leads us to conclude that this song also is from his pen. Note particularly how the opening verses of the two psalms correspond.

As with Psalm 124 its appropriateness to the circumstances in which Hezekiah found himself is evident and we can well understand its inclusion in the songs of degrees.

Past Oppressions

"Many a time have they afflicted me from my youth up, let Israel now say; many a time have they afflicted me from my youth up: yet they have not prevailed against me." (verses 1,2, RV)

The chequered history of Israel spoke eloquently of the manner in which she had been oppressed by the surrounding nations. Yet equally powerfully that history testified also to the manner in which their God had repeatedly delivered them out of the hands of those that afflicted them. The reference to Israel's youth is an obvious allusion to their bondage in the land of Egypt (Jeremiah 2:2; 22:21; Ezekiel 23:3; Hosea 2:15).

There is also reference here to the occasion when Jacob wrestled with the angel at Jabbok. Israel's enemies had

1042

not prevailed against her and this is the same Hebrew phrase used of the angel who "prevailed not" against Jacob (Genesis 32:25). It was on this occasion that Jacob's name was changed to Israel. It is as though the blessing of Jacob was perpetuated in the nation who had wrestled with God in prayer down through the years to obtain deliverance when their God's chastening hand was upon them. Kay (*Psalms with Notes*) points out that the fact that Jacob halted (Genesis 32:31) is referred to Israel by the prophet Micah – "her that halted" (4:7) – which is perhaps particularly significant as the prophet ministered in the days of Hezekiah.

In a bold metaphor the psalm describes Israel as a man thrown on his face with his pitiless enemy as it were ploughing with long furrows along his back, leaving it lacerated and torn.

"The plowers plowed upon my back: they made long their furrows." (verse 3)

It is intended to describe the intensity of suffering that Israel had endured at the hands of those that hated her. There can be little doubt that Hezekiah, contemplating the words of this psalm, could readily apply them to the circumstances of his own days for the Assyrian had in his victorious march to Jerusalem destroyed all the fenced cities of Judah, turning them into ruinous heaps. The people of the land had been powerless to withstand this terrible onslaught (Isaiah 37:26,27).

Perhaps the prophet Micah had this psalm in mind when he wrote, "Therefore shall Zion for your sake be plowed as a field" (3:12; see also Jeremiah 26:18). In fulfilment of these words it is said that after the capture of Jerusalem by Titus, a plough was driven over the temple site and again by Hadrian following the suppression of the revolt by Bar Kokhba (AD 132-135).

Nevertheless in all these afflictions, including the dark days of the Assyrian invasion, God was faithful to deliver for He remained true to the covenant that He had made with His people:

"The LORD is righteous: he hath cut asunder the cords of the wicked." (Psalm 129:4)

1043

Throughout all the time that His chastening hand was upon them, the Lord was mindful of their suffering and time and again He showed His mercy towards them in saving them out of the hands of their oppressors. This, in another figure, is described as cutting the cords of the wicked – obviously those that bound the people of Israel to them. In the Book of Job the word for 'cords' is used to describe the rope which harnesses the ox to the plough (39:10), and perhaps the idea of servitude to their captors is the thought conveyed.

Hope for the Future

As God had delivered in the past, so the psalm gives an assurance that He would continue to do so in the future. Hezekiah took comfort and found confidence in the words of David:

"Let them all be ashamed and turned backward, all they that hate Zion. Let them be as the grass upon the housetops, which withereth afore it groweth up: wherewith the reaper filleth not his hand, nor he that bindeth sheaves his bosom." (verses 5-7, RV)

The Psalmist's prayer, with which Hezekiah associated himself, was that Zion's enemies should be confounded, turned back in shame before their malicious schemes could be brought to fruition. In the case of Sennacherib this was most certainly the case. After blaspheming the God of Israel, with his army destroyed, he was compelled to return "with shame of face to his own land" (2 Chronicles 32:21).

In reading Isaiah's account of the Assyrian oppression of the people of Judah, it appears that the words of this psalm were in the mind of the prophet although he is applying the figure of speech to Judah and not the enemies of God. Before the might of Sennacherib, "they were dismayed and confounded: they were as the grass of the field, and as the green herb, as the grass on the housetops, and as corn blasted before it be grown up" (37:27). The message was, as they had done to Zion so let it be done to them. Sennacherib had returned to his own land humiliated. The reference to "the grass on the housetops" is an allusion to the manner in which grass grew upon the tops of oriental houses. There was no depth of earth and the grass sprang up quickly only to wither and die with equal rapidity. There was no harvest; no crop grown to maturity. So all the schemes and plans of Zion's enemies were doomed to failure. There could be no harvest to reap or sheaves to be gathered in. Like the grass scorched and withered by the noonday sun, one hundred and eighty-five thousand Assyrians were left dead (Isaiah 37:36).

Is it possible that this demonstration of the transience of human life was the background to the words of Isaiah?

"All flesh is grass, and all the goodliness thereof is as the flower of the field: the grass withereth, the flower fadeth: because the spirit of the LORD bloweth upon it: surely the people is grass. The grass withereth, the flower fadeth: but the word of our God shall stand for ever." (Isaiah 40:6-8)

In the words of this psalm Hezekiah could delight, for in his own experience he had seen them fulfilled. For those who withstood Israel's God there could be no word of blessing. The song concludes with a reference to the joyous greeting customarily used by those who gathered in the harvest (Ruth 2:4): "Boaz came from Bethlehem, and said unto the reapers, The LORD be with you. And they answered him, The LORD bless thee."

This was the prospect that now lay before Hezekiah and the people of the land, but for those who sought to frustrate the purpose of God and to oppress His people, unaware that Israel's God was sovereign among the nations (Isaiah 37:26), there could be no such blessing, only confusion and shame.

PSALM 130

PSALM 130 is counted amongst what are described as the seven penitential psalms (6,32,38,51,102,130, 143) – so called because of the consciousness of sin expressed by the writers and their recognition of their desperate need of the forgiveness of God.

In some ways this psalm stands as the most profound expression of the anguish of soul experienced by a man convicted in his heart of his sin and looking to God for forgiveness, although Psalms 32 and 51, written by David after his sin in the matter of Bathsheba and Uriah the Hittite, surely rival it in this respect.

There is an interesting play upon the name of God, "Yahweh" (verses 1,3,5,7) and the title "Adonai" ('Sovereign Lord', verses 2,3,6).

The extremity of the writer's situation arose out of the fact that the sacrifices of the law could avail him nothing. His only hope lay in the mercy of God to whom he looked in earnest expectation. David was in a similar position for there was no sacrifice under the law that was appropriate to the sin of adultery and murder: the penalty was death. Their hope therefore rested in the name of God and those qualities of His character revealed to Moses:

> "The LORD, the LORD God, merciful and gracious, longsuffering, and abundant in goodness and truth, keeping mercy for thousands, forgiving iniquity and transgression and sin ..."   (Exodus 34:6,7)

Note that Brother John Thomas translated the next phrase, "destroying not utterly the guilty".

The words translated "iniquity", "transgression" and "sin" encompass every kind of wrongdoing of which man is capable (see chapters on Psalms 32 and 51) and the

Psalmist's hope lay in the fact that "with the LORD there is mercy, and ... plenteous redemption" (Psalm 130:7).

Added to this was his recognition that Yahweh was also the Sovereign Lord, He who was master and controller of all things, whose power and might extended over all the earth. It is an indication that the Psalmist was not only distressed because of the anguish of soul caused by his awareness of sin, but also that he looked to God for deliverance from the adversity he was experiencing in life: in Hezekiah's case, it was of course his sickness and the imminent threat posed by the Assyrian invader, and in the king's mind these were inextricably bound together.

The prayer is personal but at the same time the writer's words are spoken for all Israel (see verses 7,8). We know that Hezekiah was a righteous man, and apart from the matter of the ambassadors from Babylon he is afforded the highest praise for the manner of his life. Nevertheless he was the representative of the people and in him all that they were in their waywardness was reflected before God. They themselves came to regard his sickness as the stroke of God and associated it in their minds with the sin of the nation. This is surely the historical background to Isaiah 53. So in the king's thoughts also he was bearing the sin of the nation and the scourge of Sennacherib was also a direct result of the apostasy of the people.

For the purpose of exposition the psalm is best divided into three parts. The wonder of God's forgiveness (verses 1-4); the Psalmist's longing for deliverance (verses 5,6) and the final word of comfort and assurance to all Israel (verses 7,8).

The Wonder of God's Forgiveness

"Out of the depths have I cried unto thee, O LORD. Lord, hear my voice: let thine ears be attentive to the voice of my supplications." (verses 1,2)

Deep waters are a common figure in scripture for distress and suffering (see Psalm 69:1,2, etc.). Perhaps the words of the prophet Isaiah were also in the king's mind for he had prophesied of the Assyrian under the figure of the great river Euphrates:

1047

"Now therefore, behold, the Lord bringeth up upon them the waters of the river, strong and many, even the king of Assyria, and all his glory: and he shall come up over all his channels, and go over all his banks: and he shall pass through Judah; he shall overflow and go over, he shall reach even to the neck."   (Isaiah 8:7,8)

So it had come to pass and with Jerusalem surrounded the waters were truly up to the neck. Given the accumulation of troubles that encompassed the king and the nation, it could well be said that they were in danger of being overwhelmed by the flood of great waters. Yet out of the depths Hezekiah cried unto God. It is a wonderful thought that in the depths of despair our prayers may yet reach unto the highest heaven, for all of us at some time must share that desperate need for God that Hezekiah experienced.

His request that God would be attentive to the voice of his supplications is an indication of the anxieties that filled his heart at this time. The words are not original to him but are taken from Solomon's prayer at the dedication of the temple (2 Chronicles 6:40-42).

In the immediate context, Solomon's prayer is that God would "remember the mercies of David thy servant". This surely was the thought that filled Hezekiah's heart for he himself was at the point of death and he had no heir to sit on his throne. Judah was in danger of being trodden into the dust by the Assyrian and the royal throne of David laid waste. Had God forgotten His promises? His prayer was that God would prove Himself faithful to the things that He had promised.

In his extremity he found comfort in his knowledge of the character of God, in the appreciation that He was merciful and gracious, longsuffering in His tolerance of human sin and iniquity:

"If thou, LORD, shouldest mark iniquities, O Lord, who shall stand? But there is forgiveness with thee, that thou mayest be feared."   (Psalm 130:3,4)

One of our problems in thinking of human sin is to appreciate how abhorrent it is in the sight of God. We who experience it and live with it tend to take it for granted, and in a sense trivialise and minimise it. The prophet Habakkuk describes God's attitude in words that should leave us with no delusions about how repugnant He finds it:

"Thou art of purer eyes than to behold evil, and canst not look on iniquity." (1:13)
(see also Psalm 5:4,5)

It is only when we understand God's hatred of sin that we can really appreciate His love and forbearance. If He were to mark iniquity, that is record it as in a book so that it is held in remembrance before Him, then who would stand? The picture is of a court of law and if we were to appear before the bar of divine justice then we would all be condemned. None would stand – that is, be vindicated or acquitted (see Psalm 1:5; Malachi 3:2).

What joy therefore to know that there is forgiveness with God. If He were wrathful and unforgiving, if He held men accountable for every sin with no possibility of pardon or clemency, how different would all men's attitudes be towards Him. There would be fear and dread but no reverence, no sense of awe at the wonder of His love and condescension. So there is forgiveness with God that He might be feared, that is held in awe and admiration.

In Hezekiah's experience this was made known in the extension of life granted to him and the destruction of the Assyrian host:

"Behold, for peace I had great bitterness: but thou hast in love to my soul delivered it from the pit of corruption: for thou hast cast all my sins behind thy back." (Isaiah 38:17)

The Psalmist Longs for Deliverance

"I wait for the LORD, my soul doth wait, and in his word do I hope. My soul looketh for the Lord, more than watchmen look for the morning; yea, more than watchmen for the morning." (verses 5,6, RV)

The verbs 'to wait' and 'to hope' are in the perfect tense, thus incorporating both the past and the present. It was a continuing experience, and the change from 'I' to "soul" is a reflection of the concentration of his whole being in waiting and hoping for God to forgive the sins of the

1049

people and his consciousness of that sin as their representative. His hope was in the word of God, for it was that word that had revealed to him that for His name's sake God would pardon his iniquity (Psalms 25:11; 79:9). It was that word that was brought by the prophet Isaiah as the king lay on his death bed:

"Go, and say to Hezekiah, Thus saith the LORD, the God of David thy father, I have heard thy prayer, I have seen thy tears: behold, I will add unto thy days fifteen years. And I will deliver thee and this city out of the hand of the king of Assyria."   (Isaiah 38:5,6)

Note again the interplay between the name of God (Yahweh) and the title Adonai, for whereas he waits and hopes for the Lord to forgive sin, it is for the Sovereign Lord that he waits and watches for deliverance from the Assyrian threat.

The psalm was written at a specific time of trial and adversity. It was particularly true of the dark days when Jerusalem was besieged and Rabshakeh poured forth his words of contempt for Hezekiah and his God. As the watchman looks for the morning, so his "soul was towards God" (literal Hebrew; see Psalm 143:6). As those who watch through the darkness of the night for the first signs of the dawn, so is beautifully described the longing of those who watch for the breaking day that heralds God's mercy. It is an apt figure for the priests in the temple as they waited to offer the morning sacrifices and the release from their duties (to which most commentators refer the figure). Equally it can be true of those who watch over the sickness of a loved one and particularly of the sentinels upon the walls of a city. How appropriate it was that the watchmen of Zion who looked for the dawn saw not the encircling host of the Assyrians, for God had manifested His power "and when they arose early in the morning, behold, they were all dead corpses" (Isaiah 37:36).

In the depths of his despair the king had thought that the morning would bring no relief from his suffering (38:12,13), yet he had poured out his heart to his God and the result had been a morning without clouds.

"But thou hast in love to my soul delivered it from the pit of corruption: for thou hast cast all my sins behind thy back." (verse 17)

Comfort and Assurance for Israel

"Let Israel hope in the LORD: for with the LORD there is mercy, and with him is plenteous redemption. And he shall redeem Israel from all his iniquities."

(Psalm 130:7,8)

Once again Israel had experienced the salvation of their God. He did not exhaust His mercy in the day that He brought them out of the land of Egypt, but time and again they had known His redemption. There was "plenteous redemption", an abundance of grace; the power of sin, the ruthlessness of the enemy could not prevail. The word "mercy" is the Hebrew *chesed* which conveys the thought of 'covenant love'. It was God's faithfulness to His covenant with David that had been the foundation of Hezekiah's hope. It was his meditation upon the psalms of David that had sustained him in his darkest hours. It is to these psalms now that he turns as he speaks these words of comfort to the people of Israel. The language of verses 7 and 8 is based on the words of David (Psalms 25:22; 34:22; 131:3) and there is great emphasis upon the word "He". It is He alone who has power to save and ultimately He will break the power of sin and deliver His people from all its consequences. Note particularly the quotation from Psalm 131, for it establishes a connection between this song and that which follows, although in terms of time the second psalm was written first.

Conclusion

We have traced the background of this psalm and interpreted it in the light of the experiences of Hezekiah. Nevertheless, it has been well said that the psalm expresses the longings of faithful men in all circumstances of extreme adversity when they are moved to cry "out of the depths". We can understand how the psalm would have been appropriated to the times of Israel's captivity and how, if it were not amongst the songs of degrees, we might have thought that this was its historical setting.

1051

We appreciate also how suitable the psalm is to reflect the feelings of present-day believers as they wait for the coming of the Lord Jesus. We too, oppressed by the world and striving in our conflict with sin, watch for the morning of that perfect day. We rejoice in the knowledge that there is forgiveness with God and in the language of Isaiah 62, the background of which is again Hezekiah's circumstances, we enter into the spirit of the prophet's words:

"I have set watchmen upon thy walls, O Jerusalem; they shall never hold their peace day nor night: ye that are the LORD's remembrancers, keep not silence, and give him no rest, till he establish, and till he make Jerusalem a praise in the earth."

(verses 6,7, RV with margin)

PSALM 131

THIS short but beautiful psalm is another of the psalms of degrees attributed to David. Most commentators doubt the authenticity of the superscription, but recognise that the sentiments expressed are appropriate to such a man. We have no reservations about the Davidic authorship and find the arguments of the critics typical of the manner in which they look for ever later dates for the writers of the Psalms.

David's Humility

What is truly remarkable about the confession in this psalm is that whereas to profess humility is usually to deny it, here the writer asserts his lowliness without losing it. We have a wonderful statement of the spirit that David showed at a particular time in his life, to which Hezekiah aspired, and which was seen to perfection in the Lord Jesus Christ.

It has been pointed out that the rapidity and earnestness of the language of this psalm point to a particular time in the life of the writer. For this reason we believe it to be a mistake to apply the confession of humility to David's life as a whole.

It cannot be denied that throughout his life David exhibited a meekness and quietness of spirit before God that was truly extraordinary. It can be traced from the time of his anointing by Samuel, through his time in the royal court, during his period of exile to his years as king over Judah and all Israel. Twice he refused to take the life of the Lord's anointed, choosing to wait until that time when God would be pleased to exalt him. He recognised the right of Shimei to curse him and refused to allow Abishai to take action against him, and throughout his reign he was ever conscious of the need to put the interests of the people of Israel before his own. Nevertheless it was one particular occasion in his life that called forth the sentiments of this psalm.

Things too Wonderful

> "LORD, my heart is not haughty, nor mine eyes lofty; neither do I exercise myself in great matters, or in things too wonderful for me." (verse 1, RV)

The word translated "haughty" means literally 'to exalt or lift up oneself' in the heart, for this is the seat of all human emotions and as a man "thinketh in his heart, so is he" (Proverbs 23:7). "Haughty eyes" are included in the list of things that God hates (Proverbs 6:17, AV margin) and there is a progression of thought in the words of the psalm. That which is nurtured in the heart will reveal itself in proud looks and eventually manifest itself in ambitious schemes intended only to magnify self. This David steadfastly refused to do and the psalm is an expression of complete and absolute trust in God. The key to interpreting verse 1 lies in our understanding of the words translated "too high for me" (AV), and "too wonderful for me" (RV). What were these things? The Hebrew word used in this instance is frequently translated 'wonder', 'wondrous' and 'wonderfully' as well as in a variety of other ways. Careful use of a concordance will establish that the word is most often used of the works of God, and we believe that David is speaking in this sense when he describes his heart as not being haughty or his eyes lofty. What was too great and too wonderful for David to exercise (from a root 'to go to and fro') his mind? Surely it was the deep things of God; the questions that arise in a believer's mind when he considers all that God has done for him. Who has not stopped in wonder and perplexity and asked, in the light of the fact that God has called us to His kingdom and glory, 'Why me'? Life in the Truth presents us with so many imponderables and we can but stand in awe of the mysteries of the work of God for our salvation, knowing that in wisdom He has done them all.

God's Covenant of Promise

The occasion in the life of David which resulted in the writing of this psalm was, we believe, when God made an everlasting covenant with him.

Following Nathan's revelation concerning the covenant, David sat before the Lord and said:

"Who am I, O LORD God, and what is mine house, that thou hast brought me hitherto? And yet this was a small thing in thine eyes, O God; for thou hast also spoken of thy servant's house for a great while to come, and hast regarded me according to the estate of a man of high degree, O LORD God. What can David speak more to thee for the honour of thy servant? for thou knowest thy servant. O LORD, for thy servant's sake, and according to thine own heart, hast thou done all this greatness, in making known all these great things. O LORD, there is none like thee, neither is there any God beside thee, according to all that we have heard with our ears." (1 Chronicles 17:16-20)

David was overwhelmed by the wonder of all that God had done for him. He marvelled at the divine initiative that had chosen him and had made such tremendous promises concerning the future of his house. We can well imagine how a man of a different calibre might have puffed out his chest and thought what a special man he was; how much better than his contemporaries that God had chosen him above them. His heart would have been filled with pride, his look haughty as he exercised his mind in the contemplation of what great things God had done for him and not for others. Not so David, however, for he was filled with a sense of awe and reverence. It was not pride that he felt but a deep and profound lowliness of heart in his appreciation that the ways of God were beyond his comprehension. For the manner in which He had shown such condescension to him, who was of low estate, was beyond his ability fully to understand.

It was the spirit of Job, who wrestled with God over the calamities that had overtaken him. He was convinced that he had a case to present before the Almighty, but was brought to recognise His majesty and omniscience and confess his own inadequacy:

1055

"Behold, I am vile; what shall I answer thee? I will lay mine hand upon my mouth. Once have I spoken; but I will not answer: yea, twice; but I will proceed no further."   (Job 40:4,5)

He was compelled to accept the wisdom and omnipotence of God, acknowledging that though all things worked together for his good, the manner of God's work in his life was something that could not be challenged, despite the fact that it was beyond his understanding.

"Who is he that hideth counsel without knowledge? therefore have I uttered that I understood not; things too wonderful for me, which I knew not."   (42:3)

All this David accepted in recognising the will of God and the right of God to do whatsoever He would. As he was to say on another occasion, considering a different aspect of the work of God:

"Such knowledge is too wonderful for me; it is high, I cannot attain unto it."   (Psalm 139:6)

In acknowledging that there are things that are beyond our understanding because of the finite nature of our thinking we must, however, not be misled as to those things that are needful for us to know for our salvation to be accomplished. These are all well within the compass of our human understanding. The first principles of the Gospel are all of them essentially simple and straightforward and well within the ability of any normal individual to grasp. Through Moses God said:

"For this commandment which I command thee this day, it is not too hard (margin, wonderful) for thee, neither is it far off."   (Deuteronomy 30:11, RV)

Like a Weaned Child

David develops the thoughts of the first verse with an illustration of the child weaned of its mother's milk:

"Surely I have stilled and quieted my soul; like a weaned child with his mother, my soul is with me like a weaned child."   (Psalm 131:2, RV)

The picture is of the weaned child on its mother's breast. Apparently children in the east were sometimes not weaned until the age of three, so we can imagine the fretting and crying associated with the process. Now, however, the child lies content; it has yielded to the will of the parent and finds solace and comfort in the assurance of the mother's love. So David could rest confidently in the knowledge that God, in His wisdom, was in control of every situation and always acted for the ultimate good of those who put their trust in Him. When things that once seemed indispensable were taken away (like the mother's milk), when the heart was filled with doubts and anxieties, David had learned to "rest in the LORD, and wait patiently for him" (Psalm 37:7). He had stilled the unrest of his soul and calmed the disquiet of his heart. David does not mean that he had experienced this inner turmoil at the time that God made His covenant with him, but rather that through the experiences of life he had come to learn to depend upon God in all the circumstances in which he found himself. Consequently, he was able to show that complete trust in God's wisdom when He revealed His will to him, although all the implications of God's intentions were too wonderful for him to comprehend. They could only be for his good and for the ultimate outworking of God's purpose in the earth.

Hezekiah

Given the dire situation in which he found himself, we can well understand how Hezekiah would have meditated upon this psalm. His own personal troubles and the dreadful threat posed by the Assyrians must have caused him great anxiety as he pondered the work of God in his life and also the prospects for the people of Israel as a whole. We believe that he learned the lessons from David's example. Surely the manner in which he had stilled his soul and put his complete trust in God, although he could not perceive the outcome of the matter, is demonstrated by his response to the taunts of Rabshakeh.

"But the people ... answered him not a word: for the king's commandment was, saying, Answer him not."

(2 Kings 18:36)

His words of encouragement to the people were:

"Be strong and courageous, be not afraid nor dismayed for the king of Assyria, nor for all the

1057

multitude that is with him: for there be more with us than with him."   (2 Chronicles 32:7)

When, after the mighty deliverance that God had wrought and the extension of life granted to him, he reflected upon his experiences, it was in the words of this psalm that he would write, "I quieted myself until morning". He too had learned the lesson of complete resignation to the will of God.

We know that later when the ambassadors came from Babylon, the heart of the king was lifted up and he brought wrath upon Judah and Jerusalem (2 Chronicles 32:25). The word used to describe Hezekiah's haughty spirit is the very word of Psalm 131 (verse 1), but surely this lapse by the king was soon repented of and he came again to recognise the need to rest in the Lord:

"Then said Hezekiah to Isaiah, Good is the word of the LORD which thou hast spoken. He said moreover, For there shall be peace and truth in my days."
                    (Isaiah 39:8)

The Lesson for Israel

When God made His covenant with David, while appreciating the significance for himself, the king also recognised that it had tremendous repercussions for the people of Israel. So it was in that confidence that David could write:

"Let Israel hope in the LORD from henceforth and for ever."   (Psalm 131:3)

Hezekiah quoted these words in Psalm 130 (verse 7), demonstrating how deeply he had meditated upon these words of David. The message of both David and Hezekiah to the people of Israel was that they too should learn to develop that spirit of resignation to the will of God and wait patiently for the outworking of His purpose.

In that confidence we too wait for the coming of the Lord Jesus.

PSALM 132

IT is not difficult to appreciate how Hezekiah would have treasured the words of this psalm and included it amongst his songs of degrees. The words of verses 10-12 would have been particularly appropriate to his circumstances:

"For thy servant David's sake turn not away the face of thine anointed. The LORD hath sworn in truth unto David; he will not turn from it; of the fruit of thy body will I set upon thy throne. If thy children shall keep my covenant and my testimony that I shall teach them, their children shall also sit upon thy throne for evermore."

The word "anointed" does not refer simply to David, but to all those who would rise in his line and sit on his throne. For God to turn away the face of His anointed would have been for Him to refuse his requests and to drive him from His presence, withholding His grace and favour from him. In the days of his sickness and confronted by the Assyrian threat, Hezekiah would have made these words a part of his earnest entreaty that God would deliver him from the adversity in which he found himself. Furthermore, the promise that God would perpetuate the line of David so that he should never want a man to sit on his throne, would have been a poignant reminder to him that at that time he had no heir. His own faith and determination to remain faithful to his God would have sustained him in the hope that ultimately his children would ensure the everlasting stability of the throne and kingdom of David. These words, of course, are an expression of the conviction that the promised Messiah would come eventually; they would have their ultimate fulfilment in the Lord Jesus Christ.

Although the circumstances of his life were different, Hezekiah found in his own experiences a re-enactment of David's spiritual aspirations.

Authorship and Background

The psalm carries no indication of the identity of the writer but most would agree that the words of verses 3-9, in particular, must be those of David himself. Yet it must be recognised also that these words appear to be a quotation, and the psalm is about David and the covenant that God made with him but written by another hand. The psalm is quoted by Solomon in his prayer at the dedication of the temple (2 Chronicles 6:41,42), but while it speaks clearly of the time when the ark of God was brought to its resting place in Zion, there is no mention of the house that Solomon built. This suggests that the psalm was written by a contemporary of David who was particularly close to him and who shared his spiritual aspirations – someone of the stature of the prophet Nathan who revealed the details of the covenant to David, or Ethan the Ezrahite who wrote Psalm 89.

The two events that form the substance of the psalm are God's choice of Zion as His resting place, confirmed by David bringing the ark of the covenant to the tabernacle he had prepared for it, and God's faithfulness to the covenant that He had made with David.

David's Yearning for God's House (verses 1-6)

The psalm opens with a prayer that God would remember David and all his afflictions. It is an indication that throughout his life David had suffered as a consequence of his faithfulness to his God. Paramount amongst all his spiritual ambitions was his desire to build a house for God. When David gave the charge to Solomon his son to build this house (1 Chronicles 22:6) he said of his own endeavours, "Now, behold, in my trouble I have prepared for the house of the LORD ..." (verse 14). In all the vicissitudes of life he had allowed nothing to deflect him from that purpose, even when he was told that he personally would not be permitted to carry out the work.

We have no record in the historical narrative of the vow to which Psalm 132:2 refers, but the earnestness and determination of David's intentions is clearly seen in the words with which he addressed all Israel:

> "I had in mine heart to build an house of rest for the ark of the covenant of the LORD, and for the footstool of our God, and had made ready for the building."
>
> (1 Chronicles 28:2)

This resolve is expressed in the words of verses 3-5 of the psalm:

> "Surely I will not come into the tabernacle of my house, nor go up into my bed; I will not give sleep to mine eyes, or slumber to mine eyelids, until I find out a place for the LORD, an habitation for the mighty God of Jacob."

The reference to a dwelling place for God is an indication that David knew his scripture and had a marvellous insight into the purpose of God. He knew that God, from the beginning, had spoken of the place that He would choose to dwell among men. This was something that was known and treasured by men of faith down through the ages.

Abraham was prepared to offer up Isaac in the place of which God had told him (see Genesis 22:2,3,4,9). This place was known to men of God thereafter. It was referred to by Moses when he sang his song of victory after Israel's deliverance from Egypt (Exodus 15:17,18) and was emphasised in Deuteronomy 12:

> "Unto the place which the LORD your God shall choose out of all your tribes to put his name there, even unto his habitation shall ye seek, and thither thou shalt come." (verse 5)
>
> (see also verses 11,14,18)

So David knew from the scripture the "place" that God would choose to make His dwelling, and when the plague was stayed at the threshing floor of Ornan the Jebusite God revealed to him the exact location where the house should be built in which He would cause His name to dwell (1 Chronicles 21:18-22:5).

Note also the reference to the mighty God of Jacob that occurs twice in the opening verses of the psalm (2 and 5). With the limited scriptures available to him (see chapter on Psalm 119), David seems particularly to have dwelt on the life of Jacob. He would recall the origin of the title (Genesis 49:24-26) taken from Jacob's blessing on Joseph which spoke of hands made strong by the hands of Jacob's God, of the help and blessings of God that would be showered on the head of one who was separate from his brethren. Psalm 34 revolves around the life of the patriarch and his anxiety over the reaction of his brother Esau to his return from Padan-Aram. The guardian care of the angels (Genesis 28; 32; 48:15,16, etc.) was something that David could readily associate himself with in the days of his flight from Saul, and indeed in the troubles that beset him throughout his life. The title "God of Jacob" spoke of His providential hand; of the comfort and consolation that He offered and of the ultimate blessing that He bestows on His faithful servants. So the title is used only by David (see 2 Samuel 23:1; Psalms 20:1; 24:6; 94:7; 146:5) and in those psalms and prophetic utterances associated with Hezekiah's reign (see Psalms 46:7,11; 76:6; 81:1,4; 84:8; Isaiah 2:3; 49:26; 60:16).

Shared Enthusiasm

It was of course David who was the prime mover in the initiative to bring the ark to Zion. However, his zeal for the project was something that enthused the nation as a whole (2 Samuel 6:2,15; 1 Chronicles 13:1-3). It was nevertheless, as we have seen, not something that was done on impulse for even as a youth, as he tended the flock at Bethlehem, he and his companions had spoken together of the time when they would be able to accomplish this purpose:

"Lo, we heard of it at Ephratah: we found it in the fields of the wood. We will go into his tabernacles: we will worship at his footstool."   (Psalm 132:6,7)

Ephratah is the ancient name for Bethlehem (Genesis 35:19; Ruth 4:11; etc.). Commentators generally find great difficulty in this verse, some assuming that the implication is that the ark itself dwelt in Bethlehem, for which there is no evidence in the historical books. Most resolve their difficulty by assuming again that there must have been another Ephratah (a 'fruitful place') near to

Kirjath-jearim ('city of woods') from whence David brought the ark out of the house of Abinadab. Interestingly, however, Kay (*The Psalms with Notes*) points out that the Hebrew word translated "fields" occurs seven times in the book of Ruth to describe the land around Bethlehem and he translates the second sentence of verse 6 as, "We found it in the forest-field." He infers from David's words in 1 Samuel 17:36 about killing a lion and a bear that his home was skirted by forest and open countryside and other writers appear to confirm his view on the topography of the area surrounding Bethlehem. This view of course precludes the necessity to apply the words to Kirjath-jearim. Regarding the word rendered "found", *Gesenius' Hebrew Lexicon* devotes nearly a whole page to the variations of meaning that the word carries. Amongst them are: 'to obtain knowledge', figuratively 'to find out by thinking'; and although rarely so used, 'to wish to find.' In our view the original suggestion that the reference is to their conversations and discussions about the ark while watching over the sheep near Bethlehem cannot be discounted, and the change from the singular to the plural is easily understood if we accept that the psalm was written by a close associate of David.

With all his heart David longed to bring the ark of God to its final resting place that he and all those who shared his love for God might enter into His habitation. Note the reference to worshipping at His footstool, for it is used particularly of the place of God's rest. When David at the end of his life spoke of the preparations that he had made for Solomon to build the house of the Lord, he referred to the place of God's habitation as the footstool of our God (1 Chronicles 28:2). Isaiah, speaking of the day of God's kingdom, writes:

> "The glory of Lebanon shall come unto thee, the fir tree, the pine tree, and the box together, to beautify the place of my sanctuary; and I will make the place of my feet glorious." (60:13; see also Ezekiel 43:7)

If we might reverently put it so, God resided over the mercy seat, between the cherubim and the soles of His feet touched the ground and hallowed it. It was to this place that men were to come to worship, to prostrate themselves before Him who was the epitome of holiness. The thought, however, is greater than this, for the writers are reflecting upon the unimaginable greatness of God, the great Uncreate, the Creator of heaven and earth. So the prophet takes us to the heart of the matter:

"Thus saith the LORD, The heaven is my throne, and the earth is my footstool: where is the house that ye build unto me? and where is the place of my rest? For all those things hath mine hand made, and all those things have been, saith the LORD: but to this man will I look, even to him that is poor and of a contrite spirit, and trembleth at my word." (Isaiah 66:1,2)

The God of Israel fills all space; He inhabits the heavens and the earth. So the ark resting in Zion was but a figure of His final resting place. No house built by man was capable of containing Him; nothing that human hands could construct would provide a dwelling place adequate for His presence, "For all those things hath mine hand made". The wonderful truth is that God's ultimate resting place is not to be a literal building made with stones but a house composed of living beings, a spiritual house made up of all those faithful men and women who, through the ages, have put their faith and trust in Him (Ephesians 2:19-22).

So the prayer had been, "Arise, O LORD, into thy rest; thou, and the ark of thy strength" (verse 8). These were the words that Moses spoke in the wilderness when the ark set forward on its journey (Numbers 10:35,36). They are quoted in Psalm 68 (verse 1) and there are allusions to the words in other psalms (78:61). The implication of the words in this psalm is that after all its journeys the ark had come to its final resting place in Zion, although the transition from the tabernacle of David to the temple of Solomon remained. Hence the quotation of the psalm at the close of Solomon's prayer at the dedication of the temple (2 Chronicles 6:41,42).

In the circumstances of which the psalm speaks it was necessary that the priests that ministered before the Lord should be clothed in proper attire (Leviticus 6:10). That clothing was to be a fitting representation of the inner holiness and righteousness that was appropriate to all

1064

who undertook this office (Isaiah 61:10: Revelation 19:8), and speaks of the redeemed in the day of the Lord Jesus when all his saints shall shout for joy as the people of Israel did in that day.

We have already commented on the appropriateness of the words of verses 10-12 to Hezekiah's circumstances in the opening paragraph of this chapter, although verses 11 and 12 belong properly to the next section of the psalm.

The Answer of God (verses 11-18)

This final section of the psalm is God's answer to the prayer contained in verses 1-10. It is a wonderful reiteration of the terms of the covenant that God made with David. Notice particularly the manner in which some of the requests of the first half of the psalm are addressed:

Request	Response
verse 1	verses 11,12
verse 8	verses 14,15
verse 9	verse 16
verse 10	verses 17,18

A comparison of all the relevant scripture makes it clear that the record of the words of the covenant, recorded in 2 Samuel 7 and 1 Chronicles 17, does not include all that was spoken to David either on that or subsequent occasions. In his prayer at the dedication of the temple, Solomon reminds God of the promise that He had made to his father. He appears to be quoting the very words of God, but while the substance of Nathan's words is the same the manner of expressing them is different (1 Kings 8:25). Similarly there is no record of God swearing an oath, but nevertheless it is clear that He had. Literally the words of verse 11 have been rendered, "The LORD hath sworn to David. It is truth. He will not swerve from it" (verse 11, *Speaker's Commentary*). Psalm 89 confirms the fact that God had sworn with an oath (verses 3,4,34,35), emphasises the faithfulness of God (verses 1,5,8,24), and provides a wonderful divine commentary on the records of 2 Samuel and 1 Chronicles (verses 28-37).

After the affirmation that God had chosen Zion for His habitation (Psalm 132:13; see also Psalm 78:67-72) – note

1065

that the ark had previously dwelt at Shiloh, Bethel (Judges 20:27), Mizpah (21:5), Kirjath-jearim (2 Samuel 7:2) and finally in the house of Obed-Edom – it is God who speaks in the remainder of the psalm (verses 14-18):

"This is my rest for ever: here will I dwell; for I have desired it. I will abundantly bless her provision: I will satisfy her poor with bread. I will also clothe her priests with salvation: and her saints shall shout aloud for joy. There will I make the horn of David to bud: I have ordained a lamp for mine anointed. His enemies will I clothe with shame: but upon him shall his crown flourish."

Zion was to be the religious centre of the nation and ultimately of the whole world (Psalms 2:6-8; 72:8-11, etc.). Jerusalem was (under David), and yet will be the city of the great King (the Lord Jesus Christ, Psalm 48:2; Matthew 5:35). It is impossible to read this psalm with understanding, without being filled with a sense of wonder and awe at the purpose of God yet to be consummated gloriously in the person of the Lord Jesus Christ at his return to the earth.

Associated with the reign of God's anointed are not only spiritual blessings but also material bounty for the poor, who are to be satisfied with bread (Psalm 72:4,12,13,16). Interestingly, it was after the feeding of the five thousand that the people would have taken the Lord Jesus by force and made him a king (John 6:5-15). Surely they recognised in this miracle a Messianic act. Mary, the mother of the Lord Jesus, refers to the words of verses 15 and 16 of the psalm in her song of praise when she appears to bring both the spiritual and material blessings together: "He hath filled the hungry with good things" (Luke 1:53). Notice also that there is a subtle change between the request of verse 9 and the answer of verse 16, with the word "salvation" being substituted for "righteousness".

Hezekiah would have found the words of the psalm relevant to his own situation, for he had provided a "great store" (2 Chronicles 31:10) which must have sustained the inhabitants of the city during the Assyrian siege.

There in Zion God would make the horn of David to bud.
The horn is a symbol of strength. It speaks also of
sovereignty and dominion (Psalm 112:9; Micah 4:13 and
the Gentile horn powers of Daniel 7). David's throne and
kingdom would be established for ever, for the horn of
David (Psalm 89:17,24; Luke 1:69) would be made to bud.
Kay (*The Psalms with Notes*) renders the passage as,
"There will I make a horn branch forth to David" and the
words are undoubtedly taken up in the prophecies of
Jeremiah (23:5; 33:15) and Zechariah (3:8; 6:12), which
speak of the righteous branch who will sit on David's
throne and be both king and priest. All these passages
have an obvious fulfilment in the Lord Jesus Christ and
the emphasis upon priesthood is also a factor to be found
in Psalm 132.

God has ordained a lamp for His anointed and a light
shining in a house was a sign of prosperity and glory. In
this context the burning lamp is a symbol of the
preservation of the dynasty of David (2 Samuel 21:17; 1
Kings 11:36; 15:4; Psalm 18:28); that light would never be
extinguished, although through the dark night of Gentile
oppression the throne itself would be overthrown.

Although the occupant of David's throne was the
anointed of the Lord, it needs to be remembered that the
word was first used of the priesthood (Leviticus 4:5; 6:22,
etc.). The final verse of the psalm (verse 18) describes the
royal Son who sits on David's throne as wearing the high
priest's mitre. His enemies will be clothed with shame
(compare verses 9 and 16) but upon his head the crown
shall flourish. The word rendered "crown" is that used in
Exodus to describe the "holy crown upon the mitre" of the
high priest (29:6; 39:30). The word translated "flourish"
means literally 'to sparkle or glitter' (*Cambridge Bible*)
and is cognate to the word used to describe the plate of
gold bearing the inscription, "Holiness to the LORD", which
is called "the plate of the holy crown" (39:30). Clearly then
the one who will sit on David's throne for ever is both king
and priest. Of the one whom David described as "my Lord"
it was written: "The LORD hath sworn, and will not repent,
Thou art a priest for ever after the order of Melchizedek"
(Psalm 110:4). Zechariah speaks of the man whose name

is the Branch who "shall be a priest upon his throne" (Zechariah 6:12,13).

When the words were spoken to Zedekiah that declared the doom of Judah's kingdom, he was told to remove the diadem (i.e., the mitre) and take off the crown for they should be no more until he came whose right it was (Ezekiel 21:25-27).

When he comes to rule over all the earth it will be to take both the mitre and the crown, for he shall sit as a priest upon his throne.

PSALM 133

YET another psalm attributed to David is included by Hezekiah in his songs of degrees. This short, beautiful song breathes the fragrance associated with the union of brethren bound together in a common bond of fellowship. It is the togetherness of those who share a unity of purpose and intention; who have a relationship based on their allegiance to their God and their desire to worship Him in common accord. They live in harmony for they have come together to praise the God who has done great things for them.

It is not, however, a general description of brotherly love and affection. Rather as the word "Behold", with which the psalm opens, implies it is referring to a specific event in the life and experience of David.

The two most obvious occasions to which the song has been applied by those who accept the Davidic authorship are firstly when, after a period of civil war, the tribes united in acknowledging David as their king (2 Samuel 5). Secondly, it has been referred to the time after Absalom's rebellion when, as "one man", the people of Israel were united in their desire to bring back David as the throne (2 Samuel 19:9-15).

We feel, however, that neither of these two events quite fit the situation. They were both primarily civil and political amalgamations whereas the spirit of the psalm speaks, we believe, of a spiritual association. We suggest that the psalm could more appropriately be applied to the time when, after a period of unrest, Adonijah sought to seize the throne and Solomon was anointed king. It needs to be remembered that David was still alive at this time and ceded the throne to Solomon. In this connection 1 Chronicles 28 and 29 should be read with their emphasis on building the house of the Lord and the

1069

manner in which David addressed the people. The peace and harmony that accompanied the beginning of Solomon's reign and the spiritual heights to which all Israel were raised when, under the king's direction, they began preparations to build the temple, was we think unequalled in any other period of the history of the kingdom:

"Then Solomon sat on the throne of the LORD as king instead of David his father, and prospered; and all Israel obeyed him. And all the princes, and the mighty men, and all the sons likewise of king David, submitted themselves unto Solomon the king. And the LORD magnified Solomon exceedingly in the sight of all Israel, and bestowed upon him such royal majesty as had not been on any king before him in Israel."

(1 Chronicles 29:23-25)

If this is indeed the background to the psalm, what a wonderful prophetic picture it gives us of the perfect unity and concord of the Christ-body in the kingdom age and how relevant to his own days would Hezekiah have found it in the celebration of the great Passover to which he invited all his brethren in the northern kingdom.

In the first year of his reign Hezekiah held this great convocation (2 Chronicles 30) to which were invited not just the people of Judah, but messengers were sent "throughout all Israel, from Beersheba even to Dan" (verse 5). Although some "laughed them to scorn" (verse 10), "divers of Asher and Manasseh and of Zebulun humbled themselves, and came to Jerusalem" (verse 11) to be joined also by some from Ephraim and Issachar (verse 18).

The reference to Hermon and Zion would speak of God's bounty bestowed on both northern and southern kingdoms alike. Note that this was not a political occasion; it had nothing to do with recognising the sovereignty of Hezekiah; it was purely a call to join in the worship and praise of the God of Israel, and significantly it is recorded:

"So there was great joy in Jerusalem: for since the time of Solomon the son of David king of Israel there was not the like in Jerusalem." (verse 26)

Behold How Good it is

There can be no greater source of happiness than for
brethren do dwell together in unity. It is a delightful
experience: to cast aside all bitterness and resentment; to
bear no grudge in the heart but to share one another's joys
and sorrows; to be of one mind; to work together in
common accord. This is the ideal for which we strive in our
fellowship one with the other, in our endeavours to serve
our Lord Jesus Christ. It is something that in this present
mortal life we must often feel we have failed to achieve.
This is not necessarily through any fault of our own, for
sometimes the attitudes adopted by others can make it
difficult to maintain the harmony for which we strive. It is
for this reason we believe that although the psalm has a
message for us today in setting before us the ideal, it is
primarily a picture of that perfect unity that we shall
know in the kingdom when, endowed with spirit nature
and the fully developed mind of Christ, we shall all be
truly one in him. In the national unity that he witnessed
in the days of Solomon, David was moved to describe the
ultimate delight of those who seek the wisdom "that is
from above (which) is first pure, then peaceable, gentle,
and easy to be intreated, full of mercy and good fruits,
without partiality, and without hypocrisy. And the fruit of
righteousness is sown in peace of them that make peace"
(James 3:17,18).

Like the Precious Ointment

"It is like the precious ointment upon the head, that
ran down upon the beard, even Aaron's beard: that
went down to the skirts of his garments."(Psalm 133:2)
The reference is specifically to Aaron and to the occasion
when he was consecrated as high priest by the pouring
over his head of the holy anointing oil (Exodus 29:5-7).
When the ceremony was performed he was clothed in the
priestly garments that were "for glory and for beauty"
(28:2). It has to be appreciated that when Aaron was
clothed in all his priestly attire, with all the spiritual
implications of those garments, then he stood before God
as a representative man. Upon his shoulders and on his
breast he bore the names of the twelve tribes of Israel

(28:9-12,17-21). All that Israel was intended to be met in him and all his ministrations were conducted on behalf of the nation as a whole. He was in this respect an emblem of the nation and they were one in him.

The holy anointing oil was also a symbol of unity, for the tabernacle and all the furniture, together with their vessels, were sanctified by it before it was poured on Aaron's head; the unity of worship that bound them together being emphasised thereby (Exodus 30:22-33). Poured over his head, the oil would have flowed over his shoulders and down his beard to cover also the breastplate. There is some doubt as to the significance of the word rendered "skirts" – some would render it 'collar' – but the sense of the words is not affected by the change. "When, therefore, the precious oil was poured on his head, it flowed (typically) upon all the tribes. An 'odour of fragrance' was diffused over the whole body" (Kay, *The Psalms with Notes*).

Like the Dew of Hermon

"Like the dew of Hermon, that cometh down upon the mountains of Zion: for there the LORD commanded the blessing, even life for evermore." (verse 3, RV)

All writers agree that Hermon was renowned for the copiousness of its dew. G. A. Smith (*The Historical Geography of the Holy Land*, page 65) states: "The dews of Syrian nights are excessive; on many mornings it looks as if there had been heavy rain." It has to be remembered, however, that Hermon was approximately two hundred miles from Zion and it is unlikely, as many suppose, that the dew of Hermon had any physical effect upon the dry and arid country of the south. Surely the point is that the profusion of dew that watered the northern Hermon was a token of the blessing of God upon His people. Dew is refreshing and invigorating, and the blessing of unity is likened to the effect of the dew on the vegetation on which it fell. It was as though the dew of Hermon fell also upon the mountains of Zion encompassing all God's people. The fact that it was the northern tribes who were most inconsistent in their allegiance to David ("the envy of Ephraim", Isaiah 11:13), would give added weight to the

1072

emphasis upon the dew of Zion being as the dew of Hermon. Just as it was one priest who stood for the people of Israel, so it was one dew that represented the blessing of God on all His people.

Dew, of course, spoke of resurrection (see Psalm 110:3; Isaiah 26:19) and the prophet Hosea brings both of the psalm's metaphors together when he writes: "I will be as the dew unto Israel ... and his smell (Kay, 'scent') as Lebanon" (Hosea 14:5,6). Those who came to Zion from the northern kingdom in the days of Hezekiah were indeed as the dew of Hermon, refreshing the hearts of all who were like-minded in Jerusalem as they came to keep the feast of Passover.

For a more detailed exposition of the significance of dew in scripture see *Eureka* by Brother John Thomas, Volume 1, pages 140-142.

It was from there, the mountains of Zion, that God had commanded the blessing. This place, in which God has chosen to dwell, stands for all His servants as the symbol of those eternal blessings enshrined in the covenants of promise. It is here that the Lord Jesus Christ will sit on David's throne exercising dominion over all the earth. Here the blessing, even life for evermore, will be enjoyed in perfect unity in the presence of the one who was anointed "with the oil of gladness above (his) fellows" (Psalm 45:7).

PSALM 134

THIS last of the songs of degrees is a fitting conclusion to the collection of psalms that bear that title. It carries no indication of authorship, but it would seem appropriate if Hezekiah himself had written it, given the fact that this series of songs was brought together by the king to commemorate the deliverance from the Assyrian host and his own salvation from death. During those dark days of crisis, it was his yearning for the house of God that was uppermost in his heart. It was to worship God in His temple for which he longed throughout those grim days of personal and national catastrophe (Isaiah 38:20-22).

The psalm consists of three verses only. The first two are a call to those who ministered to the Lord in the temple to do so with diligence. The third is the response of those ministers to this demand in pronouncing the priestly blessing on the people.

"Ye Servants of the LORD"

"Behold, bless ye the LORD, all ye servants of the LORD, which by night stand in the house of the LORD. Lift up your hands in the sanctuary, and bless the LORD." (verses 1,2)

As in Psalm 133, the word "behold" calls attention to an activity that was both needful and a cause of rejoicing. The continuous praise that ascended in the temple to the throne of God was a witness to the wonder of all that God had accomplished on their behalf, and was reflected in the substance of the previous fourteen psalms.

The reference to the servants of the Lord is clearly not to the people generally, but to those priests and Levites whose responsibility it was to minister in the temple precincts. The word rendered "stand" is that commonly

1074

used to describe the performance of these duties (see Deuteronomy 10:8; 18:7, etc.). Hezekiah, from the beginning of his reign, showed a keen interest in the rituals and services of the temple and he instructed the Levites to cleanse the house of God after the neglect of the previous generation, reminding them that God had chosen them to stand before Him to serve Him (2 Chronicles 29:3-11). Again, when he arranged for the Passover to be kept the priests and Levites stood in their place according to the Law of Moses (30:15,16).

The Lord Jesus, of course, does not need to stand daily to offer up sacrifices, for having offered one sacrifice he sat down on the right hand of God (Hebrews 10:11,12).

Those who ministered stood by night and we can understand that the temple would not have been left unattended during the hours of darkness. Apart from the performance of their priestly duties, there would have been a need of watchmen. Edersheim (*The Temple, its Ministries and Services*) and Delitzsch (quoted by Perowne, *Psalms,* Volume 2) both describe in some detail the procedure that was followed at night in Herod's temple in the days of the Lord Jesus, and whether this was based on earlier practice in Solomon's temple it is not possible to say. However, our own conviction is that it does not seem appropriate that this wonderful group of psalms should conclude with a reference to a necessary, but somewhat mundane, duty. The use of the word "stand" would also seem to preclude this interpretation. Would it not be more fitting if ceaseless praise were to be sung, both day and night, to the God of Israel by the temple choirs?

"And these are the singers ... for they were employed in that work day and night."   (1 Chronicles 9:33)

As their voices were lifted up in continuous praise they were exhorted to lift up their hands also, in the attitude of prayer, towards (see RV) God's sanctuary – that most holy place where the ark of the covenant, the symbol of God's presence in the midst of His people was to be found.

Surely it was in this profound spiritual exercise that they would truly "Bless the LORD".

It should be mentioned that the AV and RV margins render the words differently, i.e., "Lift up your hands in holiness". If this reading is accepted, although generally rejected by most textual authorities, there is an interesting connection with the words of the Apostle Paul in his First Epistle to Timothy:

"I will therefore that men pray every where, lifting up holy hands, without wrath and doubting." (2:8)

Prayer now is not just in Zion but everywhere, for where true worship is offered 'every place is hallowed ground'.

The Priestly Blessing

"The LORD bless thee out of Zion; even he that made heaven and earth." (Psalm 134:3, RV)

The response from the temple is to recite the first words of the priestly blessing (Numbers 6:24), with the addition of the words "out of Zion". The emphasis is upon the fact that the Lord is the Creator of the heavens and the earth and that consequently all power and authority reside with Him. His blessings are sure for He is faithful that promised. It is fitting that the songs of degrees should conclude with these words, for throughout the dark night of Assyrian aggression the taunt of Rabshakeh had been that the God of Israel was no different to the gods of the nations that had fallen before them (2 Kings 19:10-13). Hezekiah's response had been to spread the letter before the Lord and pray:

"O LORD God of Israel, which dwellest between the cherubims, thou art the God, even thou alone, of all the kingdoms of the earth; thou hast made heaven and earth ... Of a truth, LORD, the kings of Assyria have destroyed the nations and their lands, and have cast their gods into the fire: for they were no gods, but the work of men's hands, wood and stone: therefore they have destroyed them. Now therefore, O LORD our God, I beseech thee, save thou us out of his hand, that all the kingdoms of the earth may know that thou art the LORD God, even thou only." (verses 15-19)

(see also Psalms 115:15; 121:2; 124:8)

PSALM 135

THE writer has a note in the pages of his copy of the *Cambridge Bible* on the psalms, written by a previous owner. It says of Psalm 135, "The writer wanders freely over the whole range of the sacred books". This is a reflection of the general view of most commentators who, following Delitzsch, describe it as "a mosaic of fragments". Beyond doubt the writer brings together a wealth of scriptural references, principally from earlier psalms and the books of Exodus and Deuteronomy, but it would be wrong to conclude that there is anything haphazard about his use of scripture.

There is no indication of authorship and most writers make no attempt to determine when, or by whom, the song might have been written, the presumption being that it must belong to some period after the exile. Although it is not one of the songs of degrees it has a close affinity with the preceding psalm (as does the next, Psalm 136). The exhortation to the priests and Levites who stand to minister in the temple (Psalm 134:1,2) is repeated in the opening words of this psalm (verses 1-4) and reflected again in its closing words (verses 19-21).

The psalm also has close links with the language of Psalm 115 and the following examples should be noted:

Psalm 135	Psalm 115
verse 6	verse 3
verses 15-18	verses 4-8
verses 19-20	verses 9-11

We have established in our previous studies that both Psalms 115 and 134 belong to the reign of Hezekiah. It seems appropriate therefore to recognise both Psalms 135 and 136 as temple hymns that were written in the time of Hezekiah, perhaps by the king himself. Their substance is

1077

consequently related to the same historical events as the songs of degrees which preceded them. The lessons learned from these events are the subject of the writer's meditations on the word of God and, as has been observed, his thoughts range over the whole of the scriptures available to him. The psalm falls into five sections:

1. The Lord is to be praised because He has chosen Israel to be His peculiar people (verses 1-4).
2. God's power manifested in nature (verses 5-7).
3. God's power manifested in history (verses 8-12).
4. Those whom the nations worship are no gods and are powerless to save (verses 13-18).
5. All Israel called to unite in the worship of their God (verses 19-21).

Israel – His People

As with Psalms 112–114, this song opens with a Hallelujah and as with Psalm 134 those that stand to minister in the sanctuary and in the temple courts are to praise God for His goodness. This they had come to appreciate more fully as a consequence of His deliverance from the Assyrian and the blessings poured forth upon Judah. They were to sing praises to His name, for it was in the manifestation of all that was represented by it that His goodness had been made known to them. They were to sing praises to His name for it was pleasant (verse 3). The Hebrew is ambiguous, perhaps deliberately so, for it could mean that God's name is pleasant or lovely, which it undoubtedly is (Psalm 54:6), or it could mean that it is pleasant to sing praises to His name:

"Praise ye the LORD: for it is good to sing praises unto our God; for it is pleasant; and praise is comely."

(Psalm 147:1)

In any event it must always be pleasant to sing the praises of that lovely name.

This manifestation of the goodness of God revealed in His name was to be seen particularly in the manner in which He had "chosen Jacob unto himself, and Israel for his peculiar treasure" (Psalm 135:4).

The thought is drawn from the book of Deuteronomy:

1078

"For thou art an holy people unto the LORD thy God: the LORD thy God hath chosen thee to be a special people unto himself, above all people that are on the face of the earth."   (7:6; see also Exodus 19:5)

Note that the words "a peculiar treasure" in Exodus 19:5 are a translation of one Hebrew word, which is also rendered "special" in Deuteronomy 7:6 and "my jewels" in Malachi 3:17 (see AV margin). As the passage from Exodus makes clear, the reason that Israel were to be a peculiar treasure above all people was because "all the earth is mine". So they were to be a kingdom of priests and an holy nation for it became their responsibility to witness for God in the earth (verse 6). They were to show God to men and to bring men to God.

This was something that they failed lamentably to do, yet it remains a task that they will fulfil in the kingdom age, for –

"Many people and strong nations shall come to seek the LORD of hosts in Jerusalem, and to pray before the LORD. Thus saith the LORD of hosts; In those days it shall come to pass, that ten men shall take hold out of all languages of the nations, even shall take hold of the skirt of him that is a Jew, saying, We will go with you: for we have heard that God is with you."

(Zechariah 8:22,23)

Nevertheless, there were at least two occasions in their history when Israel did rise to the greatness of their calling. The first was in the reign of Solomon (1 Kings 10:1-9) and the other was in the reign of Hezekiah (2 Chronicles 32:23). This latter reference is particularly relevant given the historical background to the psalm referred to above.

God's Power Manifested in Nature

The awesome manifestation of power that had destroyed the Assyrian host had so impressed the writer of this psalm that he could only reflect in wonder at the might of Israel's God, who reigned supreme in the midst of all that His hands had made:

"For I know that the LORD is great, and that our Lord is above all gods. Whatsoever the LORD pleased, that did

he in heaven, and in earth, in the seas, and all deep
places."
(Psalm 135:5,6)

There is great emphasis on the word "I" in verse 5.
Perhaps the writer speaks for all Israel as he stresses that
special knowledge of the great Uncreate that was unique
to this people who were His peculiar treasure. They knew
from experience, for He had revealed His name to them,
both in the holy oracles and in the showing forth of His
character in the history of the nation. The gods of the
nations were "no gods" and the Lord, unchallenged, did
according to His will in heaven and earth, in the sea and
all deep places. The language would appear to be drawn
from the book of Exodus (20:4) and is intended to
encompass all creation.

The prophet Jeremiah was acquainted with this psalm
and he quotes it (verse 7) on two occasions in his prophecy
(10:13; 51:16). In the first of these it is in the same context
as the psalm, contrasting the reality of Israel's God with
the nothingness of idols (verses 14-16). All nature is under
His control. Cloud vapours are lifted out of the oceans
from the most remote quarters of the earth. Some suggest
that the phrase means 'from the horizon', as if the clouds
rise from it as they come into view (see 1 Kings 18:44). He
makes the lightning and the rain for both are associated
together and He brings the wind also out of His treasuries.
Strong gives the meaning of the Hebrew word as
'depositories', for all these things come out of His
storehouse. When the Lord answered Job out of the
whirlwind (Job 38) He gave us a remarkable insight into
the wonder of His supremacy and controlling hand in all
nature. Verses 22 and 23 are particularly relevant:

"Hast thou entered into the treasures of the snow? or
hast thou seen the treasures of the hail, which I have
reserved against the time of trouble, against the day of
battle and war?"

Kay (*The Psalms with Notes*) describes it beautifully when
he speaks of "the great laboratory of Nature".

God's Power Manifested in History

As fire and hail, snow, vapour and stormy wind all fulfil
His will (Psalm 148:8), so also God has manifested His

power in history for the deliverance of His people. The greatest example of this was, of course, the salvation of His people from the bondage of Egypt when He "smote the firstborn of Egypt, both of man and beast" (Psalm 135:8; see also Exodus 12:29). He showed signs (RV) and wonders before Pharaoh and all his courtiers and princes (verse 9; see also Exodus 5:21; 7:10) and demonstrated His sovereignty by smiting many (RV) nations and great kings (verse 10; see also Deuteronomy 4:38; 7:1,2; 9:1).

Prominent among these were Sihon and Og, two of the most formidable, named that they might stand for all (verse 11; Deuteronomy 3:21; see also 2:30; 3:1; Numbers 21:21-23,33-35).

Thus it was that God gave His people the land of Canaan for an inheritance. The emphasis again is upon the fact that they were "his people" (verse 12), and this tremendous manifestation of God's power in history in establishing them in the land was a sign and a token to Hezekiah and the faithful of his day that they were still His peculiar treasure and He was their God.

The Vanity of Idol Worship

The taunt of Rabshakeh had been that none of the gods of the nations had been able to deliver them from the might of Assyria, and he claimed that Israel's God would be no more effectual than they in withstanding the power of Sennacherib (Isaiah 37:11-13). Hezekiah in his prayer had acknowledged that whereas the gods of the nations were but vanity, the God of Israel was Creator of the heavens and the earth and He alone reigned supreme (Isaiah 37:14-20).

Now in this psalm the writer turns to acknowledge the sovereignty of God:

"Thy name, O LORD, endureth for ever; and thy memorial, O LORD, throughout all generations. For the LORD will judge his people, and he will repent himself concerning his servants."   (Psalm 135:13,14)

The reference is to the words used by God when He revealed Himself to Moses at the burning bush (Exodus 3:14,15; see also Psalms 30:4; 102:12,13).

His name is His memorial; it is a constant reminder of all that He is and all that He has revealed Himself to be throughout the generations of human history. The words of verse 14 are almost a verbatim quotation of Deuteronomy 32:36. The context there makes it clear that the reference is to the manner in which, when God judges His people and sees the extremity of their situation, He will not execute the fierceness of His anger but will repent of the evil that He might have brought upon them and deliver them from their troubles. Psalm 54 brings together the thoughts of both verses:

"Save me, O God, by thy name, and judge me by thy strength." (verse 1)

So it had come to pass in the experience of Hezekiah and the inhabitants of Jerusalem. Their God, when all seemed lost, had manifested Himself in strength and destroyed in a night the Assyrian host. In the consciousness of the reality of their God and the appreciation that the gods of the nations were but the work of men's hands who could not speak, or see, or hear, for there was no breath in their mouths, the Psalmist repeats (Psalm 135:15-18), with some variations, the words of Psalm 115 (verses 4-8).

His conclusion is that those who make them and put their trust in them are, like them, vanity – creatures of no substance; empty and of no value in relation to those things that are of eternal worth. The message is for all generations. We know that covetousness is idolatry (Colossians 3:5) and the gods of this world still claim their human sacrifices as men pursue the material things of this world. If we look for fulfilment and satisfaction in the things of this life to the detriment of those eternal treasures that God offers in the Lord Jesus Christ, then we too are putting our trust in things that have no lasting value, that are to perish with all those who put their trust in them.

Call to Praise

The psalm concludes (verses 19-21) with a call to all Israel to "Bless the LORD". Again the words are constructed on the pattern of Psalm 115 (verses 9-11; see also 118:2-4), and all sections of Israelitish society are invited to join in this outpouring of praise – the people generally, the priests, the Levites and the God-fearers, those Gentiles who had attached themselves to the worship of Israel's God. The words establish a link with the sentiments of the last of the songs of degrees (Psalm 134). As there the call was for God to bless His people out of Zion, so here the call is for His servants to respond, by blessing the Lord out of Zion, His dwelling place. Thus the voice of praise would be heard far and wide as all the earth wondered at the salvation that God had wrought on behalf of His people.

The final 'Hallelujah' is thought by most authorities to belong to the psalm that follows (136).

PSALM 136

EVEN a cursory reading of this psalm should convince us that it is closely connected with that which precedes it. A brief comparison of the substance of the two is even more compelling:

Psalm 135		Psalm 136
verses 1-4	Call to praise God	verses 1-4
verses 5-7	God's power manifested in nature and creation	verses 5-9
verses 8-11	God's power manifested in the Exodus	verses 10-20
verse 12	God gave them the land	verses 21-22
verses 13-18	The impotence of idols contrasted with the living God	verses 23-25
verses 19-21	Final call to worship	verse 26

We believe again that it is associated with the events of Hezekiah's reign. Perhaps the call to bless God with which Psalm 135 ended is met in the words of this psalm which, more than any other, is obviously designed for liturgical purposes.

Each phrase of the psalm is followed by the words, "For his mercy endureth for ever", and it was evidently intended to be sung antiphonally with different parts of the Levitical choir responding to the theme of the song with this emphasis upon the mercy of God.

The word rendered "mercy" is the Hebrew *chesed* that we understand to refer to the covenant love that God bears towards His people. In it they can rest with confidence, for it is an everlasting love from which nothing can separate them.

It would appear that this form of words in "the praises of Israel" was first instituted by David (1 Chronicles 16:41) and later followed by others: Solomon (2 Chronicles 7:3), Jehoshaphat (20:21) and Hezekiah (Psalm 118:1-3,29) for example.

The structure of the psalm is broadly indicated above in the comparison with Psalm 135, but for greater clarity we suggest it be approached in the following way:

Verses 1-3	Introductory call to praise and thanksgiving
Verses 4-9	God manifested in creation
Verses 10-15	Deliverance from Egypt
Verses 16-20	In the wilderness
Verses 21-22	Israel given the land
Verses 23-26	Final ascription of praise

Call to Praise and Thanksgiving

Psalm 136 is a song of deliverance. It was sometimes referred to as 'The great Hallel' in distinction to Psalms 113-118, which were known as 'the Hallel'. Evidently they were sung in connection with the feasts of the Lord, but there is much confusion amongst writers as to their precise use. If the refrain is omitted then the first three verses would read:

"O give thanks unto the LORD; for he is good. O give thanks unto the God of gods. O give thanks to the Lord of lords."

This is an obvious reference to the Book of Deuteronomy (10:17) and the context there helps us to appreciate the Psalmist's thought. The destruction of Sennacherib's host had been likened to a Passover deliverance (Isaiah 31:5) and it is this factor that directs the thread of thought developed in this song. The emphasis in Deuteronomy 10 on God's mighty acts in delivering His people from Egypt would have struck a chord with those who, so recently, had witnessed the overthrow of the Assyrian power.

"He is thy praise, and he is thy God, that hath done for thee these great and terrible things, which thine eyes have seen." (verse 21)

God the Creator

The emphasis in Psalm 136 moves to the creative power of
God, to demonstrate that there is indeed none other but
He "who alone doeth great wonders" (verse 4). This is a
further illustration of the way in which the writer has
meditated upon earlier psalms, particularly those written
by David (see Psalms 72:18; 86:10). It is by wisdom that
He made the heavens (Proverbs 3:19; Jeremiah 10:12). We
can but stand in awe at the wonder of His work, the
precision with which He has made all things both living
and inanimate:

"Who hath directed the Spirit of the LORD, or being
his counsellor hath taught him? With whom took he
counsel, and who instructed him, and taught him in the
path of judgment, and taught him knowledge, and
shewed to him the way of understanding?"

(Isaiah 40:13,14)

The verses that follow are based upon the record of
Genesis chapter 1 and are clear examples of the wisdom
and understanding that were brought to bear in these
works of creation.

Deliverance from Egypt

The mighty power that in the beginning created all things
was manifested in the deliverance of God's people from the
bondage of Egypt. Before the majesty of God Pharaoh was
powerless and the Psalmist relates the great things that
He accomplished on behalf of His people (verses 10-15).
Note the similarity of language with Psalm 135 (verses 8-
12). The record is straightforward and describes the
historical events associated with the salvation wrought on
that occasion. The reference to a strong hand and a
stretched out arm (verse 12) carries our thoughts back to
the words of the books of Exodus (13:9) and Deuteronomy
(4:34), and reminds us that Yahweh is described as "a man
of war" (Exodus 15:3). None but He could have saved this
people from the bondage in which they languished. Note
that the word translated "overthrew" is an unusual word
and is the same as that used in Exodus 14:27. Literally it
means to 'shake off'. Pharaoh was, as it were, hurled from
his chariot into the sea.

In the Wilderness

The point of the psalm is not to dwell on the unfaithfulness of Israel in their forty-year sojourn in the wilderness, but rather to emphasise the goodness of God and the many mighty acts that He performed on their behalf. Thus the reference to the manner in which He led His people through the wilderness (verse 16) is intended to direct our thoughts to the words of Deuteronomy 8:

> "Who led thee through that great and terrible wilderness, wherein were fiery serpents, and scorpions, and drought, where there was no water; who brought thee forth water out of the rock of flint."   (verse 15)

Kings renowned for their prowess in war had been unable to withstand Him. Sihon, king of the Amorites and Og, king of Bashan were notable examples of those who had fallen before His might (Psalm 136:17-20). So He had brought them to the borders of the Promised Land.

Israel Given the Land

Here God had given the land to Israel His servant for a heritage (verses 21,22).

The description of Israel as God's servant is one particularly associated with the times of Hezekiah and is emphasised in the prophecy of Isaiah in chapters connected with his reign (41:8,9; 43:10; 44:1,2,21; 48:20; 49:3). These references take on an added significance when we read amongst them passages that clearly apply to an individual (for example, 42:1-6). We see in such passages allusions to Hezekiah, the king himself, who was representative of the nation and the embodiment of all that Israel was intended to be. Beyond Hezekiah we see the Lord Jesus Christ, the true servant of God, the one who assumes the mantle of the suffering servant in the later chapters of this prophecy.

To Israel, God had given this land for an inheritance. It had been in their possession from the time of the Exodus and though dispossessed and scattered it will yet be theirs for an everlasting inheritance (Genesis 17:8, etc.), for His mercy endureth for ever.

1087

Final Ascription of Praise

Whenever Israel was brought low, the thoughts of His faithful servants turned to their establishment as a nation when God had delivered them from the bondage of Egypt. Their prayer was that God would once again save them out of the hand of their enemies.

In the destruction of the Assyrian host they had seen cause to remember all that God had done for them in the events of the Exodus described in this psalm. Some think that the reference to God giving food to all flesh (verse 25) is a corruption or dislocation of the text. But they fail to appreciate the manner in which Gentile power recognised the God of Israel after the victory won over Sennacherib (2 Chronicles 32:23). Not only so, but many Gentiles joined themselves to Judah and worshipped the God of Israel (see Psalm 87 and Isaiah 56).

It was therefore appropriate that Israel's God be recognised as the provider of all living things, for ultimately all the earth would recognise His sovereignty – a truth of which the events of Hezekiah's days were a dim, but nevertheless real, portent.

How fitting it was that the psalm should end, not with a reference to the covenant name of God that was particularly relevant to Israel, but with a title that acknowledged His universal rule over all the earth:

"O give thanks unto the God of heaven: for his mercy endureth for ever."   (Psalm 136:26)

PSALM 137

THERE can be no doubt that this psalm was written against the background of a period of captivity. It is not surprising that almost all writers apply it to the time of captivity in Babylon, brought to an end by the decree of Cyrus (c. 536 BC). This view, although the most obvious and natural way to interpret the psalm, has some difficulties associated with it. For instance, the song is not written in Babylon but by one who has returned to the land and is recalling the mockery and abuse experienced there. It would appear that Jerusalem was standing and had not yet experienced the destruction caused by Nebuchadnezzar in 586 BC. Again, the call for God to bring judgement on Edom and Babylon suggests an imminence that history does not support. The record of the fall of Babylon before the armies of the Medes and Persians, both scriptural and historical, does not lend itself to the tone of the psalm.

An alternative period of captivity is suggested by J. W. Thirtle in his book *Old Testament Problems* (pages 130-140) and this is developed by Brother H. A. Whittaker in his books, *Isaiah* and *Hezekiah the Great*.

Thirtle suggests that the psalm belongs to the period in Hezekiah's life following the extension of life granted to him by God. He argues that before this time there was a greater deportation than in the days of Nebuchadnezzar. He quotes as evidence the Taylor Cylinder which contains the record of Sennacherib's invasion of the land, telling how he carried away 200,150 of the inhabitants of Judah. Various passages in the psalms and the prophecy of Isaiah are cited to describe how these exiles were allowed to return after the destruction of the Assyrian army (see Isaiah 35:10; 43:14-21; 48:20, etc.).

1089

Jerusalem, of course, was not destroyed by the Assyrian and these exiles could look back with longing to the city they had left behind and which they held dear in their hearts.

The reference to Babylon would need to be understood as referring to the Assyrian power whose kings, Tiglath Pileser, Shalmaneser, Sargon and Sennacherib all assumed the title of King of Babylon. As a consequence, Isaiah 13 and 14 are interpreted as referring to Assyria, quoting verses 24 and 25 of Isaiah 14 as evidence:

"The LORD of hosts hath sworn, saying ... I will break the Assyrian in my land, and upon my mountains tread him under foot."

In connection with the judgement pronounced upon Edom, Thirtle refers to Isaiah 34:1-6 and 63:1-6, both of which are associated with the reign of Hezekiah. The references to the Chaldees in some of these passages would need to be understood in the sense that the exiles were deported to live amongst them, very much as the people we know as Samaritans were brought from northern lands and resettled in Israel.

The present writer finds much of Thirtle's argument compelling yet remains uncertain which of the two backgrounds is the correct one. Readers must decide for themselves, but in any event the message of the psalm is not affected whichever of the two we adopt.

By The Rivers of Babylon

We usually associate the rivers Euphrates and Tigris with the land of Babylon. Ezekiel mentions the Chebar (1:1; 3:15) and the *Cambridge Bible* points out that Babylon was intersected by numerous canals. It was a land of streams. Jeremiah speaks of it as dwelling upon many waters (Jeremiah 51:13). It was renowned for its parks and gardens and we can appreciate how the exiles would have gathered on the banks of these watercourses, perhaps sheltering from the heat of the sun and finding such places appropriate for prayer and meditation. To sit down upon the ground was a common method of expressing grief and mourning, and as they beheld the vast plains through which the rivers of Babylon flowed they would have felt the contrast between this monotonous expanse and the hills and mountains of their native land. In these circumstances their hearts would have been moved as they wept for Zion; wept for the neglect and wickedness that had brought this calamity upon them; shed tears in abundance for the longing they experienced for the city that was so dear to them.

In their hearts they could not bring themselves to sing the songs of Zion, so they hanged their harps upon the willows. They had brought their harps evidently intending to use them in singing of their homeland and the city they loved, but overcome by despondency and sadness they were compelled to lay their instruments aside. The willow was a tree that grew in abundance on the banks of the watercourses (Isaiah 44:3,4) and although some would dispute the species of tree mentioned, it would be a pointless exercise for us to pursue the arguments presented.

The dejection and gloom seen in the situation of these exiles stands in contrast to the joy of the 144,000 who stand on Mount Zion "harping with their harps" as they sing a new song before the throne (Revelation 14:2,3; see also 5:8,9).

Their own sense of melancholy was, however, not the only reason that they had hung their harps on the willows:

"For there they that carried us away captive required of us a song; and they that wasted us required of us mirth, saying, Sing us one of the songs of Zion."

(Psalm 137:3)

The word translated "wasted" is described as obscure. Suggested meanings are, 'spoilers', 'tormentors' (see RV margin), literally 'they who were mocking us'. It is a description of the malice of those amongst whom they lived. It was not, as it were, a simple call to cheer up and accept their lot. Rather, beholding their misery it was a call to them, in a scornful, derisive manner, to sing some of the songs of Zion. It is clear from the words that follow that they were referring to the temple hymns (2 Chronicles 29:27), and the demand was made to emphasise the contempt in which they held, not only the exiles, but the God whom they worshipped.

1091

To such scorn and derision there could only be one response: they hung their harps on the willows. They could not comply with the taunting demands of those who mocked them:

"How shall we sing the LORD's song in a strange land?" (Psalm 137:4)

They were strangers, having nothing in common with those amongst whom they were compelled to live. Perhaps the demand was made against the background of some festive occasion and was for them to sing to their God as all about them sang their melodies to gods of wood and stone. The Lord's songs belonged to His house and only there could they be sung appropriately.

To have complied, whether for the amusement of their tormentors or to participate in their festive celebrations, would have been an act of profanity comparable to the manner in which Belshazzar used the consecrated vessels at his feast (Daniel 5:2).

These are, of course, sound words of advice for us on our pilgrimage, for we too dwell in a strange land. We do not espouse the world's values; our spiritual aspirations cannot be shared with those who show no desire to know the God we worship. We may in our own assemblies rejoice together and sing the praises of our Heavenly Father. But there can be occasions when we sing inappropriately, forgetting that our hymns are for worship and not simply for our personal enjoyment or to fulfil our desire to sing. We may permit those who seek to learn of our God to join us on suitable occasions. Nevertheless, we cannot allow those who seek only to deride and pour scorn on us to participate in our worship. There are times when we too, metaphorically speaking, must "hang our harps upon the willows".

"Give not that which is holy unto the dogs, neither cast ye your pearls before swine, lest they trample them under their feet, and turn again and rend you."

(Matthew 7:6)

Not that these exiles would forget Jerusalem, for it represented everything that they held most dear. Although their tongues were silent and their fingers still, in their hearts they treasured those sacred things that they had left behind. If they should forget Jerusalem, then let their hands lose their ability to pluck the strings, and by cleaving to the roof of their mouth their tongue lose the capacity to speak or sing (Psalm 137:5,6).

The Children of Edom & the Daughter of Babylon

As they remembered Jerusalem, they prayed that God would not forget the hostility of the Edomites towards them, or the barbarous manner in which the daughter of Babylon (whether Chaldeans or Assyrians) had treated them.

The ancient rivalry between Jacob and Esau was perpetuated in the history of the two peoples. Although Edom had been subject to Israel in David's days (2 Samuel 8:13-14), from the days of Joram (2 Kings 8:20-22), approximately 160 years before the times of Hezekiah, they had become the ruthless and pitiless enemy of Judah. They were ever watchful to take advantage of Judah's troubles. Like a bird of prey they were ready to swoop on the carcase, although it would appear that they were never the primary aggressor. Most certainly they were ready to support both the Assyrian and Babylonian invasions:

"Remember, O LORD, the children of Edom in the day of Jerusalem; who said, Rase it, rase it (literally, 'lay it bare'), even to the foundation thereof." (Psalm 137:7)

God's judgements upon Edom for their cruel and callous attitude towards God's people runs through the writings of the prophets (see Isaiah 34; 63:1-4; Jeremiah 49:7-22; Ezekiel 25:12-14; chapter 35; Joel 3:19; Amos 1:11,12; Obadiah).

Those who visit that ancient land testify how effectively God's judgements have been carried out. We believe, however, that Edom, because of the profanity of Esau, stands as a type of the world in general, and some of the scriptures that describe God's judgements upon her speak also of the day when God's anger will be poured out on this present evil world. Isaiah 34 in particular lends itself to this understanding as it moves from Edom, the people of His curse, to embrace all nations (verses 1-6).

Perhaps this is true also of Babylon, the city being personified under the figure of the "daughter of Babylon". This city founded of old by Nimrod (Genesis 10:8-10) has ever stood for the pride and arrogance of man. It is the great enemy of God's people, an important city for successive human empires (Assyrians, Chaldees, Persians, Greeks), and it lives on in the symbolic language of the Apocalypse.

In the words of the psalm, "O daughter of Babylon, who art to be destroyed; happy shall he be, that rewardeth thee as thou hast served us" (verse 8). The words are written to describe the reaction of the exiles who had suffered at the hands of their oppressors, but remain true of God's servants in every generation who have suffered at the hands of the religious and political tyranny represented by this city.

The tense of the verb "to be destroyed" speaks of the city as if this destruction were already accomplished: literally, 'that art destroyed'; thus describing the irrevocable end of this great enemy of God and persecutor of His people.

The language of the last verse of the psalm has been the cause of much unease, the suggestion being that it is incompatible with the language and teaching of the New Testament:

"Happy shall he be, that taketh and dasheth thy little ones against the stones."
(verse 9)

Some imaginative attempts have been made to resolve this apparent difficulty. For instance, it has been pointed out that the Hebrew text rendered "stones" means literally 'the rock'. Because the Greek word *petra*, by which Edom became known, means just that, it is argued that the "little ones" are to be identified with "the children of Edom" of verse 7 who, because of their subordinate role, became "the little ones" of Babylon, dashed against their own rock. However attractive such a view might seem, it has to be acknowledged that the Hebrew word translated "little ones" means literally 'babes or infants', and providing an explanation in this psalm does not take away the fact that similar language occurs in other psalms and these things actually happened to the people of Israel and Judah (see Hosea 10:14; 13:16).

We need to remember the cruel and barbarous nature of ancient warfare. It was not unusual for victorious armies to carry out a policy of genocide and human history is littered with similar acts of savagery. It ill becomes modern critics of the word of God to express revulsion at language such as this, given the atrocities that have been committed in modern times. It is significant that as the Assyrians treated Israel, so it came to pass in the day of their destruction (Nahum 3:10). Such was the nature of that ancient world that it would not have been possible for appropriate and righteous retribution to be poured out other than by nations that lived by the same standards.

PSALM 138

THIS is the first of a group of eight psalms ascribed to David. The Septuagint adds the names of Haggai and Zechariah to the title, but it is generally accepted that there is no reason to doubt the Davidic authorship. It may be that the names of these post-exilic prophets were added because they used the psalm and applied it to the circumstances of their own days.

As far as the background is concerned, the psalm offers no clues as to the time when it was written and it could reasonably be applied to almost any period in David's life.

It is suggested that this group of psalms were brought into temple use in the days of Hezekiah and they do seem to be generally appropriate to the circumstances of his reign.

The psalm can conveniently be divided into three sections:

1. A personal declaration of praise for God's goodness and faithfulness (verses 1-3).
2. An acknowledgement that ultimately all nations will recognise and sing of the glory of the Lord (verses 4-6).
3. An assurance that whatever troubles might befall David, God will perform that which He has promised (verses 7-8).

God's Goodness and Faithfulness

David does not name the one to whom he ascribes praise:

"I will praise thee with my whole heart: before the gods will I sing praise unto thee." (verse 1)

Some ancient versions insert 'the Lord' after "thee", but this is unnecessary as there can be no doubt as to whom David is addressing. It is the Holy One of Israel and out of

1096

the fullness of his heart praise overflows. It is with his whole heart, with undivided loyalty, a complete dedication to the God who had blessed him so abundantly. His devotion was not something that was confined to his private moments, although such times are precious, but also he sings his praises before the gods. Commentators are completely divided as to the significance of the word "gods". Some ascribe it to the gods of the nations – not that David thought they had any form of existence, but as a witness before all that worshipped them that would lead eventually to the nations also singing the praises of his God.

Others, particularly Christadelphian writers, interpret the word as an allusion to the angels, and while acknowledging that this is a reasonable suggestion we believe that the reference is to the Judges of Israel, the princes of the land who exercised authority over the people (Psalm 82; Exodus 21:6; 22:8,9,28).

So both privately and publicly David was prepared to sing the praise of his God, for he was not ashamed of Him in whom he had put his trust:

"I will worship toward thy holy temple, and praise thy name for thy lovingkindness and for thy truth: for thou hast magnified thy word above all thy name."

(verse 2)

The reference to the "temple" does not mean, of course, that David could not have written the psalm for this term is used of the tabernacle, God's dwelling place (1 Samuel 1:9; 3:3; Psalm 5:7, etc.).

David's desire to worship towards God's temple, emphasised in this psalm and Psalm 5, quoted above, is picked up and echoed by Solomon in his prayer at the dedication of the temple (1 Kings 8:30,33,35,38,42,44). What is significant about Solomon's prayer is the manner in which he recognised the surpassing grandeur of the God of Israel who was pleased to dwell in the midst of His people, although the heaven and heaven of heavens could not contain Him. How much less this house which he had built (verse 27).

It would appear that Solomon had meditated upon this psalm, for the emphasis in his prayer is upon the manner in which God had kept His word of promise to His servant David, and who kept covenant and mercy with those who walked before Him with all their heart (verses 20-26; compare Psalm 138:1,2).

There is perhaps an indication here that David wrote the psalm shortly after God had made His promises to him. This view is supported by the words: "Thou hast magnified thy word above all thy name." Some find this statement difficult, for God's name represents all that He is and has revealed Himself to be. His word, it is argued, would be encompassed within the name. While this is true, it is missing the point being emphasised. The promise He had made regarding a son who should sit on David's throne for ever transcended everything that He had previously revealed. In that covenant was encapsulated the whole purpose of God. In that sense He had magnified that word of promise above all His name, for in its fulfilment everything that the name represented would be consummated.

"In the day when I cried thou answeredst me, and strengthenedst me with strength in my soul." (verse 3)

In all David's distress God had proved faithful. He had answered his prayers and in the experiences of life, knowing that God was with him, he had found an inner strength that enabled him to face all the trials and adversities that befell him with confidence. The Hebrew word translated "strengthenedst me" is a bold use of a term that elsewhere is used in a bad sense and translated "shall behave himself proudly" (Isaiah 3:5). It is emphasising that inner strength that the Psalmist felt because of his consciousness of God's presence. It was akin to the strength of the arrogant man who trusted in himself, whereas his strength was derived from the Lord his God.

All Nations Recognise the Glory of Israel's God

"All the kings of the earth shall praise thee, O LORD, when they hear the words of thy mouth. Yea, they shall sing in the ways of the LORD: for great is the glory of the LORD. Though the LORD be high, yet hath he respect unto the lowly: but the proud he knoweth afar off."

(verses 4-6)

It was always God's intention that Israel should be a witness to him in the earth. As a kingdom of priests (Exodus 19:5,6) they should have shown forth the glory of their God and brought men to Him. Scripture is a solemn witness to the manner in which they failed to fulfil their responsibilities. On only two occasions in their history do they seem to have risen to their calling: that is during the reigns of Solomon (1 Kings 10:23,24) and Hezekiah (2 Chronicles 32:22,23).

So it was that David looked to the day when all nations would finally recognise the wonder of the promises that God had made to His servants, and rejoice in the way in which through the ages He had worked out His purpose with His people Israel. Note the manner in which the ways of God are paralleled with the acts of God in Psalm 103 (verse 7). Then would they join their voices with his and sing in joyful acclaim of the greatness of God's glory. Might not this song have been inserted into the Psalter at this place in contrast to the manner in which the exiles had been unable to sing the Lord's song in a strange land? (Psalm 137:3,4). The great truth is that although He is the high and the lofty one that inhabits eternity, He condescends to those who are of low estate, who are of a contrite and humble spirit (Isaiah 57:15; Psalm 113:4-7).

However, let not the proud think that God is unaware of their arrogance, for all those who are of a haughty spirit are known to Him. He sees and observes them, distant though they might imagine themselves to be, and unlike the lowly in spirit they shall remain afar off for they can have no fellowship with Him and cannot enter into His presence.

His Confidence in the Providence of God

David knew that the work of God, both in his life and in the affairs of His people, was not complete. As he looked to the future with its unknown perils his prayer was that God would revive him or keep him alive in the midst of his troubles; preserve him by stretching forth His hand against his enemies. His confidence was that God would

1099

save him with His right hand (verse 7; see also Psalm 17:7).

> "The LORD will perfect that which concerneth me: thy mercy, O LORD, endureth for ever: forsake not the works of thine own hands."
> (verse 8)

That work that God had begun in him he desired to see accomplished. Paul expressed a similar thought in respect of the believers at Philippi:

> "Being confident of this very thing, that he which hath begun a good work in you will perform it until the day of Jesus Christ."
> (Philippians 1:6)

David's longing was for the promises that He had made to be brought to fulfilment. His emphasis upon the mercy (covenant love) of God that endures for ever is a clear indication of this. That which he confidently asserts now becomes the closing prayer of the song. "Forsake not", he cries; literally, 'do not relax'. He prays that God will carry forward that work which He had begun with His people Israel, that it might be brought to that grand consummation of all His work in the earth.

PSALM 139

THIS psalm must surely rank amongst the most magnificent in the entire Psalter. It reveals a close and intimate relationship between God and the writer who dwells on the omniscience (verses 1-6), omnipresence (verses 7-12) and omnipotence of God (verses 13-18). It is not possible to read this psalm without feeling a sense of one's own inadequacy to comment on the superlative use of language by which the writer was moved by the Spirit to express his appreciation of the reality of God.

The psalm is ascribed to David and we feel confident that it could only have been a man of his spiritual stature who would have been used by God to communicate that consciousness of the Deity that pervades the psalm. Few writers are prepared to accept the Davidic authorship, principally because of the occurrence of some Aramaic words which they believe point to a late date. This is a specious argument which relies on supposition rather than hard facts. In any event, the spiritual significance of the psalm does not rest on any particular event in David's life and its message is unaffected whoever the author might have been. Indeed, we suggest that the psalm is in fact wholly messianic and it is quoted (verse 15) by the Apostle Paul in his Epistle to the Ephesians (4:9) with reference to the Lord Jesus Christ. The psalm is introspective in character, and man is shown to be the special creation of God who lives continually in His sight and in all the circumstances of life is unable to escape His presence. Significantly there is no confession of sin, only a request that God would try him and search his heart to ensure there was no wickedness in him (verses 23,24).

The all-pervading sense of God's knowledge, presence and power might lead some to think that His power over man is absolute. However, the psalm maintains a balance throughout between men's thoughts and actions for which they are always responsible, and the providential control of God over all the affairs of life.

In the last section of the psalm (verses 19-24), the writer ponders God's tolerance of the wicked and expresses his abhorrence of all those who hate God.

The Omniscience of God

The Psalmist reflects on God's perfect knowledge of all aspects of his life and thoughts:

> "O LORD, thou hast searched me, and known me.
> Thou knowest my downsitting and mine uprising, thou
> understandeth my thought afar off."   (verses 1,2)

The word "me" does not appear in the Hebrew text. As a consequence the act of searching is emphasised more emphatically and the divine scrutiny has revealed all the thoughts and intents of his heart. Again there is great emphasis on the word "thou" in verse 2 and the sense is that it is He alone, and no other, that is able to discern this absolute knowledge of His creatures. This knowledge encompassed his whole life. Whether he was resting or working (see Deuteronomy 6:7), God had understanding of all the thoughts and inclinations of his heart. These God knew "afar off", or literally 'long before'. Before the heart conceived them God, who neither time nor space affect, was aware of the 'hidden motions' of the heart.

> "Thou compassest my path and my lying down, and
> art acquainted with all my ways. For there is not a word
> in my tongue, but, lo, O LORD, thou knowest it
> altogether."   (verses 3,4)

The word rendered "compassest" means 'to winnow or sift', and this presents a graphic figure describing that searching examination of human behaviour that God alone is capable of undertaking. It encompasses all aspects of life, both the paths we walk or our daily activities, and our times of rest or lying down. He is acquainted with all our ways, for they are the object of the most searching and discriminating investigation. Indeed, before the very words are uttered, God knows what we mean and the thoughts that lie behind them, for:

"Thou hast beset me behind and before, and laid thine hand upon me."   (verse 5)

Again there is a striking metaphor behind the language used. The Hebrew word translated "beset" is used of the besieging of a town. In effect, it is as if God has surrounded us, enclosed us in such a way that there is no possible escape from His searching gaze. Not only does God encircle us but He holds us firmly in His hand. He has laid His hand upon us in the sense that we are never free from that authority that He exercises over us, "for in him we live, and move, and have our being" (Acts 17:28).

Faced by such infinite knowledge, such an awareness of the reality and nearness of God in all the circumstances of life, the Psalmist can only conclude this opening section of his song with an exclamation of reverent awe:

"Such knowledge is too wonderful for me; it is high, I cannot attain unto it."   (verse 6)

It is beyond human understanding. It is exalted, raised up in such a way as to be completely inaccessible to men. By way of illustration, the Hebrew word translated "high" is used of an impregnable city (Deuteronomy 2:36). Truly with the Apostle we can say:

"O the depth of the riches both of the wisdom and knowledge of God! how unsearchable are his judgments, and his ways past finding out! For who hath known the mind of the Lord? or who hath been his counsellor?"
(Romans 11:33,34)

The Omnipresence of God

Just as God knows all things, so also He is everywhere present by His spirit. Man can never hide himself from God. "Whither shall I go from thy spirit? or whither shall I flee from thy presence? (verse 7). As far as the writer of this psalm is concerned, we must not think that he personally is contemplating how he might escape from God. Throughout, he is dwelling on the fact that because God is all embracing in knowledge, presence and power, this is a source of comfort to those who seek Him. Remember particularly our suggestion that the psalm is totally messianic in its character, and the Lord Jesus more than any other would have reflected on these attributes of his Father. He would have found consolation in the knowledge that it was an utter impossibility for men to prevent God from accomplishing His purpose in him.

This is not to say, however, that the words do not stand also as a warning to men who think, foolishly, that they can hide from God. The classic examples are, of course, Adam and Eve who hid themselves from the presence of the Lord God among the trees of the garden (Genesis 3:8), and Jonah who rose up to flee from the presence of the Lord (Jonah 1:3,10). Note that the word for "presence" means literally 'face' (see Genesis 4:14,16; Exodus 33:14,15, etc.) and refers to God's manifestation of Himself to men.

There is nowhere that God is not present by His spirit:

"If I ascend up into heaven, thou art there: if I make my bed in hell, behold, thou art there. If I take the wings of the morning, and dwell in the uttermost parts of the sea; even there shall thy hand lead me, and thy right hand shall hold me."   (verses 8-10)

The prophet Amos echoes the words of the psalm:

"Though they dig into hell, thence shall mine hand take them; though they climb up to heaven, thence will I bring them down."   (see 9:2-4; also Jeremiah 23:24)

Although he might scale the heavens or make his couch in the grave, there was no escape from the presence of God. We are carried from one extreme of space to the other and it is a sobering thought that not even death itself offers a haven from the wrath of God, for He is able to raise up those who are accountable to Him.

With a vivid and dramatic figure of speech, the Psalmist cries that even if he were able to travel from the east at the speed of light to the farthest reaches of the west it would be to no avail. The sea is a reference to the Mediterranean, which being to the west of the land is used as a figure of all that lies in that direction. The dawn spreading from the east over the heavens is represented as winged. Kay (*The Psalms with Notes*) comments: "Mounting up with the speed of the morning-dawn, and rushing on to the furthest west." Were this possible he still could not evade the overriding control of God, for even then His hand would lead him and there would be no relaxation of the right hand of His power.

"If I say, Surely the darkness shall cover me; even the night shall be light about me. Yea, the darkness hideth not from thee; but the night shineth as the day: the darkness and the light are both alike to thee."

(verses 11,12)

It is as impossible to hide from God in the darkness as it is to escape His presence by moving from place to place.

The word rendered "cover" means literally 'to break or overwhelm'. It is only used on three other occasions in the Old Testament, two of these being in Genesis 3:15 (translated "bruise"). The connection with the breaking of the power of sin by the Lord Jesus opens up an interesting train of thought. How often is it that men imagine they can forget God and shut Him out of their lives? They choose to walk in darkness; they willingly allow themselves to be overwhelmed by the serpent's power. Thus they delude themselves, imagining that by this means, they have escaped the scrutiny and judgement of God. Nevertheless, the light of God's word will prevail for the darkness and the light are both alike to Him (see John 3:19-21).

The Omnipotence of God

The next section of the psalm is especially appropriate to the Lord Jesus Christ (verses 13-18). As indicated above, the Apostle Paul quotes from this part in his Epistle to the Ephesians: "Now that he ascended, what is it but that he also descended first into the lower parts of the earth?" (4:9).

It is the language of God manifestation. God came down in the person of His Son for the salvation of men and then with the work accomplished ascended up on high again. (For an exposition of the verse see *Epistle to the Ephesians* by Brother John Carter). Here in the psalm there is a prophecy of the birth of the Lord Jesus Christ. It is completely missed by the majority of commentators, yet it speaks to us unmistakably of the manner in which the

Holy Spirit operated on the womb of Mary to bring to the birth the only begotten Son of God. It was in this act of divine intervention in the affairs of men that God, in the language of theophany, came down:

"For thou hast possessed my reins: thou hast covered me in my mother's womb. I will praise thee; for I am fearfully and wonderfully made: marvellous are thy works; and that my soul knoweth right well."

(verses 13,14)

The word "for" connects this passage with what has gone before. It is a recognition that God has this intimate knowledge and understanding of man because He has created him, and in the person of the Lord Jesus this is particularly true because his life was foreordained and God had revealed all that was to befall him. The word "thou" is emphatic and that translated "possessed" means literally 'made or formed'. The reins or kidneys are regarded as the seat of the emotions. Thus it is that He who created man in the beginning has a perfect knowledge of the intricacies of human thought patterns, and a precise understanding of what moves men to perform the things they do. As the *Cambridge Bible* (page 789) expresses it, "Thou knowest me, for Thou didst create me".

Arising out of the thoughts of verse 13, the following verse should be regarded as a parenthesis. The Psalmist reflects in wonder and amazement at the marvellous work of God that has produced such a complex creature as he has come to recognise himself to be.

The words which follow are of course true of David and of all men. They are nevertheless the words quoted by the Apostle Paul in the Epistle to the Ephesians and they are particularly true of the Lord Jesus, emphasising the manner in which he shared our human nature:

"My frame was not hidden from thee, when I was made in secret, and curiously wrought in the lowest parts of the earth. Thine eyes did see mine unperfect substance, and in thy book they were all written, even the days that were ordained, which day by day were fashioned, when as yet there was none of them."

(verses 15,16, RV with margin)

By his "frame" the writer means his bones or his skeleton, formed in secret, covered or hidden in the womb. The phrase "curiously wrought", meaning literally 'wrought with care', brings to mind the description in the book of Exodus of the girdle of the ephod – a cunningly woven band of gold, of blue, purple and scarlet, and fine twined linen (28:8, RV). As the girdle was embroidered with threads of different colours, so the veins and arteries of the body form a complex and intricate pattern. It was formed in the lowest parts of the earth, a way of describing the darkness of the womb, where hidden from the sight of men the embryo was mysteriously fashioned (note that the word translated "substance" in this instance is different from that used in verse 15).

It would be natural to grasp at the idea of the embryo being imperfect and refer it to the nature of the Lord Jesus that he shared with us. This truth is, in any event, implicit in the fact that he was born of a woman. The word, however, does not carry the significance of marred or flawed. Rather, it means incomplete in the sense that the embryo is as yet undeveloped. From the foetus there would develop the complete person and, referring particularly to the Lord Jesus, all that he would become was written in God's book. It was foreordained, the pattern of the life that he should live clearly revealed in the pages of scripture. This does not mean that it was impossible for him to sin, but it reflects the overriding power of God who knows the end from the beginning. It was in the knowledge of that which was written concerning him that the Lord Jesus could say: "Lo, I come: in the volume of the book it is written of me, I delight to do thy will, O my God" (Psalm 40:7,8).

It speaks to us also of the providential hand of God in our lives, for all our ways too are written in His book and we need to recognise that the circumstances we experience are under the control of our Heavenly Father.

In contemplation of these wonderful truths the Psalmist is moved to cry:

"How precious also are thy thoughts unto me, O God! how great is the sum of them! If I should count them,

> they are more in number than the sand: when I awake,
> I am still with thee." (verses 17,18)

The words about counting are obviously not to be taken literally. It is a figure of speech intended to convey the thought that the human mind could never grasp or discern the totality of all that God is. It is like plumbing the depths of a bottomless well and each fresh discovery is held precious by all those who love God. The Hebrew word translated "sum" is the plural of 'fullness' and it is intended to emphasise that absolute knowledge of God is unfathomable by man.

His last thought as he closes his eyes in sleep is of his God and when he awakes he is still in His presence. How true these words are of those who die in the Lord. He is their last thought, and when in that resurrection morn they are awoken out of sleep they are still in His presence. This was, of course, especially true of the Lord Jesus: "Into thine hand I commit my spirit" – his last thought; "Thou hast redeemed me, O LORD God of truth" – his next conscious moment (Psalm 31:5).

Why Does God Tolerate Wickedness?

> "Oh that thou wouldest slay the wicked, O God: depart from me therefore, ye bloodthirsty men. For they speak against thee wickedly, and thine enemies take
> ' thy name in vain." (verses 19,20, RV with margin)

From the sublimest of thoughts the Psalmist turns to consider the wicked who still prosper in the earth, although God is all powerful and everywhere present. Surely He will not tolerate them indefinitely but will rise up and destroy them? The Psalmist would have them depart from his presence lest their company should influence him, or he himself be swallowed up with them in the inevitable time of judgement. They are men of blood for they do not shrink from murder and violence in the pursuit of their ambitions. They have no fear of God for they cloak their actions with a pretence of righteousness. They take His name in vain as they swear falsely to achieve their evil ends. Truly they are God's enemies and David is filled with righteous indignation. He feels a deep sense of grief and anger at their behaviour (see Psalm 119:53,136,158).

"Do not I hate them, O LORD, that hate thee? and am not I grieved with those that rise up against thee? I hate them with perfect hatred: I count them mine enemies."
(Psalm 139:21,22)

The world that we live in puts us under all kinds of pressures. It is an evil world from which our God seeks to deliver us. Surrounded by human wickedness we must strive to separate ourselves from it and show our abhorrence of it in the lives we strive to live.

Note though that it is in an appreciation of his own weakness, the possibility of self-deception, that David asks God to subject him to that scrutiny of which the earlier verses have spoken. It is not in a spirit of presumptuous self-confidence that he has expressed his hatred of those that hate God. He would still know that searching of heart by Him who is all knowing and understands the deepest thoughts and intents of his heart:

"Search me, O God, and know my heart: try me, and know my thoughts: and see if there be any wicked way in me, and lead me in the way everlasting."
(verses 23,24)

PSALM 140

THERE is a close affinity between Psalms 140-143, all of which are ascribed to David. Nevertheless, while accepting the fact that the psalms are connected, there is a strange reluctance amongst orthodox commentators to accept the Davidic authorship. For no apparent reason they give a late date to the psalms and suggest that the author was copying David's style in an endeavour to illustrate events in his life. They variously claim to recognise the hatred of Saul, the slander and enmity of Doeg and the rebellion of Absalom. We believe that the first two suggestions might have some substance to them, although of course they were actually written by David in the situations described.

More accurately we suggest that they were written by David during his time in the royal court and in the events that made it necessary for him to flee as a fugitive. They were written therefore not about specific individuals, but concerning the opposition of self-seeking men, of whom Doeg was a type, who hated David and all that he stood for and were determined to bring about his demise.

Psalm 140 falls neatly into five stanzas and we follow this pattern in our consideration of it.

A Prayer for Deliverance (verses 1-3)

We have written previously in our reflections on other psalms of the difficulties that David experienced when he was taken into the royal court. He was surrounded by powerful and influential men who did not share his spiritual aspirations. They were interested only in their own political ambitions and as David grew in popularity they saw him as a threat to the fulfilment of their aims in life. They were therefore ever ready to pander to Saul's obsessive hatred; to encourage him in his fanatical desire

1110

to kill David and to slander him at every opportunity by spreading virulent untruths about his motives and actions.

It is against this background that David prays to be delivered from the plots of arrogant and unscrupulous men:

"Deliver me, O LORD, from the evil man: preserve me from the violent man; which imagine mischiefs in their heart; continually are they gathered together for war."

(verses 1,2)

The word translated "man" can be understood collectively and that this is the sense is evident by the words that follow. They are violent men not averse to bloodshed if the circumstances appear to warrant it. Secretly and deliberately they devise evil in their hearts. They stir up strife continuously. The word rendered "war" is a plural of intensity and means literally 'bitter strife'.

"They have sharpened their tongue like a serpent; adders' poison is under their lips."   (verse 3, RV)

Two metaphors are combined: the sword and the serpent's tongue. The lying tongue is compared to a sword in other psalms (55:21; 57:4; 59:7; 64:3), as is the serpent's bite (58:3,4). They are deliberately plotting to inflict a grievous wound on him by their slander. It is as though the viper's poison gland was hidden under their tongues. Note that these words are quoted by the Apostle Paul in his Epistle to the Romans (3:13).

Renewed Prayer for Protection (verses 4,5)

As he had prayed for deliverance out of the hand of his enemies, so now David repeats his prayer. He recognises that if, under the hand of God, it was necessary for him to remain in those difficult and dangerous circumstances he was completely dependent upon his God to keep and preserve him from those who sought to harm him. They were determined to "overthrow (his) goings": literally, 'to trip him up or to cause him to stumble'. To this end, as the hunters set snares and traps for the animals they wished to catch, so these proud and arrogant men were scheming to catch him as he went about his daily tasks. They had "spread a net by the wayside" – that is, in the way that he

1111

was accustomed to go. This, of course, was also the tactic of the Pharisees with the Lord Jesus, for they "took counsel how they might entangle him in his talk" (Matthew 22:15). The fact that the Psalmist refers to his adversaries as proud is an indication that he saw them not just as his enemies, but also as the enemies of his God whose purposes they thought to thwart.

Further Appeal to God for Help (verses 6-8)

Against such men there was only one who could help him in his time of need:

> "I said unto the LORD, Thou art my God: hear the voice of my supplications, O LORD." (verse 6)

His confidence lay in that special relationship that he had with his God, for He was the strength of his salvation (verse 7) or to express it colloquially, 'my strong deliverer'.

God had provided him with protection in the past and he was sure He would continue to do so now. He would cover his head as with a helmet. This is a figure of speech used to describe the manner in which God would deflect the slanders and insults that they sought to heap on his head (Isaiah 59:17; Ephesians 6:17; 1 Thessalonians 5:8).

The figure of speech is maintained, for this God would do in the day of battle – literally 'the day of armour'; the time when armour would be required. Although actual weapons were not being used, his detractors were still fighting a war with him and their words of calumny and defamation were intended to be just as effective as if they had attacked him with drawn sword:

> "Grant not, O LORD, the desires of the wicked: further not his wicked device; lest they exalt themselves."
>
> (verse 8)

May all their evil schemes be brought to nothing, for if they were successful in their intentions then they would surely exalt themselves. This would be to the detriment of the people of Israel generally, and once again David is showing himself to be a true shepherd of the flock.

Divine Retribution (verses 9-11)

In differing circumstances different approaches are required of God's servants. Thus the Apostle Paul exhorted the Ecclesia at Rome:

"Dearly beloved, avenge not yourselves, but rather give place unto wrath: for it is written, Vengeance is mine; I will repay, saith the Lord. Therefore if thine enemy hunger, feed him; if he thirst, give him drink: for in so doing thou shalt heap coals of fire on his head."

(Romans 12:19,20)

We must give place to the wrath of God, recognising that He will ultimately dispense appropriate judgement as the situation requires. Our responsibility is to treat those who treat us shamefully, not as enemies, but with kindness and consideration. By this means, if they are not won by our example their sin against us is aggravated and they heap coals of fire upon their heads.

In David's situation, however, the actions of these men went far beyond personal wrong to David. They were revealing themselves to be the enemies of God. They were not unbelievers, they were of Israel and were sinning against the light. There is nothing in David's words to indicate that he would not have fed them if they were hungry. Nevertheless, he recognised that if their mischief were to prosper it would hinder the outworking of God's purpose and be to the disadvantage of His people. In these circumstances there could be only one response:

"As for the head of those that compass me about, let the mischief of their own lips cover them. Let burning coals fall upon them: let them be cast into the fire; into deep pits, that they rise not up again. Let not an evil speaker be established in the earth: evil shall hunt the violent man to overthrow him." (Psalm 140:9-11)

The mischief that they were intent on causing was to recoil upon their own heads. Like Sodom in its inveterate wickedness, they too were to suffer the judgement of God. The word rendered "deep pits" is found only here in the Old Testament. Some suggest that it means 'whirlpool'. The RV margin has "floods" and the suggestion is that if they should escape the rain of fire, let them be swept away

1113

by the floods of water "that they rise not up again". Their overthrow was to be final; there was to be no remedy.

For such men to be established in the earth would be a disaster. This David knew and he had prayed in another Psalm:

> "Let the sinners be consumed out of the earth, and let the wicked be no more." (104:35)

The evil that they sought to impose upon others would pursue them relentlessly. The *Cambridge Bible* has "with thrust upon thrust" to emphasise the uncompromising and unremitting way in which they would eventually come to their end (Psalm 35:5,6).

Confidence in God (verses 12,13)

In the midst of this difficult and trying situation David retained his confidence in God. He was not filled with doubt and uncertainty about the outcome of the circumstances in which he found himself, for he knew from his own experience and from the assurances given in God's word that God would protect the weak and poor and deliver them out of the hand of those who oppressed them. The present trials would not continue indefinitely but eventually right would prevail. For this cause the righteous would give thanks unto His name. The upright would dwell in God's presence: initially in the peace and prosperity that would be enjoyed in the land when their God dwelt among them; ultimately in the kingdom age when God would make His tabernacle with men.

PSALM 141

NOWHERE is the affinity of this group of psalms of David (138-145) more apparent than in the similarity that exists between this psalm and that which precedes it. Here again David speaks of those who seek to defame him by slander and devious cunning schemes. They prosper in the royal court of Saul and they are ultimately responsible for encouraging the king in his delusions and causing David to live the life of a fugitive.

Not only did they seek to vilify him by libellous accusations, they were also not averse to resorting to flattery (verse 4) if they thought that thereby they could enmesh David in their evil designs. In this situation David had only one means of support. He put his trust in his God and besought Him to so work that all the plans of his enemies should be brought to nothing.

The psalm falls into three sections. Verses 1-5, and verses 8-10 are pleas that God would help him to escape out of the hand of all those that hated him. Between them is a passage (verses 6,7) that has caused great difficulty to commentators in seeking an interpretation that is in keeping with both the words that precede and those that follow it. This confusion is summed up by Perowne (*The Book of Psalms,* Volume 2, page 450):

> "To translate each sentence by itself is no difficult matter, but it is almost hopeless either to link the sentences plausibly together, or to discover in them any tangible clue to the circumstances in which the Psalmist was placed."

Appeal to God to Hear Him

"LORD, I cry unto thee: make haste unto me: give ear unto my voice, when I cry unto thee. Let my prayer be

1115

set forth before thee as incense; and the lifting up of my
hands as the evening sacrifice." (verses 1,2)

He was anxious that as he had called upon God (see RV),
He would be swift to answer his cry (Psalms 22:19; 38:22;
40:13). It would appear that David was thinking of his
prayer as a sacrifice, for the words "be set forth" mean
literally 'to be prepared or set in order', and the term is
used of the temple service in the days of Hezekiah (2
Chronicles 29:35). The reference to incense could be an
allusion to the daily offering of incense by the priests
(Exodus 30:7,8), but the connection with sacrifice suggests
that the reference is to the frankincense burned as a
memorial for a sweet smelling savour when it was mixed
with the portion of the meal offering (Leviticus 2:1-11).
The lifting up of the hands is, of course, a gesture of prayer
intended to indicate that the heart too was lifted up to
God. The fact that it is likened to the evening sacrifice
suggests that perhaps the imagery was intended to
encompass both the morning and evening sacrifices, for
the meal offering was offered in conjunction with the daily
burnt offerings (Exodus 29:38-42).

Incense ascending in a fragrant cloud is a symbol of
prayer (Revelation 5:8; 8:3,4). Perhaps the reference to the
evening and morning sacrifices is an indication that
David, aware that he would soon be compelled to become
a fugitive, poured forth his heart in prayer at these
particular times, conscious of the truth that God would
hear his servants wherever they might be (Malachi 1:11).
The fact that his prayers rose as a sweet smelling savour
is an indication of his close association with God, for this
was a sign of covenant relationship – sin forgiven and
sacrifice and praise acceptable to Him.

Nevertheless, David was aware of his own frailty and
weakness, the need to stand firm before all the
blandishments of ambitious and worldly-minded men:

"Set a watch, O LORD, before my mouth; keep the
door of my lips. Incline not my heart to any evil thing,
to practise wicked works with men that work iniquity:
and let me not eat of their dainties." (Psalm 141:3,4)

David was concerned lest he be influenced by the profane
and unwholesome speech of those who surrounded him.

1116

Perhaps also he was anxious not to break out in bitter words of recrimination concerning his persecutors, or worst of all in words of reproach against his God because of the adversity in which he found himself (see also Micah 7:5).

How could God keep his mouth in this way? Was not David responsible for the words that he spoke? The responsibility was indeed his, but he recognised the providential hand of God and acknowledged that He could direct his paths in such a way that he would be kept from the evil influences of those about him.

So also he would be kept from falling into the temptation of seeking to live that life of ease and luxury that they enjoyed and was based on wickedness and violence (Proverbs 4:17). In his anxiety to keep himself from the influence of these evil men, David acknowledged how much he needed the support of righteous men:

"Let the righteous smite me; it shall be a kindness: and let him reprove me; it shall be an excellent oil, which shall not break my head: for yet my prayer also shall be in their calamities."   (verse 5)

David had prayed that he might not be led astray by the blandishments of the wicked and it would appear that on occasions this had been a very real temptation to him. He would therefore develop a spirit that was ready and willing to accept the reproof of the righteous. It is not easy to acknowledge the correction of the godly when we are in danger of going astray. Pride and self-assurance in the way we have chosen can make it very difficult to accept that we are putting ourselves in danger of falling into sin. Sometimes the criticisms of our brethren are not offered in the most conciliatory of ways.

Nevertheless, we must develop the spirit that recognises that the wounds inflicted by the correction of the righteous are a kindness, and such reproof is as "ointment and perfume" that "rejoice the heart" (Proverbs 27:9). The Proverbs are full of sound advice on this matter (13:18; 15:5,31; 28:23) and the message is summed up in the words of chapter 27:

"Faithful are the wounds of a friend; but the kisses of an enemy are deceitful."   (verse 6)

The last part of Psalm 141:5 is difficult and the suggestion of Perowne (*The Book of Psalms,* Volume 2, page 453) seems to give the sense of the Hebrew best:

"For even in their wickedness (whilst it continues and whilst I suffer from it) shall my prayer continue."

(see also RV)

We leave verses 6 and 7 until we have considered the last section of the psalm.

A Further Plea to God

The conjunction "For" (AV, "But") with which verse 8 begins, appears to connect, not with the verses we have deferred considering, but with the prayer of verses 1-5:

"For mine eyes are unto thee, O GOD the Lord: in thee do I put my trust; leave not my soul destitute. Keep me from the snare which they have laid for me, and from the gins of the workers of iniquity. Let the wicked fall into their own nets, whilst I withal escape."

(verses 8-10, RV)

There is an urgency and expectancy about his prayer. His eyes are ever towards Yahweh his sovereign Lord (Psalm 25:15). He has placed himself under His protection and his plea is that He would "pour thou not out my life" (RV, margin). In other words, 'let me not perish'. The phrase reflects the truth that the life is in the blood and illuminates the words of Isaiah 53 (verse 12) concerning the sacrifice of the Lord Jesus Christ.

The prayer of Psalm 140 (verse 5) is repeated. He would be delivered out of all the snares and traps that the wicked had laid for him, whether by slander or enticement. His prayer was that their plots should recoil upon their own heads and that in consequence he might escape as they were caught in their own snares.

We turn our attention now to the apparent difficulty presented by verses 6 and 7.

The Judgement of the Wicked

There is a consensus of opinion amongst commentators that it is best to follow the translation of the RV:

"Their judges are thrown down by the sides of the rock; and they shall hear my words; for they are sweet.

As when one ploweth and cleaveth the earth, their (margin) bones are scattered at the grave's mouth."

(verses 6,7)

The judges are the rulers or princes of the people. It was they who in the royal court were primarily responsible for persecuting David. We do not believe that the words about casting them from the side of the rock are to be taken literally. It was a common form of punishment in ancient times and David is speaking figuratively of the day that would surely come when they would receive their just deserts. In that day the people generally, who like David had suffered at the hands of these evil and corrupt men, would rejoice in the words that he had spoken and they would be sweet unto them.

Like the stones or clods that were turned up by the plough, a day would come when their bones would be scattered over the earth, as it were at the mouth of the grave. It is a picture of an army that had suffered a catastrophic defeat – bodies lying untended and uncared for. It is an interesting speculation, but how many of those princes in Israel that sought to do David harm would have fought with Saul in his last battle with the Philistines, and how many of them were left dead on the battlefield, receiving in this way the reward for all the evil that they had purposed against the Lord's anointed?

We do not normally subscribe to the view that psalms were altered or added to at a later date to fit circumstances, but in this instance we wonder if David added these words to his earlier song after Israel's defeat at the hands of the Philistines. In any event, it is a solemn warning to all who for personal advantage, or indeed any other reason, would defame or slander their brother.

PSALM 142

THIS psalm bears the inscription "Maschil of David". This is the last of thirteen psalms that carries this title and as previously indicated it means literally 'for instruction'. The psalm therefore has lessons for those who read it and was written for the benefit of those who would learn from David's experiences. It also has some historical information at its head which helps us to determine when precisely David wrote this song. It is "A Prayer when he was in the cave" and writers are divided as to whether it is the time when David came to the cave of Adullam (1 Samuel 22:1) or the occasion when he cut off Saul's skirt in the cave of Engedi (1 Samuel 24). For reasons that will become apparent as we proceed, we believe that it was the time David came to the cave of Adullam.

The psalm can be divided into three sections. In the first, in a spirit of great despondency David makes his troubles known before the Lord (verses 1,2). Yet although filled almost with a sense of despair, he is conscious of the fact that God is aware of his situation and knows the paths he treads (verses 3,4). He recognises that the Lord is his only hope of escape from his enemies and he looks to Him for deliverance (verses 5-7).

David in Distress

"I cried unto the LORD with my voice; with my voice unto the LORD did I make my supplication. I poured out my complaint before him; I shewed before him my trouble." (verses 1,2)

Notice that the emphasis is upon the fact that David cried aloud. It was not merely silent prayer that David uttered, but he lifted up his voice. David at this time was alone and the fact that he was moved to cry aloud is an indication of

1120

the intensity of distress that he felt. The word "cried" carries the significance of need in great anxiety and distress (Psalm 107:13,19) and his anguish finds relief in the pouring forth of his complaint. This was not a grievance against God, for the word translated "complaint" means the outcome of conversing within oneself. In other words, the inner turmoil that he was experiencing led him to lay his cause before the Lord.

God Knew all His Ways

"When my spirit was overwhelmed within me, then thou knewest my path. In the way wherein I walked have they privily laid a snare for me. I looked on my right hand, and beheld, but there was no man that would know me: refuge failed me; no man cared for my soul." (verses 3,4)

It was not that God needed David to tell Him of his situation, for He was fully aware of all the circumstances in which he found himself. Rather David would ease the ache that he felt in his heart by unburdening himself before the Lord. In this way he found consolation in the knowledge that his troubles were shared. We know this to be true on the human level for so often a sympathetic ear, even one that has heard it all before, can soothe the heart that is weighed down with trouble. How much more so when we open our hearts to our Heavenly Father who is aware of all the circumstances of our lives and knows our deepest need, and every requirement for us to find that peace of heart and tranquillity of spirit for which we long.

Notice that when David utters these words he is completely alone. His spirit was overwhelmed. Literally, it fainted within him; it was as if darkness enveloped his soul (Perowne). There was no man to stand at his right hand, the natural place to look for support (Psalms 16:8; 109:31; 121:5), and no man cared for his soul (literally, 'enquires as to my soul', see Jeremiah 30:17). There was no one to care for his needs or to seek to alleviate them. In his extremity David turned to the Lord his God who knew the path on which he trod and all the evil schemes of his enemies as they sought to ensnare him. The word "thou" has great emphasis and is best expressed in English by

1121

repeating the word: 'Thou, thou knewest my path.' It was a matter of wonder and awe to David that God took knowledge of his ways in this manner. "Refuge", cried David, "failed me". There appeared to be no place of safety; nowhere that he could flee for refuge.

The fact that David was alone is the key to the historical background. There is only one occasion in David's days as a fugitive when he was completely and utterly alone as far as human help was concerned, and that was when he took flight and dwelt with the Philistines (1 Samuel 21). When he was expelled by Achish because the king thought that he was mad, David came to the cave of Adullam and, in the first instance, he must have come there alone (1 Samuel 21:13-15; 22:1).

David's Prayer for Deliverance

David would remind God of his past faithfulness and the verbs (verse 5) are in the perfect tense, describing "what he has done in the past and is still doing" (*Cambridge Bible*): literally, 'I have cried ... I have said'. The word for "refuge" (verse 5) is different from the one used in verse 4. Whereas the former signifies a place to flee to, the latter speaks of a shelter, a secure place where safety is assured. It is also translated as "hope" and "trust". Not only was God his refuge but He was also his 'portion'. Deprived by the jealousy of Saul of his inheritance in the land, he found in his God more joy and satisfaction than anything this present life had to offer (see Psalm 16:5,6).

> "Attend unto my cry; for I am brought very low: deliver me from my persecutors; for they are stronger than I." (verse 6)

It is said of this verse that it is a mosaic of phrases that occur in other psalms of David. Given that this is one of David's earlier songs, it is more likely that the repetition occurs in those psalms rather than this. Given the manner in which we are all sometimes able to recognise language characteristic of particular brethren, it is not surprising that even under the guidance of the Spirit David is permitted to use words and phrases that are distinctive to himself.

"Bring my soul out of prison, that I may praise thy
name: the righteous shall compass me about; for thou
shalt deal bountifully with me."   (verse 7)

The use of the word "prison" presents some with difficulty,
but we are not intended to take it literally. It speaks of
confinement and if we consider the time that David had
spent among the Philistines, with his movements
curtailed and under the constant observation of those who
from the beginning distrusted him, we can appreciate that
as he came alone to the cave of Adullam it would have
been with a sense of oppression and that overwhelming
darkness of spirit of which he had spoken earlier (verse 3).

But it was here at the cave of Adullam that there was
the beginning of that change in David's circumstances that
was to bring him eventually to the throne. God heard his
prayer and it was at this place that there gathered to
David "his brethren and all his father's house", together
with "every one that was in distress, and every one that
was in debt, and everyone that was discontented" (1
Samuel 22:1,2). It might be thought that these were the
dregs of society, but that would be wrong. Almost certainly
these were men who like David had suffered at the hands
of unjust judges; who had been taken advantage of by
princes in the pursuit of their worldly ambitions, and they
numbered about four hundred men. Here was the answer
to David's prayer. Here were men who recognised him as
the Lord's anointed and among them he could praise God's
name as they compassed him about. The straightforward
understanding would appear to be that as they gathered
themselves to him, so they could join in his thanksgiving.
The RV margin, however, reads, "the righteous shall crown
themselves because of me" and this rendering is supported
by many writers who understand it as a figurative way of
describing their rejoicing at David's deliverance.

The fact that those who resorted to David numbered
about four hundred men is of some significance and might
well have been understood by him as a token of God's
blessing.

David's flight to dwell among the Philistines was
caused by the actions of one man – Doeg the Edomite (1
Samuel 21:1-10). Significantly, when Esau came to meet

Jacob on his return from Padan-Aram he was accompanied by four hundred men (Genesis 32:6). He came in peace, and was this an assurance to David that he need no longer fear the actions of that wicked man who sought his life and who was responsible for killing all the priests that were at Nob?

Whether that is so or not, there can be no doubt that it was here in the cave of Adullam that David's situation changed, for God answered his prayer. He came alone in a spirit of despair, but his heart was fortified as he was joined by this company of loyal men and he could acknowledge that God had indeed dealt bountifully with him.

PSALM 143

PSALM 143 is the last of the seven so-called 'Penitential Psalms' and the writer is clearly deeply affected by the knowledge of his sinfulness and its consequences in his life. The song falls into two sections (verses 1-6 and 7-12), divided by the familiar 'Selah', each of the sections then being divided into three couplets.

It bears the heading, "A Psalm of David" and some copies of the Septuagint add, "when his son was pursuing him". There is no reason to doubt the Davidic authorship and although there is no means of verifying the authenticity of the reference to his flight from Absalom, the tone and content of the song lend themselves to the latter years of David's life and can be understood as written against that background. Our understanding of the psalm is nevertheless not affected if this suggested historical setting is in fact incorrect.

David's Sin and its Consequences
We know from the record of David's sin in the matter of Bathsheba and Uriah the Hittite (2 Samuel 12) that God told David, through the prophet Nathan, that the sword would never depart from his house. Evil would be raised up against him from within his own household, with his wives taken before his eyes and given to his neighbour (verses 10,11). All this was particularly true of Absalom's rebellion (2 Samuel 16:21).

It is evident from the first four verses of the psalm that the calamity that had now overtaken him, and the attitude of his enemies towards him, was regarded by David as a direct consequence of his sin. Absalom's uprising and the manner in which those that hated David gathered themselves about him, fits perfectly the tone of the psalm:

"For the enemy hath persecuted my soul; he hath smitten my life down to the ground; he hath made me to dwell in darkness, as those that have been long dead. Therefore is my spirit overwhelmed within me; my heart within me is desolate."   (verses 3,4)

Although he recognised that the things that had befallen him were a punishment for his sin, David also perceived that those who were gathered against him were moved in their antagonism, not just to depose him, but to frustrate the purpose of God. In this respect they were not just his enemies but God's. Their attitude towards him is reflected in the words of verse 3, for the enemy would tread down or crush his soul. It is a play upon the curse on the serpent (Genesis 3:15). The situation, however, is reversed and David is regarded as the serpent seed that needed to be destroyed (see also Psalm 41:9). It would appear that they thought their cause to be right and that David, if allowed to continue on the throne, would bring ruin on Israel. It has to be remembered that at the time leading up to Absalom's rebellion David was a sick man (see Psalm 41 again). When the crisis finally broke and David was forced to leave Jerusalem, it would appear that there had been a measure of recovery. Nevertheless, he would still have been recuperating and filled with a spirit of lethargy that was totally uncharacteristic of him when he was fully in command of all his powers.

Like Hezekiah in an earlier psalm (88:4-6), he was filled with a spirit of despair, as one for whom there was no future. Such was the calamity that had overtaken him, it was as if he had been buried alive in the darkness of the grave with those that, forgotten by God and man, were dead for ever. The phrase, "those that have been long dead" means literally 'the dead of eternity' – those that "sleep a perpetual sleep" (Jeremiah 51:39), those for whom the grave is an everlasting abiding place, their house of eternity (Ecclesiastes 12:5, "long home").

This is a powerful testimony to the reality of the death state and it is interesting to note the attempts of some writers, while acknowledging the sense of the Hebrew, to argue that the passage is not relevant to our understanding of life after death.

David felt that he had been overwhelmed by the events that had overtaken him. Literally, his spirit fainted within him and the desolation of his heart speaks of a sense of paralysis that had engulfed him (desolate, or 'motionless', *Cambridge Bible*) so that he knew not where to turn.

In God Only was Help to be Found

Conscious that these calamities which had overtaken him were a consequence of his sin and that he was experiencing the chastening hand of God, David appreciated that there was none to whom he could turn other than the Lord his God whom he had come to know and love:

> "Hear my prayer, O LORD, give ear to my supplications: in thy faithfulness answer me, and in thy righteousness. And enter not into judgment with thy servant: for in thy sight shall no man living be justified." (verses 1,2)

As at the time of his transgression David looked not to the Law of Moses for deliverance but to his knowledge of the revealed character of God:

> "The LORD, the LORD God, merciful and gracious, longsuffering, and abundant in goodness and truth, keeping mercy for thousands, forgiving iniquity and transgression and sin ..." (Exodus 34:6,7)

It is again to the faithfulness and righteousness of God that he looks. Because God is faithful He cannot be false to that which He has revealed Himself to be. For "if thou, LORD, shouldest mark iniquities, O Lord, who shall stand? But there is forgiveness with thee, that thou mayest be feared" (Psalm 130:3,4).

The principle is carried over into the New Testament for, "He is faithful and just to forgive us our sins, and to cleanse us from all unrighteousness" (1 John 1:9).

David's plea is that he will not be called to give account for his sins, for he recognises the absolute holiness of God and that no man can be justified or righteous in His sight. Paul uses this passage in his arguments in the Epistles to the

Romans (3:19,20) and Galatians (chapter 2) to demonstrate that all the world (all flesh) is guilty before God.

Notice that David refers to himself as "thy servant" and that at the conclusion of the psalm he again affirms, "I am thy servant" (verse 12). This is not just an expression of humility, but a recognition of a special relationship that he had with his God: not just that he was devoted to His service, which he undoubtedly was, but also that he stood in this capacity because of the covenant God had made with him. If David's prayer after the promise that God would make him a house is read (2 Samuel 7:18-29) it will be observed that on ten occasions David refers to himself as God's servant, and in the context in which this occurs it cannot be without significance.

In pleading that he might not be called to the bar of judgement, David is calling upon God to recognise that although he himself was a sinner, they who sought his life were also guilty before Him and whereas David was His servant, they were enemies of God and antagonistic towards His purpose.

Reflections on Past Mercies

In his distress, as he cried unto God to hear his prayer and deliver him out of the hand of his enemies, David's thoughts turned to all that God had performed in past times and longed for a fresh manifestation of His power:

> "I remember the days of old; I meditate on all thy works; I muse on the works of thy hands. I stretch forth my hands unto thee: my soul thirsteth after thee, as a thirsty land." (verses 5,6)

In one respect the remembrance of the blessings of former days compared with the troubles that he was now experiencing, would have added to the sense of distress that he felt. But in another way the knowledge of past blessings would have been a source of comfort to him, giving him assurance that if he opened his heart to God He was still powerful to deliver as in days of old. Thus he stretched forth his hands in prayer, thirsting for God, as parched land dried up by continuous drought longed for the refreshing rain from heaven – rain being an apt symbol of divine blessing (Psalm 68:9).

David's Prayer

The content of his prayer is the substance of the second section of the psalm (verses 7-12):

"Make haste to answer me, O LORD; my spirit faileth: Hide not thy face from me; lest I become like them that go down into the pit. Cause me to hear thy lovingkindness in the morning; for in thee do I trust: cause me to know the way wherein I should walk; for I lift up my soul unto thee." (verses 7,8, RV)

In his extremity he looked for a speedy response to his prayer for if God were to hide His face, that is withdraw His presence, the light of His countenance, then David would be as a dead man. He longed for God to pierce the darkness that enveloped him as the dawn breaks the blackness of the night, that he might rejoice once more in the sunshine of God's blessing. He had put his trust in God and he longed for Him to teach him the ways in which he should walk to avoid those dangers that threatened his throne and the fulfilment of those wonderful promises that God had made to him:

"Deliver me, O LORD, from mine enemies: I flee unto thee to hide me. Teach me to do thy will; for thou art my God: thy spirit is good; lead me into the land of uprightness." (verses 9,10)

To escape from the clutches of his enemies he would have God to hide him. The Hebrew verb 'to hide' means 'to cover or conceal' and it is suggested that by the change of one letter the significance would be, 'unto thee have I fled for refuge' (*Cambridge Bible*) – a change that is supported by the Septuagint.

He would have God to instruct him and it is interesting to note that David is recalling the words of an earlier psalm (25), written against the background of his flight from Saul. It would seem that he had meditated once again upon the words of this song, for it colours so much of what he has to say. There also the emphasis is upon David's conviction of his sinfulness and the wonder of God's forgiveness (verses 7-11).

Also, the need for God to teach him of His ways, that he might have a better understanding of the providential working of His hand, is stressed (verses 4,5); together with the need for that quality of meekness that would make him amenable to the sweet influences of God's word (verses 3,4,8,9,12).

David's prayer is, "Let thy good spirit lead me in a level land" (Psalm 143:10, literal translation). The term "level land" or "plain country" (see Deuteronomy 4:43) is geographical, used as a metaphor to describe a way of life free from all the obstacles and encumbrances which now confronted him. It is reminiscent of the words of the prophet Isaiah:

"Prepare ye the way of the LORD, make straight in the desert a highway for our God." (40:3,4)

Also the words of Proverbs:

"In all thy ways acknowledge him, and he shall make straight thy paths." (3:6, RV margin)

David's confidence that God will answer his prayer is reflected in the last two verses of the psalm. The verbs are all in the future tense to emphasise his belief that God would manifest Himself on his behalf:

"For thy name's sake, O LORD, Thou wilt revive me; in Thy righteousness Thou wilt bring my soul out of trouble. And in Thy mercy Thou wilt smite my foes, and wilt uproot all who harass my soul; because I am Thy servant." (verses 11,12; Kay, *The Psalms with Notes*)

Note another reference to Psalm 25 – "For thy name's sake, O LORD" (verse 11). It is because of His faithfulness to that which He has revealed Himself to be (Exodus 34:6,7) that God will quicken or revive His servant. He will lift him out of that slough of despond into which he had fallen by delivering him from the hand of those that hated him. Note again that it is for His righteousness' sake, for God is ever true to what He has shown Himself to be.

For his enemies, hardened and impenitent men, determined to oppose David and in their antagonism to him show themselves also to be the enemies of God, there can be no reprieve. They were traitors to the cause of truth and had forfeited their right to live. Commentators generally think the words to be contrary to the spirit of the New Testament, but they have failed to see the larger picture. This is not a personal cry for revenge, but a recognition that ultimately the wicked will be destroyed out of the earth: "But those mine enemies, which would not that I should reign over them, bring hither, and slay them before me" (Luke 19:27).

The Lord Jesus Christ

Our considerations have led us to think of the Lord Jesus when he will finally sit on David's throne and all the rage and vain imaginations of the nations will be frustrated by the power of God. We suggest, however, that the words of David in this psalm were in the thoughts and meditations of the Lord Jesus when he hung upon the cross.

Think first of David's declaration that "in thy sight shall no man living be justified" (verse 2). Was any man ever more conscious of that fact than the Lord Jesus when he was crucified? He carried the whole burden of human sin and was totally aware of the fact that if he failed there could be no life for any man; nothing but that perpetual sleep in his house of eternity of which verse 3 had spoken. As David's enemies had gathered together to destroy him, so "Herod, and Pontius Pilate, with the Gentiles, and the people of Israel, were gathered together, for to do whatsoever thy hand and thy counsel determined before to be done" (Acts 4:27,28).

The Lord Jesus had committed no sin. He of all men did not deserve to die; he had never known the shame that guilt brings. He had shared all our experiences, being tempted in all points like as we, but had never shared with us that separation from God that is the inevitable consequence of sin. Yet we believe that on the cross, in ways that are perhaps beyond our understanding, he was given an insight into just what this meant for those whose sins he carried. From the sixth hour to the ninth hour there was darkness over all the earth (Luke 23:45). It was as if God drew a veil over the experiences of the Lord Jesus during that period of time. Recalling Abraham's experience, it was "an horror of great darkness (that) fell upon him" (Genesis 15:12). It spoke of death and separation from God and it was at the ninth hour as the darkness lifted that the Lord cried: "My God, my God, why hast thou forsaken me?" In some way he had entered into our experiences and these things are reflected in the words of the psalm: "He hath made me to dwell in darkness, as those that have been long dead" (verse 3). The consequence – "Therefore is my spirit overwhelmed within me; my heart within me is desolate" (verse 4).

It was immediately after this, only moments before the Lord gave up the spirit, that he cried, "I thirst". It was not a cry of physical deprivation, but an indication of his longing for God. This again is reflected in the psalm: "My soul thirsteth after thee, as a thirsty land" (verse 6).

Thus the spirit of Christ speaks to us through the experiences of David and the words that he left on record for our learning and instruction.

PSALM 144

A LTHOUGH ascribed to David, most commentators describe this psalm as a late composition made up of a mosaic of quotations from earlier songs of David and therefore regarded as his. They fail to see a real continuity of thought in the psalm and describe verses 12-15 as being the only part of the compilation that might be original to the writer, although on balance most feel that this too is borrowed, probably from an unknown psalm.

Our own study of the psalm led us to the conclusion that, although their expertise in Hebrew is helpful in leading us to an understanding of the words and phrases written, the barrenness of their thinking in seeking a historical setting for the psalm is staggering. In our own thinking we had come to the conclusion that the background to the psalm is to be found in the events surrounding David's ascent to the throne over all Israel (2 Samuel 5) and it was with some satisfaction that we eventually found a reference in Perowne (*The Book of Psalms*, Volume 2, page 464) to the fact that –

> "Qimchi, who holds the Psalm to be David's, refers it to the events mentioned in 2 Samuel 5, when having been acknowledged by all the tribes of Israel as their king ... and having completely subjugated the Philistines, he might look forward to a peaceful and prosperous reign."

Some copies of the Septuagint add, "against Goliath" to the title and the Targum of verse 10 reads, "from the evil sword of Goliath". Perowne dismisses these points with the comment: "It is scarcely necessary to remark how improbable such a view is." We suggest, however, that herein is one of the clues that lead to a proper understanding of the circumstances that moved David to write this psalm.

Historical Background

2 Samuel 5 tells us how after a period of civil war (2 Samuel 3:1), the death of Abner brought matters to a head and all the elders of Israel came to David in Hebron and anointed him to be king over all Israel (verse 3). Seeing in these events a possible opportunity to take advantage of the situation, the Philistines came up twice to the valley of Rephaim to confront David but on each occasion the Lord delivered them into his hands (verses 17-25). As we consider the words of the psalm it will be seen how fitting they are to these circumstances.

Quotations from Earlier Psalms

In our view the weight placed upon quotations from other psalms is overemphasised. There are, we believe, two psalms that form a backcloth to David's words: Psalm 18 in particular and also Psalm 8. Similarity of language with other psalms is a characteristic of all of David's writings and is of little value in determining which was written first.

The references to Psalm 18 are beyond dispute and that psalm bears the superscription:

"A Psalm of David, the servant of the LORD, who spake unto the LORD the words of this song in the day that the LORD delivered him from the hand of all his enemies, and from the hand of Saul."

It was evidently written early in David's reign, probably when he reigned as king in Hebron. The psalm is repeated with minor variations in 2 Samuel 22 in the context of the end of David's life, and we can appreciate its appropriateness to that particular time in the king's reign. Psalm 144 must therefore have been written a few years later in the midst of the events described above, and it is not difficult to appreciate why David's thoughts would have revolved around that particular psalm. We list opposite for easy reference the allusions to Psalm 18 that we have identified in Psalm 144.

Psalm 144		Psalm 18
verse 1	"The LORD my strength"	verse 1
verse 1	"Which teacheth my hands to war"	verse 34
verse 2	"My fortress; my high tower, and my deliverer"	verse 2
verse 2	"My shield" – translated "buckler"	verse 2
verse 2	"Who subdueth my people under me"	verse 47
verse 5	"Bow thy heavens, O LORD, and come down"	verse 9
verse 6	"Cast forth lightning, and scatter them: shoot out thine arrows, and destroy them"	verse 14
verse 7	"Send thine hand from above ... deliver me out of great waters"	verse 16
verses 7, 11	"The hand of strange children"	verses 44, 45
verse 10	"It is he that giveth salvation unto kings"	verses 33, 34,50

Psalm 144 is, of course, very much shorter than Psalm 18. Apart from the references given above, the general mood of the first eleven verses of the song is nevertheless wholly in keeping with the tenor of the longer psalm, and given the circumstances in which they were written it is easy to understand why David's thoughts should have revolved around his earlier song which itself was based upon previous scripture (see Psalm 18 – *The Praises of Israel*, Volume 1).

The other psalm to which there is an obvious reference is Psalm 8, verse 3 being a quotation of verse 4 of that song. Psalm 8 was composed to celebrate "the death of the man between the camps"; that is the Philistine champion Goliath and the relevance of the comments of the Septuagint and the Targum become apparent, given the threat from the Philistines that confronted David as he became king over all Israel (see Psalm 8 – *The Praises of Israel*, Volume 1).

David's Confidence in God

As David was crowned, his thoughts must have carried him back over those difficult years that he had

1135

experienced, from the day that Samuel had anointed him to be king, his early successes in battle with the Philistines when God had taught his hands to war and his fingers to fight (verse 1), his years as a fugitive when he was hunted by Saul. Sometimes it seemed as if every man's hand was against him. It was of that time that he could write:

> "My goodness, and my fortress; my high tower, and my deliverer; my shield, and he in whom I trust."
>
> (verse 2)

The word translated "goodness" is the Hebrew word *chesed*, sometimes rendered "lovingkindness" and descriptive of that love that God had towards those who had come into a covenant relationship with Him. In a bold figure, David describes his God as the One who had encompassed him with loving kindness in delivering him from all his adversity. The places in which he had taken refuge, the weapons of defence that he carried, he sees as figures of the care and protection that God had afforded him in the midst of all his troubles. Now, at last, the throne was his, for God had subdued the people under him (verse 2); all the rebellious elements in Israel's ranks had finally submitted themselves to his authority.

The Philistine Threat

After a turbulent period of unrest in Israel that lasted throughout David's seven-year reign in Hebron, it was not surprising that the Philistines should have thought it timely to test the strength of the new king. David won two victories over their army and as always he sought guidance from his God before going forth to battle (2 Samuel 5:19,23).

In these circumstances it was natural that David's thoughts should go back to his victory over Goliath and the words he had penned in Psalm 8:

> "LORD, what is man, that thou takest knowledge of him! or the son of man, that thou makest account of him! Man is like to vanity; his days are as a shadow that passeth away."
>
> (verses 3,4)

It should be noted that there is a different emphasis in Psalm 144 from that in Psalm 8. There, considering the finiteness of man, his insignificance when compared with the wonder and majesty of God's creative work, David is moved to marvel at the fact that it is in such a transient and insignificant creature that God is pleased to carry forward His purpose in the earth. Here, appreciating the transitory nature of human life he recognises that all human endeavour is powerless before the power and might of God. Like a breath (vanity) he vanishes away; he is like a shadow that has no substance and after a brief moment ceases to be.

Having described the fleeting nature of human life in general, David makes his prayer to God to deliver him from this cruel foe – these strange children (Kay, "sons of the alien") that were gathered against him:

"Bow thy heavens, O LORD, and come down: touch the mountains, and they shall smoke. Cast forth lightning, and scatter them: shoot out thine arrows, and destroy them. Send thy hand from above; rid me, and deliver me out of great waters, from the hand of strange children; whose mouth speaketh vanity, and their right hand is a right hand of falsehood." (verses 5-8)

It is the language of theophany, of God coming down and manifesting Himself among men (Exodus 19:18; 20:18). David's prayer is that God would rescue him from the troubles in which he found himself. The reference to "great waters" is perhaps an indication that the Philistine threat was far greater than we might have imagined. After all, they came twice and perhaps there was still a measure of uncertainty about the unity of the nation so recently come together under his sovereignty. That God did "come down" is evident from the record in 2 Samuel 5 and the victories were won by David acting on His specific instructions. Perhaps there had been some diplomacy at first with an apparent agreement being reached, for David speaks of their vanity, or lies, and of the manner in which they had raised their hands in a solemn oath which he describes as "a right hand of falsehood".

A New Song

Having defeated the Philistines and established himself on the throne, David would sing a song of redemption. A new song is always a song of deliverance and David could now look forward to a period of peace and prosperity. So he sang his praises unto God accompanying himself on a harp of ten strings, for God alone could bring salvation and deliver kings. Faced with the responsibilities that now rested upon his shoulders he repeats his prayer of verses 7 and 8, entrusting his rule to the guidance of the Lord his God (verses 9-11).

What he longed for as a true shepherd of the flock was for Israel to experience a period of peace and tranquillity, in which the people could delight themselves in the joy of family life and the prosperity that comes from a time when they were no longer threatened by Gentile power:

"That our sons may be as plants grown up in their youth; that our daughters may be as corner stones, polished after the similitude of a palace: that our garners may be full, affording all manner of store: that our sheep may bring forth thousands and ten thousands in our streets: that our oxen may be strong to labour; that there be no breaking in, nor going out; that there be no complaining in our streets."

(verses 12-14)

There is much discussion amongst commentators as to the grammatical correctness of the introductory words of this passage. They offer no clear guidance and it is perhaps an example of how one can get distracted by technicalities when the general meaning of the words is obvious.

David would have the threat of war removed in order that their sons, like saplings, might be nourished and grow into strong and sturdy trees. As decorated pillars in a grand house, he describes the grace and beauty of their daughters. He looks for an abundance of crops and a multiplying of their sheep and oxen. There was to be no breach of city walls by hostile invaders and the people were to be secure in the knowledge that they would not go out to surrender to the enemy. In consequence, there would be no complaining, or wailing, in their streets. For this blessing David longed, and it was his prayer for this people over whom he had been raised up to reign. In confidence he could declare:

1138

"Happy is that people, that is in such a case: yea, happy is that people, whose God is the LORD."

(verse 15)

PSALM 145

IN this psalm we have a magnificent song of praise
extolling the greatness and power of Israel's God, seen
not only in His mighty acts but also in the love and
condescension He shows to all His creatures. God is
supreme, His sovereignty exercised over all the works of
His hands for He is the King Eternal.

It bears the title "A praise (tehillah) of David". It is the
only psalm to which this title is given and from this word
the Hebrew title of the whole of the Psalter is derived:
'Tehillim' or 'Praises', hence the title of these three
volumes of studies on the Psalms.

The psalm is alphabetic in form, each of the twenty-one
verses, of two lines, beginning with the letters of the
Hebrew alphabet in order. The verse that should have
begun with the letter 'Nun' between verses 13 and 14 is,
however, missing. This is a feature of other alphabetic
psalms where different letters are omitted (see for
instance Psalms 25, 34 and 37) and we have previously
suggested that this is not the result of carelessness but a
matter of design, although we might not always be able to
discern the purpose behind the omission. We leave further
comment until we reach verse 13 in our considerations.

As to the historical background of the psalm, it has to
be admitted that it could have been written at almost any
time during David's reign. But following, as it does, a
psalm written when David ascended the throne over all
Israel, we believe there are good reasons for linking the
two psalms together and suggest that this is in fact the
"new song" to which David referred in verse 9 of Psalm
144. The psalm falls into two sections: the first (verses 1-
13), extolling the greatness of the King Eternal and the
magnificence of His mighty works; the second (verses 14-
21) demonstrating that His glory and majesty are seen to

1140

best effect in the love and condescension that He shows to
men and to all creatures that His hand has made.

The King Eternal (verses 1-13)

In reading this psalm it soon becomes apparent that the
writer was a man who lived with an absolute conviction
that it would be his inestimable privilege to know that
immortal life that God had promised to those who love
Him. Three times in the psalm he uses the phrase "for
ever and ever" (Hebrew *le-olam va-ed* – 'to the age and
onward' – *Young's Analytical Concordance*). Thus the
opening verses of the psalm read:

"I will extol thee, my God, O king; and I will bless thy
name for ever and ever. Every day will I bless thee; and
I will praise thy name for ever and ever."   (verses 1,2)

Literally the Hebrew says, "my God, the King"
(*Cambridge Bible*) and the sense is that He who is Israel's
true King is the absolute and universal sovereign. It is
particularly appropriate that David, having just been
raised to the throne, should feel it necessary to
acknowledge this truth.

In recognition of this fact he would give honour to Him
to whom it truly belonged, extolling and blessing His
name every day in the assurance that by God's grace that
praise would be perpetuated eternally:

"Great is the LORD, and greatly to be praised; and his
greatness is unsearchable. One generation shall praise
thy works to another, and shall declare thy mighty
acts."   (verses 3,4)

A different word for 'praise' is used in verse 4 to that in
verse 2 (RV, "laud", Strong: 'to address in a loud tone').
The idea would seem to be that the praise is wholehearted;
there is no holding back, but with all one's energy, with all
one's being it is to be poured forth to Him who is
exceedingly worthy to be praised. Indeed from generation
to generation men should pass on the message of all His
wondrous acts of deliverance:

"I will speak of the glorious honour of thy majesty,
and of thy wondrous works. And men shall speak of the
might of thy terrible acts: and I will declare thy
greatness."   (verses 5,6)

David would emphasise the attributes of the great king: splendour (honour), glory, and majesty are the qualities that he associates with the sovereignty of his God. Of these things men are provoked to speak as they contemplate all His terrible acts that they could consider only with a sense of reverence and awe. David would occupy himself diligently with them (*Cambridge Bible*), rehearsing in his mind the marvellous works of God. Note also that the word translated "might" is different from that used in verse 4, being better rendered 'strong'. The two words appear together in Psalm 24: "The LORD strong and mighty, the LORD mighty in battle" (verse 8).

David's thoughts turn to the wonder of God's revealed character as it was proclaimed to Moses (Exodus 34:5-7):

"They shall abundantly utter the memory of thy great goodness, and shall sing of thy righteousness. The LORD is gracious, and full of compassion; slow to anger, and of great mercy." (verses 7,8)

The effect of remembering all that God has done in His goodness is that praise springs up like a fountain in the hearts of those who have experienced it. It is poured forth like a perpetual, never ending stream of adoration (see Psalm 19:2).

They sing of His righteousness, for therein is the assurance of His faithfulness to all that He has promised (see Psalm 143:1). The words of verse 8 are taken almost verbatim from verse 6 of Exodus 34. It is a declaration of God's forbearance towards sinners; His grace and compassion towards those that fear Him, for He is of great mercy (literally, 'great in lovingkindness'). This goodness is manifested towards all His creatures:

"The LORD is good to all: and his tender mercies are over all his works. All thy works shall praise thee, O LORD; and thy saints shall bless thee." (verses 9,10)

God's goodness encompasses all creation; not just man, but as the next line shows everything that He has made is sustained by Him and by His power fulfils His purpose in creating it at the beginning (see Psalm 104). All things, both living and inanimate, bear witness to His majesty and sovereignty by the manner in which they conform to

His laws. Ultimately all creation will be recognised as showing forth His glory, for:

"Thou art worthy, O Lord, to receive glory and honour and power: for thou hast created all things, and for thy pleasure they are and were created."

(Revelation 4:11)

At that time it is His saints, in particular, who will bless Him, those who have made a covenant with Him by sacrifice (Psalm 50:5). They are the objects of His loving-kindness, kind and pious in character, and separated unto Him from the world that they might constitute the assembly or congregation of His people.

That the Psalmist is speaking of the age to come is evident from the words that follow:

"They shall speak of the glory of thy kingdom, and talk of thy power; to make known to the sons of men his mighty acts, and the glorious majesty of his kingdom."

(Psalm 145:11,12)

As a consequence of God's saints blessing His name they will make known to the sons of men the magnificence and splendour of His kingdom. As the Apostle Paul expresses it:

"... when he shall come to be glorified in his saints, and to be admired in all them that believe (because our testimony among you was believed) in that day."

(2 Thessalonians 1:10)

Transformed into his image, their bodies fashioned like unto his glorious body (Philippians 3:21), they will proclaim throughout all the earth the wonder of God's redemptive work and the blessings that have accrued for all creation, for –

"Thy kingdom is an everlasting kingdom, and thy dominion endureth throughout all generations."

(Psalm 145:13)

It is at this juncture that the alphabetical sequence is broken by the omission of the letter 'Nun'. It must be significant also that this is the dividing point between the two sections of the psalm. Kay points out (*The Psalms with Notes*, page 448) that the 'Nun' occurs in the line following the lacuna (gap, missing portion) and that this would serve to give great emphasis to that line. He points out that the Rabbis noticed this but were then diverted by a bizarre link to Amos 5 (verse 2) which only confused the issue more. Each Hebrew letter also has a meaning. 'Nun' means 'fish' and given the connection attached to fish in the New Testament, where on a number of occasions they are used to represent believers gathered into the Gospel net, could it be the intention to draw our minds towards the love and condescension of God shown to those who seek the salvation that God offers? For a more detailed consideration of the alphabetic psalms see Psalm 34 (*The Praises of Israel*, Volume 1).

The Love and Condescension of God

From this point the emphasis is upon the glory of God revealed; not in the symbols that men associate with power and majesty, but in the love and compassion that He shows to those who are His and indeed to all living creatures:

> "The LORD upholdeth all that fall, and raiseth up all those that be bowed down. The eyes of all wait upon thee; and thou givest them their meat in due season."
>
> (verses 14,15)

It must ever be a source of comfort to those who strive against sin to know that although on occasions their frailty and weakness might lead them to fall, even in their moments of weakness God is with them. Literally, He is with those who are falling to sustain and uphold them. David, in a psalm of his old age, was able to reflect upon the lessons that he had learned in life:

> "The steps of a good man are ordered by the LORD: and he delighteth in his way. Though he fall, he shall not be utterly cast down: for the LORD upholdeth him with his hand."
>
> (Psalm 37:23,24)

It is in this confidence that the righteous show tenacity and perseverance that will never give up in the face of all the trials and temptations that beset them:

> "For a righteous man falleth seven times, and riseth up again: but the wicked are overthrown by calamity."
>
> (Proverbs 24:16, RV)

The word translated "bowed down" provides an interesting connection with the New Testament. In the Septuagint, the same Greek word is used as in Luke's Gospel to describe the woman with a spirit of infirmity, who was "bowed together" so that she was unable to lift herself up. Through the healing touch of the Lord Jesus "she was made straight" (Luke 13:11-13). The miracle stands as an enacted parable that aptly describes what the Lord Jesus can do for us in our battle with sin.

As we look to God for those spiritual blessings that He has promised, so all creation looks to Him expectantly to be provided with their meat (Psalm 104:27; Matthew 6:26). There is an important point being made. We are of more value than all the beasts of the field and all the birds of the air. So if God cares for them in providing those things that are needful for their well-being, it is a testimony to us that we need not be anxious over those spiritual blessings that He has promised, for God's care for all His creatures is an assurance to us of His faithfulness. The two thoughts are brought together in the next couplet of verses:

"Thou openest thine hand, and satisfiest the desire of every living thing. The LORD is righteous in all his ways, and holy in all his works."   (Psalm 145:16,17)

The fact that God provides for, and satisfies, every living thing is a witness (Acts 14:17) that He is true to His character. His loving-kindness in the bonds of the covenant is assured to His saints, for:

"The LORD is nigh unto all them that call upon him, to all that call upon him in truth. He will fulfil the desire of them that fear him: he also will hear their cry, and will save them."   (verses 18,19)

It cannot be coincidence that just as the letter 'Koph' introduces verse 18 with the words "The LORD is nigh ..." so also this letter is followed by the same phrase in Psalm 34 (verse 18) and within the eight verses headed by this letter in Psalm 119 it is written:

"Thou art near, O LORD; and all thy commandments are truth."   (verse 151)

1145

The same feature does not appear in Psalm 25, but the relevant words give us a remarkable insight into what it means for God to draw nigh to those that call upon Him.

> "Look upon mine affliction and my pain; and forgive all my sins."
> (verse 18)

For God to be nigh unto us in this way then, we must call upon Him in truth. It means that those to whom God is close have an understanding of the truths that He has revealed concerning Himself and His purpose. But the word also carries the idea of trustworthiness, and thus is emphasising also the need for integrity on the part of those who cry unto the Lord. There is no place for the man who is a hypocrite or double-minded.

When God promises to fulfil the desires of our hearts, it must be remembered that this refers not to the blessings of this life, when sometimes the things that we yearn for are not compatible with living the life to which we have been called in the Lord Jesus. Rather the reference is to those spiritual blessings that God offers to those who cry unto Him. In this respect, God will grant us the desires of our heart if these are the things that we truly treasure, for:

> "The LORD preserveth all them that love him: but all the wicked will he destroy. My mouth shall speak the praise of the LORD: and let all flesh bless his holy name for ever and ever."
> (verses 20,21)

Again we are reminded that this is a song of the kingdom age when the wicked will be destroyed from out of the earth (Psalm 104:35), and those who enjoy the blessings of that era will joyfully sing the praises of God's holy name.

The Transfiguration

It would not be appropriate to leave this psalm without noticing that it is truly messianic. It appears to have particular reference to the occasion when the Lord was transfigured and talked with Moses and Elijah in the mount. The three Gospel records that relate this event all speak of the disciples who shared this experience as seeing the kingdom of God come (Matthew 16:28; Mark 9:1; Luke 9:27). Note that Mark adds the words "with power". This is in keeping with our understanding of the psalm and in a wonderful way it speaks of the Lord's experience with Moses and Elijah:

"One generation shall praise thy works to another, and shall declare thy mighty acts."　　　(Psalm 145:4)

"They shall speak of the glory of thy kingdom, and talk of thy power."　　　(verse 11)

Not only so, but these two men who had been privileged to have visions of the glory of God now saw them consummated in the person of the Son of God and their experiences are reflected in the words of the psalm.

Thus Moses' vision of the glory of God is reflected in the words of verses 7-9, and the life of Elijah, who thought that he alone remained faithful to Israel's God and was fed by the ravens and by the widow of Zarephath, whose barrel of meal wasted not and her cruse of oil did not fail (1 Kings 17), is seen in verses 14-16.

Note also the word "power" used by Mark in his record, which is surely taken from verse 11 of this psalm. Further confirmation of these remarkable links is provided by the Apostle Peter when he writes of the transfiguration in his Second Epistle:

"For we have not followed cunningly devised fables, when we made known unto you the power and coming of our Lord Jesus Christ, but were eyewitnesses of his majesty."　　　(2 Peter 1:16)

PSALM 146

THIS psalm is the first of the series of five 'Hallel' psalms that brings the Psalter to a conclusion. Psalms 146-150 all begin and end with a "Hallelujah".

Commentators generally are almost obsessed with the idea that these psalms belong to the time of Nehemiah. In our view the evidence is unconvincing and we feel that the psalms as we now have them were compiled, with a few exceptions, by Hezekiah and his men as also they did with parts of the book of Proverbs (25:1). It seems particularly appropriate that the final three psalms of praise should be associated with this man who declared – after his deliverance from Sennacherib and his recovery from a life threatening disease –

"Therefore we will sing my songs to the stringed instruments all the days of our life in the house of the LORD." (Isaiah 38:20)

Psalm 146 is a wonderful expression of the folly of putting one's trust in men when compared with the assurance of the Lord's care and protection. Although it bears no indication of authorship, the language of the psalm lends itself in a most apposite way to the events of Hezekiah's days. This will become apparent as we consider the substance of the song.

After the opening ascription of praise (verses 1,2) and an exhortation not to trust in human power or wisdom (verses 3,4), the psalm emphasises the need to put one's trust in the God of Jacob (verse 5), whose omnipotence and beneficent character manifested on behalf of those who are oppressed and put their trust in Him is the seal of His eternal sovereignty (verses 6-10).

Praise the Lord

After the opening ascription of praise, no doubt a call to the congregation to lift their voices in adoration, the Psalmist speaks individually to encourage them to sing with understanding by entering into the spirit of what he has to say:

"Praise ye the LORD. Praise the LORD, O my soul. While I live will I praise the LORD: I will sing praises unto my God while I have any being."   (verses 1,2)

The similarity with the words of Hezekiah quoted above (Isaiah 38:20) need hardly be emphasised. His longing to sing the praises of the Lord in His house was the motivating force behind the life and actions of this righteous man.

Put no Trust in Man

"Put not your trust in princes, nor in the son of man, in whom there is no help. His breath goeth forth, he returneth to his earth; in that very day his thoughts perish."   (verses 3,4)

This is a message that was emphasised in other psalms associated with the life of Hezekiah (Psalm 118:8,9), and the manner in which he learned how true this was becomes evident from the circumstances surrounding the Assyrian invasion.

During his period of sickness Hezekiah would have been unable to fulfil his royal duties and, as a consequence, it would have been necessary for him to delegate authority to the princes of Judah. To these men fell the responsibility of negotiating with Sennacherib as his army came ever closer to Jerusalem. It is evident from Isaiah's prophecy that among them were devious and unscrupulous men who were more concerned with furthering their own political ambitions than in carrying out the policy encouraged by Isaiah and Hezekiah. Notable amongst them was Shebna, described as the "treasurer" and also as being "over the house". He was a man who gloried in high office and who evidently had taken to himself the highest offices of state (Isaiah 22:15-19). It was he who, with others of similar disposition, followed a policy of appeasement and rejoiced in a treaty negotiated with Sennacherib that involved buying him off with the treasures out of the Lord's house (Isaiah 28:14-15,18). It was nevertheless a treaty that they had no intention of keeping if another way could be found, and they had entered into negotiations with Egypt to form an alliance against the Assyrians (Isaiah 30:1-7; 31:1-3).

However, Sennacherib was aware of their deceitfulness and he had no intention of keeping the treaty they had made (Isaiah 36:4-6). For Hezekiah's reaction to this web of deceit by which he was surrounded read Psalm 120, the first of his songs of degrees.

What folly then to trust in princes, for in them there is no salvation to be found (Psalm 33:16,17). For all their apparent might and power they are but men (Hebrew, *adam*) soon to return to their earth (Hebrew, *adamah*), "for dust thou art, and unto dust shalt thou return" (Genesis 3:19). In that day (an echo of Genesis 2:17?) his thoughts (literally, 'purposes', 'schemes') perish. It does not matter how great a man might appear in the eyes of his contemporaries. The honour and esteem they heap upon him is all to no avail, for the nature we bear is transient and when man returns to his earth all his wisdom and intellect are lost in the nothingness of death (Psalm 49:16-20).

The God of Jacob

In contrast to those who put their trust in an arm of flesh, "Happy is he that hath the God of Jacob for his help, whose hope is in the LORD his God" (Psalm 146:5).

There is a contrast here between "his earth", which is all that human life, apart from God, has to offer, and "his God" to whom the godly man looks for his salvation. Such help that the princes of this world are able to offer is at best temporary. The salvation that God offers relates a man to those eternal things that belong to His kingdom.

Whenever the psalms speak of the "God of Jacob", it is always to offer the comfort and consolation that comes from the knowledge that His providential hand is at work on behalf of His servants, for nowhere is the guardian care of angels manifested so clearly as in the life of this man (Genesis 48:15,16).

This passage, around which the message of the psalm as a whole revolves, is particularly appropriate to the circumstances of Hezekiah's life as he experienced first a complete recovery from his sickness and was then delivered out of the hand of the Assyrians.

Such a man is happy or blessed, and this is the twenty-fifth occasion that this Hebrew phrase occurs in the Psalms. It is of course that with which the Psalter opens: "Blessed is the man ..." (Psalm 1:1).

God's Power and Character

The ground of the Psalmist's confidence in God is now developed. Compared with the frailty and transitory nature of human life, and the manner in which all men's plans and schemes perish with them, the God of Jacob is He "which made heaven, and earth, the sea, and all that therein is: which keepeth truth for ever: which executeth judgment for the oppressed: which giveth food to the hungry" (verses 6,7). Trust in God because of His power seen in creation is a characteristic of Hezekiah's prayer (Isaiah 37:15,16) and of many of the psalms associated with his life (Psalm 115:15; 121:2; 124:8; 134:3). In this fact he found assurance of the sovereignty of God over all that His hands had made, so he need fear nothing that man could do unto him. This confidence was founded not just on the almighty power of God, but also on the way in which God had used that power on behalf of His people. Therein His character had been revealed and through those attributes He had been shown to be One who kept truth for ever. God is faithful; His word can be trusted implicitly and not only so, in contrast to the promises of men, it stands for ever.

It is of interest to note that these words about the creation, so characteristic of Hezekiah, were used by the apostles in their prayer – not this time about the threatenings of Rabshakeh, but those of the Jewish Council who had commanded them not to speak or teach in the name of the Lord Jesus (Acts 4:18,24-30). Significantly it was the healing of the lame man at the gate of the temple which brought these matters to a head (Acts 3:1-6), and the emphasis throughout the record is about the fact that only in the name of the Lord Jesus was salvation to be found (Acts 4:10,12) – surely an echo of the teaching of Psalm 146.

The God of Israel had revealed Himself to be beneficent and compassionate to those who were oppressed. He gave food to the hungry, loosed the prisoners, opened the eyes of the blind, raised up those that were bowed down, loved the righteous and preserved the strangers (verses 7-9). Five times in this catalogue of virtuous actions the memorial name of God, Yahweh, stands emphatically at the head of the line to show that it is He and no other who can perform these wonderful works. Human princes fade into complete and utter insignificance compared with the wonder of the works of God.

All these acts, which are reflected in the history of Israel, were fulfilled also in the circumstances of Hezekiah and the people of Judah in the days of the Assyrian invasion.

The reference to the strangers, or sojourners (RSV), is particularly interesting for this is the only occasion when connected with the fatherless and widows that it is used in the plural. There was, of course, an influx of Gentiles into Jerusalem following Hezekiah's exaltation in the eyes of the nations (2 Chronicles 32:23; Psalm 87:4-6; Isaiah 56:3-7). They, with the fatherless and the widows, would be particularly vulnerable and were assured of the care and protection of Israel's God.

These attributes of the great Uncreate were manifested to perfection in the work of the Lord Jesus during his ministry and can be seen reflected in the miracles he performed (Matthew 14:15-21; Luke 13:16; John 9:32: Luke 13:13; Mark 7:26).

Whereas God manifests His care and compassion to the needy who cry unto Him, "the way of the wicked he turneth upside down (RV margin, 'maketh crooked)" (Psalm 146:9). Because their path is marked by corruption, God diverts their ways so that they are brought to ruin. All their plans and schemes lead them only to the grave (Psalm 1:6).

It is appropriate that just as the promises God has made stand forever, so the psalm should conclude with a recognition that His sovereignty also, unlike the dominion of earthly princes, is eternal. The day will come when His authority will be acknowledged by all people, nations and tongues. The experiences of Hezekiah, and his reflections upon them as recorded in this psalm, speak unerringly of the truth of this fact:

"The LORD shall reign for ever, even thy God, O Zion, unto all generations. Praise ye the LORD."

(verse 10; see also Psalm 145:13)

PSALM 147

ONCE again, historically, we are in the company of Hezekiah. It will be observed, with the aid of a concordance and marginal references, that there appear to be many verbal links with the book of Nehemiah. This we believe is because Nehemiah, in the circumstances in which he found himself, meditated upon the manner in which God had delivered Judah from the Assyrians and blessed Jerusalem in the days of Hezekiah. The events of those days were a source of great encouragement to him in the difficulties that he faced and not only this psalm, but others also of the same period, are reflected in his words and actions.

The psalm is one of praise and thanksgiving for the deliverance experienced and the blessings that followed. It comprises three sections, each beginning with a fresh call to praise God. Within these divisions the universal power of God, His providential care for all His creatures, and His special concern for His covenant people are all intertwined. The divisions of the song are easily identified and can be summarised as follows:

1. Praise for God as the omnipotent and omniscient sovereign of the universe who cares for and delivers those who put their trust in Him (verses 1-6).

2. Praise for God's providential care over all His creatures and the lesson to be learned by His people from this fact (verses 7-11).

3. Praise for the peace and prosperity that He has brought to Jerusalem and the privilege bestowed upon His people by the manner in which He has committed His word to them (verses 12-20).

It should be noted that the psalm revolves around two other passages of scripture (Psalm 33 and Isaiah 40).

1154

Psalm 33 is closely connected with Psalm 32, which is concerned with David's sin in the matter of Bathsheba and Uriah the Hittite. In it David sings a new song, always a song of deliverance and redemption, and there is a great emphasis upon the word of God (Psalm 33:4,6,9,11) as there is in Psalm 147 (verses 15,18,19). See also the stress placed upon the futility of human strength in both psalms (Psalm 33:13-18; 147:10,11).

Isaiah 40 obviously relates to the days of Hezekiah and verses 3-5 of the psalm are clearly based on the words of Isaiah (verses 25-31). The transience of human life and the impotence of men compared with the power of God are also features of Isaiah's message (verses 6-8,23,24).

The Omnipotence and Omniscience of God

"Praise ye the LORD: for it is good to sing praises unto our God; for it is pleasant; and praise is comely."

(verse 1)

When the psalm was sung in the temple services the first "Hallelujah" would have been the call by the precentor (leader of the singers) for the congregation to lift up their voices in praise. Good, pleasant, comely: these are the adjectives that describe what the singing of God's praises should mean to us. It should be a source of joy and the words that we sing, as an expression of our understanding, should be the foundation of that which we rejoice in:

"Speaking to yourselves in psalms and hymns and spiritual songs, singing and making melody in your heart to the Lord." (Ephesians 5:19)

Note that the expression, "praise is comely" is drawn from Psalm 33 (verse 1).

They were to sing praise and make melody to their God for:

"The LORD doth build up Jerusalem: he gathereth together the outcasts of Israel." (Psalm 147:2)

This was the cause of their rejoicing for after the long period of deprivation experienced during the Assyrian invasion and siege of Jerusalem, the blessing of God was now poured forth on the city and the outcasts, those who had been carried away captive together with those who

1155

had fled for safety to surrounding lands, had now returned.

It was, however, not just the necessary work of the reconstruction of walls and buildings that is referred to, but also the renewal and restoration of the spiritual life of the people. This was not something that could be achieved with immediate effect, but it was an ongoing process as the tenses of the verbs indicate:

"He healeth the broken in heart, and bindeth up their wounds. He telleth the number of the stars; he calleth them all by their names. Great is our Lord, and of great power: his understanding is infinite. The LORD lifteth up the meek: he casteth the wicked down to the ground."   (verses 3-6)

The Assyrian threat had been a most harrowing experience. The people of Jerusalem and of Judah generally had been filled with despair and there had come with these times of adversity a realisation that they had brought these things upon themselves by their unfaithfulness to their God. So in this psalm we see the manner in which, under the guidance of Hezekiah, they had come to feel a sense of contrition and remorse.

It may well be that the words about the Lord building up Jerusalem have more to do with the spiritual revival of the people than the actual work of rebuilding. Note how David used similar words in relation to his sin in the matter of Bathsheba and Uriah the Hittite, when there would appear to have been no threat to the actual walls of the city (Psalm 51:17). The security of Jerusalem depended upon the spiritual health of its inhabitants. So now the Lord was healing (Exodus 15:26) the broken in heart. Compare the words of the prophet Hosea who prophesied in the days of Hezekiah and his predecessors, although primarily to the northern kingdom (5:13; 6:1; 7:1).

The proverb says that "by sorrow of the heart the spirit is broken" (Proverbs 15:13). But to all those who turn to Him the Lord is nigh "and saveth such as be of a contrite spirit" (Psalm 34:18).

1156

The wonder of the love and condescension of God towards those who seek Him with a true heart is seen in the words that follow. They speak of the omnipotence of God and of powers beyond the wildest imaginations of men to comprehend, for it is He who counts the stars and calls them by their names who humbleth Himself to come down for the salvation of weak and puny creatures such as we. It was God who when He made promise to Abraham likened the numberless stars of the heavens to the grains of sand that are upon the seashore (Genesis 22:17). It is a remarkable thing that in recent years scientists have come to make this same comparison. There are as many stars in the innumerable galaxies of space as there are grains of sand upon the seashores of the earth. It is beyond our understanding, yet who told the writer of Genesis, without any of the aids of modern science, that such was the case? When we stand therefore on a bright and starlit night and see the myriads of stars, countless galaxies stretching endlessly into the boundless realms of space, what a sobering and wondrous thought it is to remember that He who can count the stars and call them all by name is also a healer of the broken in heart.

The message of the psalm is the same as that of Isaiah 40 (verses 26-29). The similarity of language is so striking that one wonders, given his close association with Hezekiah, whether Isaiah himself was the author of this psalm.

Notice that He calls them all by name; they are all known to Him. So the message for Israel was, and for us is, that if He "who hath created these things" knows the number of the stars, how much more can faithful men have confidence that every one of them is known to God. The Good Shepherd said of his sheep that they "hear his voice: and he calleth his own sheep by name, and leadeth them out" (John 10:3).

Truly our God is great and abounding in power; His understanding is infinite. "To His understanding there is no number, it is incalculable" (*Cambridge Bible*) – a sublime contrast, for He who numbers the stars is Himself the possessor of immeasurable wisdom.

This vast storehouse of power and might is used by God for the benefit of His servants. He brings it to bear in the moral government that He exercises providentially over the earth, for He "lifteth up (RV, upholdeth) the meek" and "casteth the wicked down to the ground" (Psalm 147:6). The reference is to the manner in which, because they sought Him in humility, God delivered them out of the hand of the Assyrian and humiliated those who sought to do them harm.

God's Providential Care

In the light of this deliverance the call is to "sing unto the LORD with thanksgiving" (verse 7). The opening words would appear to be a reference to the song of Miriam: "Sing ye to the LORD, for he hath triumphed gloriously; the horse and his rider hath he thrown into the sea" (Exodus 15:21) – a most appropriate recollection given the Passover deliverance from the hand of the Assyrians (Isaiah 31:5).

Again the call is to make melody to God on the harp and this was probably the cry of the precentor as another part of the temple choir took up the chorus. The theme of this section of the psalm is to emphasise the boundless care of God for all His creation. He sends the clouds which bring the refreshing rains so needful for the cultivation of the earth (Psalm 147:8). But more than that, He sends His rain upon those parts of the earth which are beyond the capability of men to cultivate, for He causes grass to grow upon the mountains and provides food for the beasts of the earth (verse 9). Particular reference is made to the young ravens that cry. The raven is especially mentioned in scripture as an example of the care of God for His creatures, probably because its home is in desolate places and it flies restlessly over wide areas in search of food (see, for example, Luke 12:24). The thread of thought in these few verses is dealt with in a much more detailed manner in Psalm 104.

As God cares for all His creatures, so also there is a lesson for men. They too are utterly dependent upon Him for their daily sustenance. They live by His permission and the things that give them a sense of security, that delude them into thinking that they are sustained by their own power, are not those in which God delights.

"He delighteth not in the strength of the horse: he taketh not pleasure in the legs of a man" (verse 10). How much might Israel have envied the military power of surrounding nations. Yet the lesson of the destruction of the Assyrian army should have taught them that it was by spiritual strength and not by war horses and warriors that their battles would be won, for:

> "The LORD taketh pleasure in them that fear him, in those that hope in his mercy." (verse 11)

Jerusalem's Peace and Prosperity

Once again the cry goes forth to praise the Lord – this time to Jerusalem (verse 12):

> "For he hath strengthened the bars of thy gates; he hath blessed thy children within thee. He maketh peace in thy borders, and filleth thee with the finest of the wheat." (verses 13,14)

The background is again the deliverance of Jerusalem in the days of Hezekiah. As a result of that divine victory the security of the city was assured. Zion's children, the inhabitants of the city, were blessed beyond measure. The figure of Zion's children is a common one in psalms associated with Hezekiah and in the prophecy of Isaiah (see Psalm 87:5,6; Isaiah 54:1, etc.). Peace was now known within the borders of the land and they were filled with the finest of wheat (Isaiah 60:17,18; 2 Chronicles 32:28,29).

As intimated earlier, it would appear that Nehemiah had meditated upon the events of Hezekiah's days and had learned the lessons. The Hebrew word translated "strengthened" (verse 13) is used by Nehemiah (3:4) for repairing the walls and gates of Jerusalem and his conviction throughout was "that this work was wrought of our God" (6:16).

Again the Psalmist reverts to the power of God manifested in nature. We remember that the creative might of God was the basis of Hezekiah's prayer for deliverance from the hand of Sennacherib (Isaiah 37:15-19). Perhaps never since the days of David had the conviction been stronger that the gods of the nations were no gods at all, and so they rejoiced in the knowledge of the sovereignty of God, not just in Israel but throughout all the earth.

The emphasis is on the power of God's word:

"He sendeth forth his commandment upon earth: his word runneth very swiftly." (Psalm 147:15)

The word is personified; it is spoken of as if it were God's messenger sent forth to perform His will. It is reminiscent of the words of Psalm 33: "For he spake, and it was done; he commanded, and it stood fast" (verse 9), which in turn recall the words of Genesis 1: "And God said, Let there be light: and there was light" (verse 3). It is by the power of that word that God's sovereignty is exercised in nature:

"He giveth snow like wool: he scattereth the hoarfrost like ashes. He casteth forth his ice like morsels: who can stand before his cold? He sendeth out his word, and melteth them: he causeth his wind to blow, and the waters flow." (Psalm 147:16-18)

All nature, sustained by God's word, speaks of the goodness of God towards all men: "For He maketh his sun to rise on the evil and on the good, and sendeth rain on the just and on the unjust" (Matthew 5:45). But for His people Israel there was a greater privilege. The God whom all nature obeyed had given to them His word in their law, and it was this that distinguished them from all other nations on the face of the earth (Deuteronomy 4:7,8):

"He sheweth his word unto Jacob, his statutes and his judgments unto Israel. He hath not dealt so with any nation: and as for his judgments, they have not known them." (Psalm 147:19,20)

These privileges brought great responsibilities. They could not escape their calling, for "You only have I known of all the families of the earth: therefore I will punish you for all your iniquities" (Amos 3:2). "Praise ye the LORD."

PSALM 148

THERE is an affinity between this psalm and that which precedes it. The closing words of that psalm might well be regarded as an introduction to this song, for the reference to Israel's privileged position with which it concluded (verses 19,20) also forms the concluding thought of Psalm 148:

"He also exalteth the horn of his people, the praise of all his saints; even of the children of Israel, a people near unto him." (verse 14)

In both instances it is Israel's nearness to their God that is being emphasised; the fact that it is they of all nations that have this closeness of relationship with the Creator of heaven and earth.

The psalm itself is a magnificent paean of praise extolling the majesty and might of the great Uncreate, all that His hands have made, both inanimate and animate being called upon to show forth His praises. The fact that it is only in the last verse that reference is made to Israel's unique association with their God is significant. It implies that after a period of devastation and loss of prestige and power, the nation was now restored to its covenant responsibilities. Once more they function as a kingdom of priests (Exodus 19:6).

This could well have been in the days of Hezekiah, for during his reign Judah fulfilled their ancient responsibility (2 Chronicles 32:22,23). However, there is no indication of authorship or of an historical setting. In this respect perhaps we should regard the psalm as timeless, for it speaks of Israel's ultimate destiny. The thrust of the psalm is that as a kingdom of priests, in the exercise of that mediatory function, they call all creation to join in universal praise, and to join with them in

1161

recognising the wonder of their God and all that He had wrought through them. It was a principle enshrined in the law, for in the day of Israel's blessing the cry was:

"Rejoice, O ye nations, with his people."

(Deuteronomy 32:43)

The thought, however, goes beyond Israel and speaks of the grand consummation of the purpose of God, when the multitude of the redeemed, made unto their God kings and priests (Revelation 5:10), will echo the sentiments of this psalm:

"Thou art worthy, O Lord, to receive glory and honour and power: for thou hast created all things, and for thy pleasure they are and were created."

(Revelation 4:11)

The psalm falls into two sections: first the heavens are called to praise (verses 1-6); then the earth and its inhabitants (verses 7-13), before the final emphasis upon Israel and her privileged position (verse 14).

Let the Heavens Praise Him

The anthem of praise begins in the heavens and sounds forth until it is answered from the earth beneath (verse 7). Angels join their voices in glad acclaim (verse 2; Psalm 103:20; 1 Kings 22:19). The psalm follows the creation record in Genesis 1. Sun and moon together with the other heavenly bodies follow (verse 3). The call reaches out to the "heavens of heavens", that is the very highest heavens (Deuteronomy 10:14; 1 Kings 8:27). It is interesting to consider the words of Paul in his Second Epistle to the Corinthians (12:2) when he speaks of himself as caught up to the third heaven. The Epistle to the Hebrews speaks of "the patterns of things in the heavens" (9:23) and in Jewish thought the tabernacle was built according to the pattern of the heavens: the first heaven answering to the court of the tabernacle; the second heaven corresponding to the holy place and the third heaven to the most holy place – the use of the plural in reference to the heavens lending itself to such a view.

Following the Genesis record, the call is also made to the waters that were above the heavens (verse 4; Genesis 1:7). This was the original arrangement in creation. It was part of the organisation of things that God pronounced "very good" (Genesis 1:31). Scientifically this may not be the present order of things – the flood of Noah's day affecting the situation. Nevertheless, in the kingdom age there will undoubtedly be a change in the climatic conditions that we experience now, and with the curse removed may there not be a return to that divine arrangement that was created in the beginning?

They are to praise "the name of the LORD":

"For he commanded, and they were created. He hath also stablished them for ever and ever: he hath made a decree which shall not pass." (verses 5,6)

The reference to God's name in this context is significant. It is by that name that He has made Himself known throughout human history. It is the unfolding purpose contained in the name that has finally brought about the situation described in this psalm, when heaven and earth and all creation send forth this magnificent song of praise. The word "he" in verse 5 is emphatic: "*He* commanded, and they were created":

"By the word of the LORD were the heavens made ... For he spake, and it was done; he commanded, and it stood fast." (Psalm 33:6,9)

Literally, 'He caused them to stand fast'. Not only in their original creation but by unchangeable laws that cannot be broken, He maintains them in their courses and orbits (Jeremiah 31:35,36; 33:25). In these truths lies the assurance:

"While the earth remaineth, seedtime and harvest, and cold and heat, and summer and winter, and day and night shall not cease." (Genesis 8:22)

Let the earth and all that is therein praise him

As God's will is done in heaven, so it shall be done on earth. All living creatures, all manifestations of God's power in nature, all that He has created will join together in unison to show forth His majesty and thereby to praise Him for what He has accomplished in the earth. It leads to a declaration of the fulfilment of that purpose that He had in creating man in the beginning.

First the great dragons that inhabit the deepest depths of the oceans are called upon to offer praise (verse 7). The word "dragon" signifies any large sea creature (Genesis 1:21), such as the great fish that swallowed Jonah. God's wonders seen in nature are called to play their part: fire, hail, snow and vapour (mists) with stormy winds fulfilling His will (verse 8). The way in which nature has been used by God both miraculously and providentially to perform His will is worthy of comment. God used a strong east wind to divide the sea (Exodus 14:21) for Israel to cross over on dry land. When Jonah fled from the presence of the Lord, He sent a great wind and caused a mighty tempest (Jonah 1:4). When Paul was shipwrecked on his journey to Rome it was that tempestuous wind Euroclydon that God raised up. If we were to look at secular history, then classic examples are the storm that was instrumental in the defeat of the Spanish Armada and the Russian winter that proved disastrous to Napoleon in his invasion of that country.

Mountains, hills, fruit-bearing and non-fruit-bearing trees, wild beasts, domestic animals, reptiles and birds (verses 9,10): clearly those mentioned are intended as representative of all that God had created, and as we are led finally to humankind it seems appropriate to regard those referred to as forming the mortal population of the earth in the Millennium:

"Kings of the earth, and all people; princes, and all judges of the earth: both young men, and maidens; old men, and children: let them praise the name of the LORD: for his name alone is excellent; his glory is above the earth and heaven." (verses 11-13)

Without any distinction as to rank, age, or sex, all are called to praise the Lord. Whereas the previous expressions of praise were manifested in the being of the creatures, in the wonder of God's creative hand and the manifestation of His power in nature, now in man it is the expression of the human will – gladly and freely given because of the blessings of God made known among them. As we consider this remarkable psalm coming finally to redeemed man, surely the point that is being made is this:

1164

"For the earnest expectation of the creation waiteth for the revealing of the sons of God. For the creation was subjected to vanity, not of its own will, but by reason of him who subjected it, in hope that the creation itself also shall be delivered from the bondage of corruption into the liberty of the glory of the children of God."   (Romans 8:19-21, RV)

The Israel of God

"He also exalteth the horn of his people, the praise of all his saints; even of the children of Israel, a people near unto him."   (Psalm 148:14)

As previously intimated, the psalm was probably written at a time of restoration when Israel was once more able to assume her covenant responsibilities. In exalting the horn of His people God had once more restored them to a position of dignity and power among the nations. As a consequence of this blessing He, their God, had become a praise to all His saints (Deuteronomy 10:21) – a people whom He had separated unto Himself that they might be holy, even as He is holy; even the children of Israel who amongst all the nations had occupied a privileged and special relationship with Him. They were a people near unto Him (Leviticus 10:3; Deuteronomy 4:7), for they were a kingdom of priests and a holy nation; they had an affinity, a closeness of association, that through the covenants that He had made bound them to Him in a bond that He will never break. In the kingdom age Israel will once again take to herself those ancient responsibilities and fulfil that destiny that God intended her to have. (Zechariah 8:23). We see beyond natural Israel, however, to the congregation of the saints, for we too are near unto Him and we shall also reign as kings and priests upon the earth. In that day all creation will praise the Lord in the fulfilment of His word and the accomplishment of the purpose that He had in the beginning when He made all things. "Praise ye the LORD."

PSALM 149

HERE is yet another jubilant chorus of joy as the closing thoughts of Psalm 148 (verse 14) are echoed and expanded:

"Sing unto the LORD a new song, and his praise in the congregation of saints. Let Israel rejoice in him that made him: let the children of Zion be joyful in their King."
(verses 1,2)

A new song is always a song of redemption, sung to celebrate an act of deliverance wrought by God on behalf of His people (Psalms 33:3; 96:1; 98:1; Revelation 5:9). Again we have no indication of authorship or historical background but the language of the psalm, and its theme, link it with that which precedes it and, as in that instance, we wonder, tentatively, whether it belongs to the reign of Hezekiah.

Certainly it celebrates a notable victory in which all Israel rejoice in the ensuing blessings and look with confidence to a future in which their God will subdue all their enemies before them. They are called to rejoice in their Maker, for they owe their very existence as a nation to Him (Psalms 95:6; 100:3; Isaiah 43:1) and they are addressed as the "congregation of the saints" (RV). The saints are the godly, those who are beloved of God because they are His covenant people and as the children of Zion (Psalm 87:5,6) they praise their King. It is not to be supposed that this indicates there was no earthly monarch sitting on the throne of David. From the time that the monarchy was established it was always recognised that he who sat on David's throne did so as the representative of the God of Israel who remained their true King. As David declared when his son acceded to the throne:

1166

"He hath chosen Solomon my son to sit upon the throne of the kingdom of the LORD over Israel."

(1 Chronicles 28:5)

The reference to the saints is a characteristic of the psalm and it should be noted that the word occurs on three occasions (verses 1,5,9).

Although undoubtedly celebrating some remarkable deliverance in the history of Israel, it is not possible to read this song without becoming aware that the act of salvation referred to became a type of the final deliverance that God would work on behalf of His people – a time when He would judge all nations and all flesh should be called upon to praise their sovereign King.

Israel's Worship

"Let them praise his name in the dance: let them sing praises unto him with the timbrel and harp." (verse 3)

That our praise of God should be expressed in dance is not a concept that many of us would feel comfortable with. Although the timbrel, or tambourine, would probably not be our instrument of choice, we could perhaps be happier with the thought of music being used for this purpose; we would probably think of it as an aid to contemplation and meditation. In this context, however, it is an expression of an overflowing joy in the wonder of God's goodness and it was a characteristic of the worship of Israel throughout the history of the Old Testament. We remember that David danced before the Lord with all his might and was seen leaping and dancing when he brought the ark to Zion (2 Samuel 6:14,16). He was not alone in expressing his joy in this way for Psalm 68 describes the rejoicing of the procession that followed David (verse 25). Further examples will be found in Exodus 15:20, Judges 11:34 and Jeremiah 31:4.

It is said that in the festivities of the Feast of Tabernacles in later times even the leading men and teachers of the people joined in the dance (*Cambridge Bible*).

There are no indications in the New Testament of dancing in the worship of the first century believers, and this leads us to the conclusion that what we are considering are different cultures that express their

1167

delight in their Saviour in different ways – Israel through the natural inclinations that were characteristic of their environment and background. We, perhaps influenced by centuries of more formal methods of worship, albeit by an apostate church, approach our Heavenly Father in a more staid and reserved fashion. Nevertheless, our joy should be no less real whatever the form in which we seek to express it.

It is a warning to us of how careful we must be not to criticise the methods of worship that might be adopted by some brethren and sisters to whom our Western culture is alien, particularly given the worldwide nature of our Faith.

The Joy of God's People

The reason for this overflowing sense of joy and elation is that God has delivered His people from those who oppressed them. This is not a once-for-all event. It is not the case that having won a great victory on their behalf He then leaves them to their own devices. Rather it is a continuing experience:

"For the LORD taketh pleasure in his people: he will beautify the meek with salvation."   (verse 4)

The pleasure that God takes in His people in the day of their reconciliation to Him is beautifully expressed by the prophet Isaiah, who perhaps had this very psalm in his mind for he speaks first of God as their Maker:

"For thy Maker is thine husband; the LORD of hosts is his name ... For a small moment have I forsaken thee; but with great mercies will I gather thee. In a little wrath I hid my face from thee for a moment; but with everlasting kindness will I have mercy on thee, saith the LORD thy Redeemer."   (Isaiah 54:5-8)

The meek are those who are of a humble and contrite spirit whose hearts are open to the sweet influences of God's word. Above all things they are teachable (see Psalm 25:5,8,9,12) and ready to submit to the will of God. These God will beautify or adorn with His salvation. For Israel, no doubt, it meant that they would enjoy all the blessings of the covenant. In the larger context of the psalm it speaks of that glorious incorruptible nature with which the people of God will be clothed in the day when the Lord Jesus will come, and these bodies of our humiliation will be "fashioned like unto his glorious body" (Philippians 3:21). In that day we shall be like him in every way, having also received the blessing from the Lord, even righteousness from the God of our salvation (Psalm 24:5; Isaiah 61:3). Because of this His saints rejoice in glory, that is the glory in which they are adorned, and sing aloud upon their beds. Their songs in the night are no longer times of reflection and tears (Psalms 4:4; 6:6), but further opportunities to sound forth the praises of their God (Psalm 149:5).

The Honour of the Saints

The verses with which the psalm concludes have been the subject of much discussion and some difference of opinion:

"Let the high praises of God be in their mouth, and a twoedged sword in their hand; to execute vengeance upon the heathen, and punishments upon the people; to bind their kings with chains, and their nobles with fetters of iron; to execute upon them the judgment written: this honour have all his saints. Praise ye the LORD." (verses 6-9)

Not unexpectedly, orthodox commentators find the words of the psalm out of keeping with their perception of the teaching of the New Testament. Almost without exception they quote the words of the Apostle Paul, "For the weapons of our warfare are not carnal" (2 Corinthians 10:4), ignoring of course those passages that are relevant, not to our present pilgrimage, but to the second coming of the Lord Jesus Christ.

Nevertheless, the writer well remembers in the days of his youth, heated arguments between brethren on the question, 'Will the saints be at Armageddon?' with this psalm being a key passage in the debate. It is a long time since we have heard the matter discussed in any detail.

We do not feel it appropriate here to consider the possible order of events leading to, and following, the coming of the Lord Jesus but clearly the psalm is emphasising the privilege and honour of those who will be associated with him in that day.

If the word "saint" be applied in the first instance to the people of Israel, then scripture tells us of them:

> "Thou art my battle axe and weapons of war: for with thee will I break in pieces the nations, and with thee will I destroy kingdoms."   (Jeremiah 51:20)

How will this be accomplished? Zechariah, speaking of the day of the Lord's coming, writes:

> "In that day will I make the governors of Judah like an hearth of fire among the wood, and like a torch of fire in a sheaf; and they shall devour all the people round about, on the right hand and on the left; and Jerusalem shall be inhabited again in her own place, even in Jerusalem."   (12:6)

The place of Israel in the outpouring of God's judgements and the subjugation of the nations of the world must not be underestimated:

> "Arise and thresh, O daughter of Zion: for I will make thine horn iron, and I will make thy hoofs brass: and thou shalt beat in pieces many people: and I will consecrate their gain unto the LORD, and their substance unto the Lord of the whole earth."
>
>   (Micah 4:13)

As we have already intimated, however, the words must also refer to the immortal saints of all ages. With our limited understanding, our conviction that we must pursue a path of non-violence in this present age, linked perhaps with a natural aversion to bloodshed, we might find these words difficult to comprehend. However, made like unto the Lord Jesus, clothed with spirit nature, we shall in that day see things from a different perspective and with a different motivation. Remember that the Lord Jesus himself will come as the Lion of the tribe of Judah and of him it is written: "Thou shalt break them with a rod of iron; thou shalt dash them in pieces like a potter's vessel" (Psalm 2:9, see also verse 12). Even more decisive are the words of Revelation 17 which describe how the ten kings who give their strength and power to the beast "make war with the Lamb, and the Lamb shall overcome them: for he is Lord of lords, and King of kings: and they that are with him are called, and chosen, and faithful" (see verses 12-14;

1170

also 19:11-21). This does not mean that warfare will be indiscriminate, for the appeal will also be made to "kiss the Son, lest he be angry" (Psalm 2:12). Nations will first be given opportunity to acknowledge the King and accept his sovereignty, for there is that which is "sharper than any twoedged sword" – the word of God which is quick and powerful in discerning the thoughts and intents of the heart (Hebrews 4:12). That word will be used effectively in that day and it is those only who will not allow the word to have its intended effect upon their hearts and minds who will know the terror of that literal two-edged sword by whomsoever it is wielded.

There is also an element of misconception regarding the Millennium reign of the Messiah. Our hope is to reign as kings and priests with him (Revelation 5:10) and we often describe this time as a period of universal peace and tranquillity for the mortal people of the earth. But as Psalm 72 makes clear this is not the complete picture, for peace is only maintained through the authority and sovereignty of the Lord Jesus and those who reign with him. Thus the psalm tells us:

"He shall judge the poor of the people, he shall save the children of the needy, and shall break in pieces the oppressor ... They that dwell in the wilderness shall bow before him; and his enemies shall lick the dust."

(verses 4,9, see also verses 12-14)

So it is that both Israel and the immortal saints will have a part to play in carrying out "the judgment written", for "this honour have all his saints". What greater privilege could there be than to be numbered among the called, the chosen and faithful associated with the Lord Jesus when he comes to fulfil the will of his Heavenly Father and consummate His purpose in the earth? We can but join our hallelujahs with those of the Psalmist: "Praise ye the LORD."

PSALM 150

W HAT could be more appropriate to conclude the praises of Israel than this call to universal praise? Each of the previous four books of the Psalms ends with a doxology and while this psalm was almost certainly intended for liturgical use in the temple, it appears to stand also as a doxology not just to Book Five but to the whole of the Psalter.

The songs of God's servants written over hundreds of years of Israel's history have led us into every aspect of spiritual experience: the burden of sin and the happiness of sin forgiven; the trials and adversities of the godly man, the wonder of God's providential hand and the confidence of deliverance; the sovereignty and majesty of God and the beauty of His holiness; His name revealed in action on behalf of His servants; the spirit of the Lord Jesus Christ made known with wonderful insights into his thinking and relationship with his Heavenly Father. The Psalms have been rightly termed 'The Fifth Gospel'.

So in this final psalm we are presented with the grand conclusion of the godly life for the individual servant of God and, after all the weary years of human sin and stubbornness and its ensuing misery, the marvellous consummation of the purpose of God in the earth:

"Let every thing that hath breath praise the LORD."
(verse 6)

The psalm is all of a piece and it would be a pointless exercise to seek to subdivide it in any way. There are ten calls to praise God:

"Praise God in his sanctuary: praise him in the firmament of his power. Praise him for his mighty acts: praise him according to his excellent greatness."
(verses 1,2)

1172

First there is a call to men to join in united praise in His sanctuary, the temple, the place where His glory resides; not only in a literal temple made with hands but also in that spiritual house, consisting of the glorified saints in whom also His holiness will dwell. But praise resounds also from heaven above, from the firmament of His power – His handiwork being the evidence of His omnipotence and power (Psalm 68:34).

Angels, in whose image man was made, who down through the ages have been His messengers and representatives in the work of salvation, join in the glad chorus. They praise Him for all His mighty acts (see Psalm 145:4,11,12) revealed and rejoiced in by His servants in the pages of the Psalms. They extol Him "according to the abundance of his greatness" (Psalm 150:2, *Cambridge Bible*. See also 1 Chronicles 29:11).

This great chorus of praise to God resounds within His sanctuary. The variety of instruments played, the trumpet, the psaltery, the harp, the tabret and pipe, stringed instruments and organs, loud cymbals and high sounding cymbals all combine together in a glorious outpouring of harmony. In Israel the instruments would have been played on different occasions by different classes of people; some by the priests, others by the shepherds, others by the maidens as they danced. So all strata of society are brought together in this united expression of incomparable joy that the God of Israel had fulfilled His purpose in the nation.

The fact that the praise is in the sanctuary, however, carries us beyond the literal temple to the saints, the household of God. As we think of the various kinds of instruments, all with their distinctive sounds, we are reminded that the followers of the Lord Jesus Christ have their own characteristics that distinguish them one from the other. The different instruments speak of the variety of capacities that each brings to this final swell of orchestrated sound, as the faithful of all ages rejoice in the consummation of God's purpose.

There could be no grander conclusion to the matter: "Let every thing that hath breath praise the LORD" (verse 6). It has all been accomplished by the redeeming work of

1173

the Lord Jesus Christ who, having put down all rule and authority and power and put all enemies under his feet, has delivered up the kingdom to his Father that finally God might be "all in all" (1 Corinthians 15:24-28).

"Worthy is the Lamb that was slain to receive power, and riches, and wisdom, and strength, and honour, and glory, and blessing. And every creature which is in heaven, and on the earth, and under the earth, and such are as in the sea, and all that are in them, heard I saying, Blessing, and honour, and glory, and power, be unto him that sitteth upon the throne, and unto the Lamb for ever and ever." (Revelation 5:12,13)

INDEX OF SCRIPTURE REFERENCES
Due to their large number, Psalm references are not
indexed when occurring within their relevant chapters.

THE PRAISES OF ISRAEL

1179

THE PRAISES OF ISRAEL

THE PRAISES OF ISRAEL

THE PRAISES OF ISRAEL

THE PRAISES OF ISRAEL

THE PRAISES OF ISRAEL

THE PRAISES OF ISRAEL

THE PRAISES OF ISRAEL

1192

SCRIPTURE INDEX

:8 .... 339, 660

6:1 676

:3 842

:4 655

:5 676

:8 274

:9,10 677

:11,12 673

7:10-16 690

:11,14 690

:14 321

8:6 659

:6,7 320

:7,8 319, 598, 781, 1018, 1048

:8 .... 321, 472

:13 594

:14 976

9:6 .... 306, 658

:6,7 690

10:5,6 677

11:1-4 544

:1-5 307

:3 658

:4 .... 307, 658, 842

:5 658

:10 428

THE PRAISES OF ISRAEL

THE PRAISES OF ISRAEL

THE PRAISES OF ISRAEL

THE PRAISES OF ISRAEL

THE PRAISES OF ISRAEL

TOPICAL INDEX

1203

H

Hair, long, 501

Hallel, the, 1085, 1148

Ham, 611

Hands, lifting of, 170

Happiness, true, 4, 199

Heaven, first, second and third, 1162

Hebrew alphabet, meanings of letters; numeric values, 992; tabulated, 982

Heman, 261, 553, 653

Hephzibar, 303; marriage to Hezekiah, 303

Hermon, dew of, 1072

Hezekiah, marriage to Hephzibar, 303; his conduit, 316; his sickness, 596, 701; his Passover, 626, 1009; Psalm of, 956; mother of, 964; his prayer re Sennacherib's letter, 1004, 1076; "the Jew", 1019; a great man, 998

Horn, of unicorn, 769

Horns and hoofs, 517

Hymn singing, 1092

Hypocrisy, 352

I

Idol worship, 952

Imprecation, against children, 1094; against David's enemies, 1130; reconciling with NT teaching, 1169

Imprecatory psalms, 230, 912

Imputation of righteousness, 200

Incense, 255

Isles, 811

Israel, a "peculiar treasure", 1078; called 'gods', 308; God's witnesses, 212

J

Jachin and Boaz, 483

Jacob, God of, 110; his vision, 110; his wrestling, 144, 221

Jael, killed Sisera, 501

Jeduthun, 261

Jeduthun (Ethan), 553, 588

Jehoram, 303

Jehoshaphat, 643

Jerusalem, City of God, 332; ploughed by Titus, 1043; ploughed by Hadrian, 1043

Jesus, superior to angels, 310

Jezebel, 303

Jonath-elem-rechokim, 385

Joseph of Arimathea, 270

Jubilee, 324, 674

Judas Iscariot, 282, 916; relationship to Christ, 390

Judges of Israel, 1097

K

Kadesh-Barnea, 974

Kibroth-Hattaavah, 609, 890

Kidron, 134

King(s) of Babylon, 1090

Kirjath-jearim, 1063

Kissing, the Son, 15; betrayal by Judas, 15

Kohathites, 284

Koph (also see *qoph*), 1145

Korah, Dathan and Abiram, 451, 458, 639, 891; judgement on, 388

Korah, sons of, 284, 316, 338, 653

L

Lachish, 316

Lacuna, 1143

Language, unknown, 629, 946

Laver of brass, 483

Legion, healing of, 464

Leprosy, 706; suggestion David suffered from, 193, 254

Levites, God their inheritance, 83

Life, its transience, 264

Light, 873

Lilies, 295

Lion, figure of God, 590; of Judah, 591; of Assyria, 592

Lunar year, 876

M

Maccabees, 642

Magnificat, 941

Mahalath, 371

Mahalath Leannoth, 692

Mahanaim, 220

Man of God, 731

Manasseh, 304, 568; birth of, 697
Manna, 609, 765, 886, 931
Marriage, of Hezekiah and
Hephzibar, 303
Maschil, 199, 356, 370, 566, 1120
Massah, 796
Meal offering, 254, 806
Meanings of Hebrew letters, 218
Meat offered to idols, 142
Meditation, 25; in the night, 240
Melchizedek, everlasting
priesthood, 157; blessing of, 954;
order of, 924, 930
Memorial table, 139
Merab, Saul's daughter, 416
Meribah, 631, 796, 894; murmuring
at, 894
Merodach Baladan, 568, 580
Meshech, 1000
Messianic psalm, 3, 100, 120, 228
Methuselah, age of, 736
Michal, David's wife, 415
Michtam, 370, 393, 425, 566
Millennium, enforced peace, 1171
Mitcham, 80
Mizmor, 819
Mizraim (Egypt), 611
Moriah, 693
Morning, 26
Moses and Elijah, 1146
Most Holy Place, 170
Music, God-given gift, 329; abuse of,
329
Music and dance, used in worship,
1167; tolerance of other cultures,
1168; used in worship, 1173
Music in worship, 261
Musical talent, of Korah's
descendants, 284
Muth-labben, 41

N

Nabal, 72
Nature of Christ, 1107
Nazarite vow, 722
Nebo, 953
New song, 801, 821, 1138, 1140,
1155, 1166

Night watches, division of, 736
Nile, 781
Nimrod, 934, 1094
Noah, 62; The Flood, 176
Northern Kingdom, 606, 615
Numbering Israel, 181
Numberless, 272
Nun (letter), missing from
sequence, 1140, 1143; meaning
of, 1144

O

Obed-edom, 140, 1008
Og, king of Bashan, 1087
Oldest Psalm, 731
Omnipotence of God, 1105, 1157
Omnipresence of God, 1103
Onomatopoeic word, 823
Optatives, 543
Orchestras, 261
Original sin, 361
Ornan the Jebusite, 180

P

Padan Aram, 225
Padishah, Persian father, 219
Palm tree, 770
Parables, 604
Patriarchs as prophets, 799, 882
Pavilion, 163
Pe, repeated in alphabetic sequence,
146, 217, 218, 982
Peace, of Jerusalem, 1012
Peniel, 144, 221
Penitential psalms, 199, 1046, 1125;
listed, 30
Pentateuch, 1
Pentecostals, 76
Perez-uzza, 141
Perfect man, the, 199
Persecution, 276
Peter's denial, 259
Petra, 430
Pharisees, setting traps, 1112
Phinehas, 893
Plagues of Egypt, 884
Poetic form, 174
Pool of Siloam, 316

Poor, care of, 79
Potter and clay, 214
Prayer, only heard if offered
  sincerely, 474
Precentor, 953
Prepare the way, 28
Prevenient grace, 76
Priest, function of, 695
Priestly, blessing, 478, 721;
  garments, 1071
Priests at Nob, 146, 220, 222
Prophets, patriarchs so called, 799
Proselytes, 1026
Prosperity of wicked, 558
Prostration before God, 795
Providence, 882
Psalm 110, quoted in New
  Testament, 920

Q

Qoph (also see *Koph*) omitted, 146
Quails, 931
Queen of Sheba, 478, 544, 546
Quoted in New Testament, Psalm
  69, 520; Psalm 110, 920

R

Rabshakeh, 317, 1015; taunts of,
  1057, 1081
Rahab (Egypt), 719
Rainbow, 178, 241
Rehoboam, 726
Reins, 155
Repeated scriptures, 95
Reuben, 497
Revelation, use of Old Testament
  quotations, 581
Rhetorical repetition, 783
Riches, dangers of, 339, 345
Rivers, of Babylon, 1090
Rock of offence, 976
Rod and staff, 139
Ruth, 436

S

Sabbath rest, 792
Saints, role in judgement, 1169
Samuel, meaning of name, 941
Sargon, King of Babylon, 1090

Satan, 915
Saul, mental derangement, 37
Scalp, 501
Scripture, repeated, 95
Scriptures, as available to David,
  991
Sea monsters, symbol of Egyptian
  power, 572
Second coming of Jesus, 810, 815
Secret place, God's, 746
Seed, 132; of the serpent, 62
Selah, 16, 323, 390, 344
Sela-hammahlekoth, 534
Sennacherib, 316, 325; his letter,
  317; destruction of his army,
  320, 331, 465; deliverance from,
  1018; King of Babylon, 1090
Serpents, 412
Servant, of God, 614
Seventy Weeks Prophecy, 925
Shalmaneser, 598; King of Babylon,
  1090
Sheba son of Bichri, 70
Shebna the scribe, 596
Shechinah (Shekinah), 570, 679
Shepherd, 135; of Israel, 173, 555,
  611, 617, 620, 641, 651, 838
Shibboleth, 511; flood, hard to
  pronounce, 511
Shields, 330, 723
Shiggaion, 37
Shimei,cursing David, 280, 1053
Shofar, 323, 721
Shortest psalm, 966
Shoshannim, 294, 482
Shoshannim eduth, 580
Shushan eduth, 423
Sihon, king of the Amorites, 1087
Silver Trumpets, 323, 625, 720, 823
Simeon, 270
Singing and dancing, 699
Sins, seven, committed in the
  wilderness, 889
Sirion, 174
Sisera, killed by Jael, 501; his army
  defeated, 505
Six-Day War, 647, 652

THE PRAISES OF ISRAEL

Snails and slugs, 413
Solomon's prayer, at dedication of
    Temple, 1048, 1060, 1064, 1097
Son of God, Israel, God's firstborn,
    13; Jesus, 14
Song(s), of Hannah, 585, 725, 941;
    of Deborah, 496, 505; of Mary,
    941; of Miriam, 1158; of Moses,
    725, 969, 972; of Degrees, 996
Sowing and reaping, 1028, 1038
Spanish Armada, 1164
Sparrow, 666
Springtime, 482
Stars, innumerable, 1157
State of Israel, 647
Stephen's apology, 487
Storms of life, 176
Stormy winds, 1164
Suffering, of Jesus, 120
Sundial, of Ahaz, 997
Superscriptions, 41, 115
Swallow, 666
Swearing deceitfully, 78, 143
Symmetry, 174

T

Tabernacle, movements of, 612;
    Moses', 748
Tabulated comparisons,
    Psalm 3 – Psalm 4, 16;
    Psalm 6 – John 12 – Hebrews 5,
    33;
    Psalm 7 – 1 Samuel, 39, 40;
    Psalm 8 – 1 Samuel 17, 42;
    Luke 10 – Isaiah 14 – Psalm 8,
    44, 45;
    Psalm 9 – Psalm 10, 51;
    Psalm 14:5,6 – Psalm 53:5,6, 69;
    Genesis 6 – Psalm 14, 72;
    Psalm 16 – Hebrews 12, 85;
    Psalm 17 – Psalm 16, 86;
    Psalm 17:15 – 1 John 3:1,2, 92;
    Deuteronomy 32 – 1 Samuel 2 –
    Psalm 18, 99, 100;
    Psalm 6 – Hebrews 5, 123;
    Psalm 28 – Psalm 31, 188;
    Psalm 38 – Psalm 39, 262;
    Deuteronomy 33 – Psalm 68,
    486;
    Judges 5 – Psalm 68, 486;
    Psalms 70 & 40 – Psalm 35, 523;
    Psalm 69 – Psalm 70, 524;
    Psalm 40 – Psalm 69, 525;
    Psalm 35 & 40 – Psalm 71, 526;
    Psalm 74 – Psalm 79, 567;
    Psalm 79:6,7 – Jeremiah 10:25,
    575;
    Psalm 79:1,8,9 – Daniel 9:18,
    575;
    Psalm 79 – Revelation 11, 580;
    Psalm 77 – Exodus 15, 599;
    Psalms 42 & 43 – Psalm 84, 662;
    Psalm 86 – Psalms of David,
    683, 684;
    Psalm 86 – Exodus, 685;
    Exodus 23 – Psalm 91, 753;
    Psalm 92 – Psalms 90 & 91, 762;
    Psalm 96 – Psalm 97, 809;
    Psalm 96 – Psalm 98, 820;
    Psalm 95 – Psalm 100, 836;
    Psalms – Isaiah, 841, 842
Targum, 41
Tarshish, 547
Taylor Cylinder (Prism), 898, 1089,
    1018; quotation from, 1020
Temple, dedication of, 111
The poor, care of, 79
Theophany, 1137
Third Book of Psalms, conclusion of,
    730
Thirtle's thesis, 41, 115
Thorns, dry, 414
Three-fold emphasis, 974
Threshing-floor, of Chidon, 141; of
    Nachon, 141; of Ornan, 180, 182
Thunder(s), secret place of, 630;
    seven, 176, 178
Thunderstorm, 174, 806
Tiglath Pileser, King of Babylon,
    1090
Tigris, 1090
Time of trouble, 60
Timelessness of God, 734
Title, Son of man, 48
Titles of Psalms, 294; Thirtle's
    thesis on, 41, 115
Tizri, 625
Tongue, a fire, 384; use of, 373
Tower, of Babel, 388; high, 420,
    442; strong, 322, 435
Transfiguration, 292, 1146

1208